A DOOR IN THE OCEAN

A DOOR IN THE OCEAN

A MEMOIR

David McGlynn

COUNTERPOINT
Berkeley

Library of Congress Cataloging-in-Publication Data is available.

ISBN: 978-1-61902-163-1

COUNTERPOINT
2560 Ninth Street, Suite 318
Berkeley, CA 94710

www.counterpointpress.com

Interior design by VJBScribe
Cover design by Debbie Berne

For Katherine, Galen, and Hayden,

my whole life

Out of chaos, beyond theory, into a life that peaks and breaks, the wave emerges. The shore where it dies lies ahead and waits, unseen. A life must peak as it rides up the shallow approach, steepen, and break. I want you to think of yourself like that, of your body and soul like that, one flesh traveling to shore, to collapse, all that way to end by darkening the sand and evaporating. Where do you go? You repeat in other waves, repeat and repeat. Each bears a message. Each has a meaning.

MARK JARMAN, *EPISTLES*

CONTENTS

A DOOR IN THE OCEAN

Good People of the World

When the meet announcer called the race to the blocks, I lowered my goggles. I jounced my shoulders and cranked my neck from side to side—a move Jeremy Woodley, my best friend, and I had learned from watching Jean-Claude Van Damme. I was in lane two; Jeremy was two lanes to my left, in four. Between us, a skinny boy in a blue Speedo from the opposing school bounced on the balls of his feet. I had no idea if I could beat him, and I didn't care either way. After the meet, he'd disappear with the rest of his team into the yellow school bus parked outside. Jeremy and I had to see each other every day. I didn't care if he and I came in last, so long as I touched the wall before him. Beating him was the only thing that mattered.

Our coach stood beside the pool in a shirt and tie, damp beneath the collar and armpits from the dank, chlorinated air inside the natatorium, and from the lather he worked himself into while running alongside the lanes. His tan forehead glistened, and his thinning hair stuck out like the bristles of an old broom. He looked at me and clenched his fist, his gold state championship ring a judging eye in the center of his hand. The rest of the team filled the bleachers behind him. The girls' hair bulged, oblong, in their silver caps, and the boys stood together in a line on the uppermost bleacher, beneath the snarling maroon-and-white bobcat painted on the cement wall. Trey Smith's head fit perfectly between the cat's teeth. "Here we go, Woodley!" they shouted in unison as they clapped their hands. "Let's go, McGlynn!" Curt Wood, on the far end, clanged a big copper cowbell.

The starter blew the whistle, and the natatorium fell silent. Water gurgled through the gutter drains, and for a moment the pool stood so still that the surface appeared to swell above the coping. "Step up, boys," the starter said into the microphone. His Texas drawl echoed through the room and sounded as though it had been piped in from far away.

I looked down the lanes as I mounted the block. Jeremy stood with

3

his back straight and his chest puffed out, his eyes fixed on the other side of the pool, as if getting there were his only concern. He filled his cheeks and let out a long stream of air. He turned his head toward me. His goggles were mirrored, his jaw set. He didn't nod, so I didn't either. He'd finished our freshman year with a faster time in the two hundred freestyle, had trained hard all summer while I was visiting my father and stepmother in California, and now, in the first meet of our sophomore season, he had every intention of putting this race, and me, to bed.

"No way," I whispered as I curled my toes over the edge of the block. "Not this time."

"Two hundred–yee-ard freestyle," the announcer said. "Take your marks."

I bent and gripped the edge of the starting block. My stomach rose into my throat, the muscles in my back and arms beginning to twitch and spasm. I felt the horn coming before I heard it, that insidious simulated gunshot that I'd begun to hear in my dreams.

When the sound came at last, I lunged.

Go!

An hour later, Jeremy and I stood in the locker room. Water lay in puddles on the floor and mold crept up the walls, turning from green to black as it saturated the grout. The tight space between the lockers, where he and I and the rest of the team peeled off our suits after coming out of the showers, smelled of chlorine and shampoo, the bloodlike perfume of rusting metal. They were talking about the boy who'd been shot and killed the previous weekend. The story had made the news because the boy had been a top prospect to play college ball, and because he was the second football player killed since school had started, only three weeks before. The shooting had happened at a high school inside the 610 Loop, the highway dividing the city of Houston from its suburbs. Far enough away to feel safe, close enough to warrant comment.

"I heard he was in line in the cafeteria, waiting for breakfast," Trey Smith, the senior captain, said. "He made fun of some girl's shirt or something, and she pulled a gun from her backpack and shot him."

Trey made a gun with his thumb and forefinger, turned it sideways, and pointed it at Mike Collins. "Bam!"

"You bitch!" Mike said, clutching his chest and falling backwards against the lockers. The rattle reverberated down the row. "You skanky punk-ass slut."

"I'm gonna get you, sucker!" Allen Swift shouted.

A cheap way to get laughs, but it worked. The meet had come down to the final relay, and we'd won it, and Trey's anchor split was his fastest in-season time to date. The head coach of the University of Arizona had already come to watch him practice. The coach from the University of Texas would be visiting in a few weeks. Trey's future spread before him like a buffet table: senior year, college, the Olympics hovering on the far horizon. Even the dumbest jokes made us laugh.

"Now the whole team's going to wear those lame black armbands," Jeremy piped in. Though we'd been on the varsity squad since our fresh-man year, we'd had to wait until we were sophomores to earn lockers among the upperclassmen. For weeks we'd tried, and failed, to participate in their conversations. Jeremy's win tonight had earned him the right to do exactly that.

I carried my shoes to the far end of the bench and sat with one foot propped on the pine, forcing my wet feet down inside my socks. Even though I told myself it didn't matter, and made a show of laughing at Trey's joke, I couldn't help feeling sullen and embarrassed: Jeremy had looked at me like he knew he could beat me, and I'd proved him right. I'd finished fourth, a full second behind him.

"They're all going to wear his number on their helmets," Mike echoed. "Take a knee in his honor after every game."

"Bullshit," Trey said. "Such complete bullshit."

Operation Desert Storm's brief, lopsided domination of the news eight months earlier had made the symbolism of paying tribute—the yellow ribbons tied around the magnolia trees along the farm-to-market roads, the proliferation of American flags—ridiculous. But at fifteen, what wasn't ridiculous? Jeremy and I could barely get through The Pledge of Alle-giance without cracking up.

Curt Wood sprayed a stream of Right Guard into his armpit until the wisps of hair turned white. Trey waved the cloud away and coughed. "Got enough on, sport?"

"It doesn't work right if I don't spray it close," Curt said.

"Man, nothing can help that," Jeremy said. He sauntered down to me.

He wore his towel draped over his shoulder. "Cheer up," he said. "You were gone for most of the summer."

"I swam in California," I said. I'd taken the county bus each morning at five, from my father and stepmother's house in Laguna Beach to the high school in Corona del Mar. Remembering those early mornings, the coastline drowned in a hazy grapelight, gave me another reason to tell myself my loss didn't matter: I'd be back in California, for good, before the season was over. Even so, I'd expected more from myself.

"Your time wasn't bad," he said. "It's only September."

I concentrated on tying my shoes. Magnanimity felt like yet another spoil of victory.

Jeremy stepped past me, past the end of the bench, and stood beneath the last illuminated fluorescent tube in the ceiling. The locker room beyond hunkered in darkness. He unfolded his big white towel and turned his back to me. "Ready, Dave? Watch, watch." He swiped the towel back and forth across his back and wiggled his rear end. "I'm Zestfully clean!" he sang. A reminder that despite the hair under his arms and the fuzz on his lip, he was still a boy. As was I.

I've scoured my memory of this day a thousand times in search of clues. At first, I hoped to discover the motive and perpetrator of the crime, but later I began to wonder if Jeremy sensed the doom gathering around him, the subtle shift in the weather. Did God—as my stepmother proclaimed during the summer—post signs visible only to those with the eyes to see? Had I missed them because I was young or because I was blind? For example, I remember the white T-shirt screened with an anchor logo he wore that night: He'd gotten it for free with a pair of Dockers. He hated it, but wore it because it was his only white T-shirt, and it looked good beneath his polos.

This afternoon is also one of the last in which I'd see my old self. One of the last moments in which I'd find horsing around in a locker room after a swim meet an uncomplicated pleasure, one of the rites of being in tenth grade and on the varsity team. My ability to laugh about a boy shot inside his school was proof of my immunity from the sprockets of the universe. It was the last time ordinariness would feel, well, ordinary. My parents' divorce and my father's immediate exit from Texas three years earlier, though painful, had felt more or less ordinary. I wasn't the only person I knew with a parent in a different state. When I remember myself on that late September afternoon—the boy lacing up his sneakers, his foot propped on the bench—I wonder whether my own future self already exists there.

Jeremy zipped up his bag and we headed outside. Autumn had officially begun, but the air was still as hot as summer. A herd of silver nimbus clouds lumbered across the sky, and mosquitoes buzzed around the dim yellow bulb above the door. My mother's red Ford idled in the lot. I could hear Annie Lennox on the radio even through the closed windows. My mother had dropped off Jeremy's sister Bekki and my sister Devin at their own swim practice, at a different pool, on her way to pick us up. Jeremy's mother would pick up the girls after their workout. My mother's perfume wafted out when I opened the passenger-side door. "How'd it go?" she asked. I shrugged and pulled the seat forward so Jeremy could climb in back. I sank into the front seat, held my hand to the air conditioner vent until my fingertips turned numb. In the side-view mirror, I saw Jeremy lean his head against the back of the seat. I turned the radio to Power 104 and cranked the volume.

The phrase "best friend" suggests an unadulterated loyalty Jeremy and I never enjoyed. It wasn't only swimming; we spent more time together than we did apart. In addition to the four hours a day we swam in the moldy six-lane pool appended to the back of our high school, we carpooled to and from workouts each morning and afternoon. During the school day, we had four of our six classes together, plus lunch. He was a lean, handsome boy, a favorite among his teachers, not above ribbing me for my slower split in the relay, my double chin, my flat-footed run. He poked his finger in my stomach and giggled like the Pillsbury Doughboy. It made the girls on the team laugh, and I hated him for that.

All the same, we were friends. We'd been on teams together since junior high, and at thirteen and fourteen, proximity was the sole requirement for friendship. We were stuck together so we stuck together. Our freshman year, when our lockers were isolated from the rest of team, we listened to the older boys howl and swear and punch each other, their voices distorted and tinny from the rows of crosshatched metal grating between us. When they remembered we were there, they drifted over to steal our deodorant or twist our tits or goad us into boxing. If we stuck up our dukes, we got punched. If we didn't, we got punched. We learned to dress quickly and keep our voices low.

One spring day after the season had ended, Jeremy and I found the locker of an older swimmer hanging open. No one else was around. We pressed our shoulders together and pissed into the locker—puerile payback for the taunts and hazes, but payback nonetheless. We laughed while we pissed, spraying through the grates into the adjoining lockers. The next week, Trey Smith, Mike Collins, and Ted Reid, our team's diver, picked us up before school and drove to the parking lot behind the donut shop. Trey told us to get out. The fog in the parking lot smelled like sugar and rising dough. "Take off your clothes," he said, and from the trunk of the car, Ted Reid produced two satin dresses, castoffs from one of their sisters. The dresses wouldn't zip all the way up. They applied lipstick and eye shadow and rouge on our cheeks. They taped to our backs signs that read, I'M A FRESHMAN, KICK ME, then replaced our shoes with long black swim fins that cracked against the ground with every step. "Leave it on all day or you're in deep shit," Mike said. Trey locked our clothes in the trunk. Jeremy and I looked at each other. We had balloons filling the breasts of our dresses and lipstick smiles that stretched from ear to ear.

In biology that morning, we waited for Blaise Houghland, the sophomore who sat at our lab table. I worried about what she'd say when she saw me wearing a dress, but at least I'd get her attention. She came in a few seconds after the bell rang, her soft, hot-rolled brown hair bouncing against the shoulders of her drill team uniform. She tilted her head to the side and smiled, all sympathy and sisterhood, not a drop of ridicule. "You guys," she said. But she sat down next to Jeremy.

The bayou behind my house wound along the backside of a dilapidated strip shopping center, behind the Burger King and dry cleaner's, and under the bridge where truant junior high students went to smoke cigarettes and suck face. A twenty-minute walk, half that if I rode my bike. Jeremy lived on the other side, in a two-story, red-brick house on a quiet cul-de-sac tucked deep within a maze filled with similarly large and boxy red-brick homes. With its wide lawn and tall fence skirting the backyard, the constable precinct patrolling the streets, his house seemed to me as impenetrable as an army fort, the kind of house the Big Bad Wolf would turn away from, gasping and discouraged. Since my father had moved out, my house, though also made of brick, had begun to show signs of neglect. The roof shingles were rotting, and lichen had rooted in the damper corners of the foundation. Cottonmouths slithered up from the bayou's muddy stream and lay coiled in the sun on our cracked patio, waiting for lunch to drop in.

Jeremy had an older sister with two children of her own and an older brother fresh from the University of Texas who worked for Charles Schwab and was living at home to save money for his wedding. His younger sister, Bekki, was thirteen, a year older than Devin. His parents both worked for big downtown petrochemical companies and exuded a calm that bespoke of security. They watched the news together every night and slept in twin waterbeds in their expansive master bedroom. I thought it was weird at first, too Ward and June Cleaver, until Jeremy explained that waterbeds were more comfortable when you flew solo. "Unless you're doing it," he said. "Then the wave is cushion for the pushin." He had a waterbed, too, and showed me how you make the wave by kicking his heels against the foot of the mattress, moaning, "Oh baby, oh yes."

His brother Greg had a subscription to *Sports Illustrated*, and we traded old issues back and forth, as if they were almanacs for manhood. Would Ohio State's winning streak hold? Would Shaquille O'Neal turn pro after his sophomore season at LSU? Would Mike Scott pitch as well now that Nolan Ryan had left the Astros? We debated sports trivia, lingo, standings, and statistics. The magazine even included a yearly lesson in sex when the swimsuit issue came out. In the locker room before swim practice, Mike had told me about the party he and Ted Reid had gone to in Klein, a little farther out than our neighborhood but part of the same hurricane of suburban sprawl that swirled around Houston. They'd arrived to find a hot tub full of girls in bikinis. "So, by the end of the night, I was doing this one girl," Mike said, like it was nothing, as though *doing* a girl was the same thing as talking to her on the phone. The idea of it was like a movie in which a car jumps across a gap in the highway and lands on the other side: not impossible, but nevertheless difficult to fathom. And before sex had become a possibility for me, it had proved itself dangerous. The inscrutable hunger that often woke me in the night had also shattered my parents' marriage, catapulting my father to a new life three states away and leaving my mother unable to speak his name without anger, resentment, disdain.

Sometimes swimming only made things worse. The boys and girls teams were scored separately, but we practiced together. We got to see Erin Montague and Nicky Delbridge in their training suits everyday, their legs tanned from lifeguarding all summer, their breasts round and firm beneath the Lycra. Even Summer Sanders' nipples were visible through her suit when she won the two hundred butterfly at the World Championships in Australia. "Ten thousand miles away, and there they are, plain as day," Jeremy said as we sat before the TV in his living room. "Ba-da bing."

"Thanks to the magic of television," I said.

But only with him could I talk this way. All the time we spent with our horns locked in battle had forged an intimacy peculiar to competitors. We knew the other had the hots for Blaise Houghland because we'd confessed only to each other. He was the only person in Houston, in the entire state of Texas, I felt I could trust. The sturdiness of his house—the long afternoons we lingered on the living room floor in front of the television, his mother dancing with a beer in the kitchen on Friday nights—made it a refuge from my own home, still recovering from the nuclear winter of my parents' divorce. My mother had re-entered marriage hastily, but definitively. No longer single meant she was no longer a single mother. She worked to convince Devin and me our family was whole again now that we had two parents living under one roof. She said it might be easier to think of my father as an uncle, someone we'd visit, but something less than a parent. We needed to look toward the future, she said. We needed to start again.

But starting again hadn't been easy. My stepfather technically lived with us in Houston, but most of his business was in Dallas and Austin. He sold industrial microscopes to tech companies, table-sized machines for assembling microchips and circuit boards. He was gone for most of the week, and on the weekends his son and daughter flew in from Dallas. On Saturdays my stepfather unloaded the equipment from the back of his van, my stepbrother and I helped him click into place the rear bench seat that had spent the week in a dusty corner of the garage, and then the six of us, our newly constituted family, trucked off to every fair, art festival, rodeo, and expo between Brenham and Galveston. We devoured pizza and turkey legs and funnel cakes, took photographs of ourselves with our faces and hands locked in wooden stocks, with our backs to the Astro-dome, dressed in Dickens-era capes and twirling Victorian parasols. My mother snapped pictures everywhere we went, as if to generate proof that she was happy.

I knew the fairs and the festivals were distractions from the fact that no amount of fun could supplant my mother's disappointment. She'd landed in the clichéd half of all marriages that end in divorce, and her second attempt felt less like a new beginning than the roughshod cobbling together of what remained of the past. My mother told me of her dreams in which strange men stood over her bed. Other nights she didn't sleep at all, and I heard her pacing the hallways. My stepfather was always on the road, trying to stay involved with a son and daughter who lived far away, whom he only saw for a few days a month. Exhaustion loomed; fuses grew short. My stepfather's temper rivaled my mother's; in their ire they were equally matched. When they wore out screaming at each other, they got on the phone and screamed at the Texas Child Support Division, at my father, at my stepfather's ex-wife.

They were most tender when they were hurt. The night my mother lunged at my stepfather and broke her wrist—he stuck his arm up to deflect her and she fell backward onto the bathroom tile—was one of their best. He carried her to the car and drove her to the hospital. She returned home with her arm in a sling and his arm around her waist. She walked inside with her head against his shoulder. Neither was to blame, they said. It was an accident. She wouldn't have fallen had the tiles not been slick. A period of quiet affection followed. My mother made tacos for dinner, and my stepfather decided to work from home for a few weeks so he could help more around the house. He'd take over the carpool until her wrist healed. I prayed it would last, even though I knew it wouldn't.

Jeremy was the only friend I'd called from my father's house in California. He was the one person I knew I'd miss if I didn't come home.

I'd returned from California in August, a week before tenth grade started, and told my mother I wanted to move in with my father and step-mother. I'd finish high school in California and come back to Houston for the same amount of time I currently spent away from it: a week or so at Christmas, three weeks in the summer. To sweeten the deal, my father had offered to pay for my plane tickets back and forth. My mother said no way, not a chance in hell. My maternal grandparents and uncles were convinced I'd been brainwashed. "You shouldn't have let him go in the first place," my grandmother told my mother.

To make matters worse, I'd come home wearing around my neck the silver cross my father and stepmother had given me for my birthday. "What's this?" my grandfather asked one afternoon. He pinched the cross and lifted it away from my skin to examine it over the rim of his eyeglasses. I had my back to the refrigerator. My mother and grandmother were skinning chicken breasts at the kitchen sink behind us. My uncles and stepfather were drinking beer on the back patio and cheering on my grandparents' terrier as it chased down a squirrel.

"It's what it looks like," I said. "A cross."

"So you joined the church?" he asked, letting the cross fall back against my neck.

"Not exactly," I said. "But I like it."

"Jesus never did a damn thing for anybody!" my grandfather shouted. My mother glanced up but didn't interrupt. My grandfather leaned closer; I could smell his Skin Bracer, the lime from his gin. He said, "That woman had her sights set on your father from the moment she saw him. Now she's aiming for you." By *that woman*, of course, he meant my stepmother, the former evangelical missionary and now children's pastor who had, in their estimation, stolen my father from our family in Texas, fled with him to California, and turned him into a religious nutcase.

Outside, my uncles cracked their knuckles and slapped their chests and talked about flying to California to kick my father's ass. My stepfather threw his hands in the air and yelled that my father and stepmother were "living a lie!" His words made me the angriest, if for no other reason than that he'd been installed in my father's place. He hung his clothes in my father's closet, and when he was home, slept on my father's side of the bed, on the same mattress, in the same linens. He never stopped talking about getting my stepbrother to move down from Dallas. His unwillingness to understand why I might want to live with my father was a fact I registered as the height of hypocrisy. When I pointed it out, my mother said, "It's different."

"How?" I asked.

"Because your stepbrother doesn't have any kind of father up there. His mother's single. You have a dad here."

The more she refused to let me move, the more desperate I became. When I talked to my father on the phone, I could hear my mother listening on the extension or outside my bedroom door. I sat inside my closet, but it wasn't private enough. I called him a few times from Jeremy's house until I grew nervous about the charge showing up on his parents' long-distance statement. So I began riding my bike to the pay phone at the supermarket. I'd call collect and say "Safeway" when the operator asked for my name. My father would deny the charges and call me back. He had the pay phone's number in his address book.

From the pay phone I called a lawyer. I asked how I could have custody transferred from my mother to my father. I stood with my hand shielding my face for fear one of our neighbors would recognize me and tell my mother where I'd been, who I'd been talking to. "It's not so easy," he said. It would require a court appearance, and I'd have to prove injury in order to overturn the terms of the original divorce decree. The process would take a year, and I'd need to meet with a psychologist. By that time I'd be nearly finished with high school. And, he said, psychological abuse was tricky to prove and there was no guarantee. "But if you can make it to California," the lawyer said, "your father doesn't have to send you back."

I started tenth grade with a plan: I'd feign surrender until Christmas and act like the whole business of moving to California was behind me. When I visited my father in December, I'd simply refuse to get on the plane to come home. I rolled up pairs of socks and underwear and shoved them inside the legs of my jeans and the sleeves of my shirts to see how much extra I could fit inside my suitcase. I discovered I could hide my favorite cassettes under the suitcase's lining. Twice I went to the Wrap & Mail Room to ship small packages to myself: photographs and books, a pair of shoes. The rest I could live without.

I told my plan to Jeremy a few days before our first swim meet. "Bummer," he said. He was nonchalant about the whole thing, dismissive. I'd been telling him of my plans to escape since before I came back from California, and so far none had come to pass. "I've already mailed myself two boxes of stuff," I said.

"Really?" he said. He looked down at the counter, opened the silverware drawer, and lifted out a spoon.

"My mom can't stop me from going to visit," I said. "It's in the divorce decree. She can get arrested if she doesn't let me."

"What about the season?"

"I'll finish it there," I said. "Mission Viejo is one of the best clubs in the country. Their pool is awesome."

"Why don't you just go now?" he asked. He put the spoon away, and turned to the ceramic jug beside the microwave. He stuck his hand down inside and came up with three Oreos. He slid one across the island to me. "You have enough money in your savings account for a plane ticket, right? Just cash it out and go."

The idea had occurred to me, but it seemed, somehow, to cross a line. I didn't like the notion of *running away*, the weakness and desperation it implied. Even though Devin and I had flown by ourselves between Houston and Orange County at least a dozen times, I worried someone would prevent me from getting on the plane, that the cops would escort me in handcuffs back to my mother, who wouldn't let me out of her sight ever again. And with each week that passed, a certain lassitude overtook me, the routines of swimming and school, going to the movies on Friday nights, the football game on Saturday. I'd begun to doubt my own resolve.

"I don't know," I said. "I don't have a ride to the airport."

"Good news, then," he said. "My dad might be buying me a car. A Monte Carlo from some guy at his work." He sifted through the basket on his kitchen counter until he found a piece of paper and a pen. He drew an outline of the car, paying particular attention to the tail fin on the trunk. It was enough for me to picture it: the tinted windows rolled down, our elbows propped on the sills, the radio cranked as we thundered down the freeway. It took me a minute to remember that he was offering to drive me to the end of our friendship. Saying good-bye to him at the airport, shaking hands at the skycap stand—the way I'd greeted and departed from my father for the last two years—seemed, just then, as sad as never seeing the Pacific Ocean again.

"The car's a total hoopty," Jeremy said. "But it's better than walking."

The last week of September, my father's company sent him to Houston for a week, where he still had business connections, and he extended his trip through Sunday so he could spend the weekend with Devin and me. My mother worried my father was coming to meet with a lawyer to try to take me back to California with him. She threatened not to let me see him until he assured her he had no tricks up his sleeve. Even then, we had to wait until the weekend.

After the swim meet on Thursday night, about an hour and a half after my mother dropped him off at his house, I called Jeremy on the phone. My mother was busy mopping the kitchen floor so it would shine when my father came over the next day, and I'd timed the call to coincide with Jeremy's mother's leaving to pick up his sister and mine from swimming. The temperature had come down with the sunset and his father and brother were tinkering with the sprinkler system in the front yard. There was no one around to tell us to get off the phone. We didn't talk about the meet; we talked about the Longhorns and our own high school's game that weekend. "You think you can talk your dad into going to the game?" he asked.

"I'll try," I said. "But I doubt it." I didn't let on that I didn't care about the game anymore. High school football was a Texas passion, but I was intent on escaping Texas.

"Lame," he said. I could hear his disappointment. We were finally allowed to sit with the older members of the team, but neither of us wanted to sit with them by ourselves. "I'll go to the next game," I said. "We suck anyway."

"We suck *royally*," he said. "Our team sucks the sweat off a dead man's balls." And like that he was back, his honking laugh fuzzing out the connection.

We hung up at 8:20. No long good-bye, no "hey, nice talking to you"—we each said "later" and the phone went dead. I went into the living room to watch the end of *The Cosby Show* before packing my bag for morning practice. I looked at the clock when I hung up the phone and again when Jeremy's mother pulled into our driveway. It was 8:40 PM. The lights of her Oldsmobile flashed through the closed mini-blinds. Devin slammed the front door behind her as she came inside. I heard the car shift into gear and Jeremy's mother and sister drive away. It was five minutes from our house to theirs.

In the twenty minutes between the end of my phone call with Jeremy and Devin's return home, two men arrived at Jeremy's house. There may have been more than two men, or only one man with several guns, but the police speculated, given the number of shots fired, that there were two of them. They tied Jeremy's ankle to his brother Greg's and forced them both to kneel on the living room carpet, side by side, near the entryway.

They held a gun to Jeremy's father's head as he sat near the fireplace. There's reason to believe, given the forensics report about the order of the shootings, and knowing Mr. Woodley, that he begged for his sons' lives, but of course there's no way to know that for sure. Greg was shot first, three times in the back of the head. Jeremy watched his brother's murder before he felt the gun's muzzle against his own head. The killers used four bullets instead of three for him. They beat his father with the handle of the gun and made him kneel beside his sons. Shot him six times. All three were shot with .22-caliber revolvers, which are quieter than other weapons and don't discard shell casings. None of the neighbors heard anything. The men let themselves out, closed the door behind them, and disappeared. They were inside the house for less than ten minutes.

My mother was awake when the phone rang. I'd gone to bed a half hour earlier, but I wasn't asleep yet. I heard her ankles crack as she moved down the hallway to answer the phone in the kitchen. The phone rang again, then once more before she picked it up. I heard her say hello. "What?" she said. "What are you saying?"

Then she called for me: "David!"

I ignored her at first. She and my stepfather often argued after I'd gone to bed; I'd grown accustomed to the sound of her screaming in the kitchen, had learned to block it out. She shouted my name again before I understood she was calling for me. "David!"

I threw back the covers, opened my bedroom door. I stood in the hallway in my underwear. "What?" I shouted back. Without my glasses, I couldn't see past the carpet. "What do you want?" I said.

"The Woodleys are dead! Oh my God, the Woodleys are dead!"

"What?" I said. The hallway was a blurred white path, my mother an amoebic specter pacing at the far end.

"That was Trey Smith's mother." She paused, then disappeared around the corner. "The Woodleys are dead!" she screamed again. "Come quick, it's on the news."

I did not go quickly. I walked slowly, cautious of what I could not see, not yet comprehending what she was saying and therefore certain that when I reached the end of the hallway, I'd learn that she had said something different. Whatever had incited this panic in her would prove benign, an overreaction. Or maybe my unconscious understood what my waking mind did not: the magnitude of what waited for me in the kitchen, the way it would reroute the course of my life, and so it moved me slowly to keep me from burning my energy too quickly. It was 10:20 on a Thursday night. I wouldn't sleep again until Saturday.

My mother had moved into the front room. She stood before the television, both hands covering her mouth. "What did you say?" I asked.

She pointed to the TV. "Look!"

The television looked like a kaleidoscope, colors swimming, tumbling over one another. I knelt down and leaned into the screen until the picture turned to a tight plaid of red, blues, and greens. The report by then had ended. My mother reached for the cable box and changed the channel, and there, filling the screen and my entire field of vision, was Jeremy's house. Yellow POLICE LINE: DO NOT CROSS tape stretched across his front yard. Siren lights flashed in the windows. The wooden sign announcing Jeremy's membership on the swimming team was nailed to the pine tree: a white circle depicting a maroon silhouette of a swimmer rising out of the water, Jeremy's name clearly visible beneath. "Police are talking to neighbors," the reporter said. "So far no witnesses have been identified."

The reporter cut back to the anchor and the weather came on. "I don't understand," I said. "What happened?"

"It's 10:27," my mother said. "The news repeats in three minutes."

Devin came in. In her pink nightshirt and bare feet she appeared to float over the tile floor. She sat down on the couch behind me, and my mother sat down beside her. "Three minutes," my mother said. "Maybe by then they'll know more."

I walked back to my room for my glasses, pulled on my shorts and T-shirt. Not until I stopped shivering did I realize that I had been. I sat on the floor in front of the television and waited for the news to start. A Chevrolet commercial came on, then one for Fancy Feast. No one said a word.

The Channel 13 logo swam up on the screen, and the anchor said they were following a breaking news story about a bizarre shooting in an upper-middle-class neighborhood in far northwest Houston. The picture cut to the reporter, the same woman from a few minutes before. She stood in front of Jeremy's house in a blue Windbreaker and read from a notepad she held below the camera's gaze. "The victims are Barry

Woodley, and his sons Greg and Jeremy," she said. "They were discovered by Lynn Woodley and her teenage daughter after they arrived home from swim team practice, about 8:45 this evening."

"Oh my God," Devin said. "It happened while we were in the car."

"A few of the neighbors we spoke with say Barry and Greg were outside when Lynn left the house at eight o'clock," the reporter said. "But so far no one reports any other suspicious activity. The victims were shot execution-style, in the back of the head. It appears to be a professional hit."

Execution-style. A professional hit. Such words belonged in a spy novel, components of an elaborate, far-fetched plot, set behind the Iron Curtain. Not in real life, not in my life. They didn't make sense. "Why would anyone want to kill them?" my mother asked. I was stuck on the *what* and hadn't yet moved on to question the *why* or the *who*.

The camera traveled back in time and showed the front of the house again, without the newslady standing in front of it, the curved cement walkway leading to the front step, the open door a creamy glow in the center of the screen. The camera panned closer and zeroed in on the sheriff, or one of his deputies, standing in the doorway with his hands on his belt, his beige Stetson pointed toward the ground. He stepped to the side, and I could see through the doorway to the foyer, the living room just beyond, the bodies lying facedown on the carpet. They were barely visible, but I could see them. Jeremy lay at the end, his left arm by his side, his face turned toward his brother. I recognized his T-shirt, that stupid Dockers T-shirt with the lame blue anchor logo.

The camera lurched forward in time and showed the coroner wheeling the bodies, each covered in blue tarps and strapped to a gurney, down the driveway. The coroner's ambulance waited with its rear doors hanging open, its siren lights dark and still.

I followed the camera through time, zooming in and out of focus, as though I was no longer a person and had instead become an amalgam of lines and shapes flickering across a screen. I'd been in bed ten minutes ago, looking forward to spending the weekend with my father in his downtown hotel room, and now I was here, on the floor, Jeremy dead in his entryway, Jeremy wrapped in a tarp, Jeremy being hoisted into the rear of an ambulance. The reporter came on screen again, her back to the house, lights still flashing in the windows. I flew past her, through the front door. I could see the furniture and the table and chairs in the dining room to the right, the stack of magazines on Greg's nightstand in the room to the left, the pair of goggles stuffed inside the still-wet latex cap buried at the bottom of the black-and-yellow Nike bag, still sitting by the backdoor where Jeremy had dropped it when he came inside.

I came back to my house, my living room, my own body. I sat sweating, my weight on my palms. My wrists ached. The phone started ringing. My mother wrapped her arm around my sister's head and hugged Devin against her shoulder. The phone kept ringing. The news went to commercial. I stood up, turned off the set.

I went to school the next morning, but the principal told the team we didn't have to go to class. Between bells, the students processed through the hallways desanguinated and silent, as if circling a field where a plane had crashed, the wreckage too hot to approach. Some cried when they saw me. Other simply stared. Jeremy and I had been together so often that once people figured out who he was, they figured me out, too. I'd felt invisible up to that point, a nobody, a dork in glasses and braces, but now I felt shrouded in an ethereal glow. As though I was involved with the murder somehow, a witness to it, the lone survivor.

The swimming team roamed the hallways in a pack, gathering in the cafeteria and later in a classroom. We sat on the floor, and our friends came to sit with us and cry. The girls on the team leaned their heads against my shoulder and cried until their tears soaked through my shirt. I wanted to cry, too, but I couldn't. I dropped my head between my knees and stared at the carpet, hoping gravity would help, but no tears came. I wanted an hour of clean grief, but instead I felt something more shameful: pleasure in the attention. In the hallway, I locked eyes with Blaise Houghland. She swam upstream through the flow of students to reach me and wrapped her arms around my neck. I felt the quiet flush of victory: I'd won her affection at last. I concentrated on the clasp of her necklace, the pale skin disappearing into the collar of her blouse, aware she was in my arms for a reason that had nothing to do with me, and that after I let go I'd probably never touch her again.

In the afternoon, I slipped back to the school parking lot with Trey, Mike, Ted Reid, and Chris Mangold, who owned the old Buick station wagon we piled into. The upholstery was a washed-out midnight blue and reeked of old cigarettes. We left the radio off and the windows rolled up, the dull sunlight magnified through the glass. I sat in back between Mike and Ted, my shoulders pressed against theirs. The heat from their skin burned through the sleeve of my T-shirt. Mike and Ted stared out the window beside them; I looked straight ahead at the dashboard, the dimming clock above the radio, my own face in the rearview mirror. Though it wasn't me, wasn't my face. I didn't recognize myself.

Chris worked through the neighborhood streets, one winding block after another stretching from Highway 290 to Highway 6, more than ten thousand houses in one subdivision. Mike and Ted lived in the middle village, Jeremy in the one farthest east. Chris turned corners without touching the brake, ran one stop sign after another. I felt Ted's bony shoulder dig into my arm when we swung left, smelled Mike's cologne when we swung right. The Buick's engine sputtered and growled. We wandered through the labyrinthine streets, dipping into the thermometer-shaped cul-de-sacs only to do a donut in the bulb and race back out again, past house after house built of red brick with wide front lawns, halos of brown needles skirting the pines. Some houses looked so much like Jeremy's that I wondered if we'd wound up on his street by chance. Which caused me to wonder: Did the killers go to the wrong house? Did they choose a house at random, stopping their car because they saw a front door left open, a television flickering inside a window? There had to be a reason, a cause, though the more the car turned and the more houses we drove past, the more reasons and causes slipped away.

Only a few people were on the sidewalks. School wasn't out yet, and it was too hot to play outside. A woman pushed a baby in a stroller. The UPS man carried a box to a doorstep. Yet how could I be sure that anyone was who they appeared to be? How could I be sure the woman wasn't hiding a gun in the stroller's back pocket, or that the UPS man wasn't leaving a bomb beside the door? Even the bicycle left lying sideward on a front lawn looked abandoned, as though the child it belong to had been snatched off the street in broad daylight. What reason did I have to believe the killing was finished, that the men who murdered Jeremy weren't in their car right now, looking for their next victim?

I leaned forward, put my head on my knees. Chris took another corner. The car leaned like a Tilt-A-Whirl.

Trey Smith sat up front, staring down at his fist, opening and tightening it as though adjusting his grip on a handful of sand. He looked hard at the man standing on the sidewalk in a white polo shirt, scribbling on a clipboard. His Sears Home Improvement van was parked against the curb. "Fucking salesman," Trey said. "Like anyone wants his shit right now."

"Want me to stop?" Chris asked, turning to look at Trey. If Trey wanted to fight, Chris was in.

Trey hesitated, but told Chris to keep driving. "Let's go see his house," he said.

We turned onto Jeremy's street. News vans lined the curb, their heavy-duty power cords snaking along the ground to the cameras. At two o'clock in the afternoon, the sky was stagnant and white. Nothing was happening, but the cameras were rolling. The police were parked across the street. I didn't like it that the cameras were filming Jeremy's house; it felt like they were preying on the tragedy, exploiting it. Somewhere below my anger lurked a dull fear that Jeremy's house showing up on the news would cause something else awful to happen. I felt I was connected to this place, that I in some way belonged to it, and the more his house showed up on the news, the more I risked the killers finding their way to me.

Chris Mangold rolled down the window and leaned his head out. "Hey!" he called. "Get the fuck out of here!"

An officer walked over and peered through the car windows. "Shouldn't ya'll be in school?" he asked.

"We're Jeremy's teammates," Trey said, leaning across Chris's shoulder. He tightened his hand around the parking brake. Trey's head was shaved, even in the off-season. He'd always been hot-tempered and quick to fight, and of all the members of the team I was most careful around him. I could see him itching to go toe-to-toe with the cop. "We can do whatever the hell we want today."

"Give me ya'lls' names," the officer said. He unbuttoned his breast pocket where he kept his steno pad.

Trey said his name was Phil Latio. Chris said his name was Mike Rotch. I gave the officer my real name. "Nice one," Chris said when the officer walked away. "Playing it straight to throw him off. Dumb fuck's too stupid to get it anyway." The officer disappeared into the house across the street from the Woodleys', and a moment later a man in a beige suit came outside and knocked on the car window. He spoke my name. "Would you come inside for a minute?" he asked. His brown mustache hid his upper lip. He wiped his forehead with the palm of his hand.

I said I didn't feel good about that. The man opened his wallet and showed me his badge. "I'm a detective," he said.

"It's okay," Chris said. "I'll come with you."

Two ears of Indian corn tied together with a yellow ribbon hung from the neighbor's front door. The chilled air in the foyer caused the hair on my arms to stand up. The house was identical to the Woodleys', only everything was reversed. The dining room was to the left instead of to the right, the kitchen was on the wrong side of the house. The neighbor herself I recognized, but only vaguely. Her daughter went to my school, but I wasn't friends with her. She brought Chris and me each a glass of water and said that Mrs. Woodley and Bekki would be staying with her for a few days. The detective held his notepad on his knee, a pen in his hand. "Did you know they were selling their piano?" he asked me. "Did he mention someone coming over to see it?" He used only pronouns—they, he. I pictured the inside of the house: The piano sat against the wall, like a desk, with picture frames arranged on top. I never once heard it played. It made sense they'd sell it. "No," I said, "I didn't know." Jeremy hadn't said anything. "Did they steal the piano?" I asked.

The detective shook his head. "You recall when you talked to him last?"

I said Jeremy and I had talked on the phone until 8:20 last night. The detective wrote this down in his notepad. "He didn't mention anything? Could you hear anything in the background?"

"He was in his room. We talked about the football game." The detective nodded, crossed and uncrossed his legs. "Didn't anyone see anything?" I asked.

"We're talking to everyone," he said. "You might be the last person who talked to him, you know that?" I nodded. He pulled a card from his jacket pocket and handed it to me. "If you remember anything else, you call me, okay?"

"Okay," I said.

Chris leaned forward. "You find who did this and you won't need to bother with a trial," he said. "I guarantee it."

The detective nodded sympathetically, then stood up. Chris and I stood up, too. He reached out his hand; Chris shook it first. He set his hand on my shoulder and steered me toward the door. "He was my best friend," I said to the detective. I felt the need to say this after offering so little to help the case. I was the last person to talk to Jeremy alive, and it didn't add up to much.

"We'll find them, son," he said, and shook my hand again. I wanted to believe him. I wanted to believe that the police, with their infinite resources and indefatigable allegiance to justice, could pull fingerprints out of water and tell the color of a car from a single tire track; I wanted to believe that this detective would toil day and night, following leads and chasing down suspects, stopping at nothing until he found the men responsible. But the way he called me son, like he knew how to handle punks like me, like I was a punk who needed handling, and the way he squinted against the afternoon glare and tried to usher me out the door, made him hard to believe.

The memorial service was on Monday. Coach decided the team should practice that morning. He'd emptied Jeremy's locker and held in his hands Jeremy's pull buoy, two foam cylinders tethered with a nylon cord. He passed it to Trey and said we should each take a turn swimming with it. He bit down on his bottom lip and began to sob. It was the hardest I'd seen anyone cry since the murders. He bent forward and rested his hands on his knees and started gagging and spitting. Eventually Allen Swift climbed out of the water, hugged him, and walked him to the bleachers.

Afterward we went out to breakfast and then drove to Trey's house, then Nicky Delbridge's house, then Chris Mangold's. We sat on the couches in each living room and tried not to wrinkle our clothes. When we grew tired of one place, we moved to another. Occasionally a television was turned on, but never for very long. Going to school was never an option.

The memorial service took place at the Woodleys' church, a plain, gray-and-white building a mile from school. The sanctuary was a large octagonal room with folding chairs, a stage up front full of flower arrangements in beveled glass vases. Mr. Woodley's, Greg's, and Jeremy's pictures had been blown up to poster-size, framed, and perched on easels. There were no caskets.

Mrs. Woodley and Bekki and Jeremy's older sister, Annie, sat up front, flanked by relatives. I sat in back with my teammates. Only the pastor spoke; no one else gave a eulogy, but during the sermon, Trey Smith began to sob. He leaned forward like he was going to be sick and pressed a wadded tissue into his eyes. He sat directly behind me, and I could hear him choking as he swallowed air. I reached back and set my hand on his knee. I wanted to appear strong and to believe that Jeremy was in a better place, as the pastor said. Even though we who were left behind were full of sorrow, Jeremy's condition had, strange though it may seem, actually improved. But I also reached for Trey's knee because I was having trouble with sorrow. I had managed to cry only once, late Saturday night in my father's hotel room, overcome with exhaustion, and I felt I needed to touch someone else's grief in order to break through my own numbness, experience grief for myself. To my surprise, Trey set his hand atop mine and held it there until the pastor finished speaking.

Mrs. Woodley, Bekki, and Annie left through the door near the stage before the pastor led the congregation in the final song. I saw only the orb of Mrs. Woodley's permed hair move among the heads before it disappeared through the dark hole of the door. The pastor said that after the service, the family was hosting a private reception. To this event I was invited.

The reception was held at the same neighbor's house where I'd talked to the detective on Thursday. Triangular sandwiches and rolled cold cuts and lemon bars cut into one-inch squares covered the dining room table. The air-conditioning had been dialed down, and with so many people crowded inside, the house felt damp and close. My stepfather showed me how to undo the top button of my dress shirt and hide it with my tie. I moved between my teammates and my mother, shoveling in plates of food because doing so seemed expected of me. "Eat up or it will go to waste," the neighbor said whenever I put down my empty plate. Bekki sat with her cousins, a cluster of unfamiliar teenagers who eyed me warily, a warning to stay back.

At the end of the reception, I found my way to Mrs. Woodley so I could say good-bye. She wore a beige, flower-print dress and gold earrings the size of coins and looked more like the mother of the groom at a wedding than a woman who had discovered the murdered bodies of her husband and sons. She was holding a cocktail plate with fruit and crackers on it, which she set on the table when she saw me. She held her arms open to me and I stepped toward her, though I did so awkwardly, my eyes on the table rather than on her. She squeezed me tightly, then pulled back and held me by the shoulders. "I love you, David," she said.

"Me, too," I said, and at that moment, looking Jeremy's mother in the eye, I vowed I'd never forget him. But I wanted to do more: I wanted a grander gesture of my fidelity, proof that Jeremy was in fact the friend I'd claimed him to be. "Maybe I could cut your grass for a while," I said. "Until the winter."

"If that's something you'd like to do," she said, "that would be wonderful. But you know you don't have to."

"I want to," I said. "I'd like that very much."

I imagined mowing the Woodleys' lawn alone, a Sisyphean hero pushing the mower back and forth across the grass, propelled by nothing more than honor, devotion. I'd give up weekends, swim practices, homecoming. The heat wouldn't be a factor. Nothing mattered more than keeping the Woodleys' yard perfectly manicured. But when word got out about my plans, Coach let the team out of practice so we could all do the job together. We arrived at the Woodleys' house on the first Friday in October, a week and a day after the murders. The sky had at last turned from white to blue, and the temperature had dropped into the seventies. The wind carried leaves away from the sycamores. Every doorstep on the block had a pumpkin on it.

Mrs. Woodley opened the garage door and showed us to the equipment. The mower sat beneath a peg board from which hung the weedwhacker, the edger, the hedge trimmer, brooms of various sizes arranged longest to shortest, three orange extension cords coiled into figure eights—a testament to Mr. Woodley's meticulous, engineer's nature. Tennis balls suspended from the garage's ceiling by transparent fishing line rested against the windshields of both cars.

I was given first dibs, and I took the mower. Ted Reid and Mike Collins fought over the weed-whacker and the edger; Curt Wood volunteered to take care of the hedges. They carried the extension cords to the front yard. I gassed the mower and pushed it through the gate to the back. The lawn was an easy mow: a big square inside a six-foot wooden fence, a dogleg that disappeared behind the garage. Four wilted flower arrangements sat in their vases on the wrought-iron patio table, their once-white petals turned the color of rotten apples. Inside the kitchen window, Trey Smith sat at the table with Mrs. Woodley. They stared intently into each other's eyes in a shared moment of trust, as though one of them was confessing a secret they'd been able to tell no one else. Mrs. Woodley reached across the table and took hold of Trey's hand. Trey looked down and nodded.

I primed the gas, set my foot on the base, and yanked the starter cord. The small engine hiccupped a puff of oily smoke and roared quickly to life. I worked as I had once envisioned: in long strips back and forth, parallel with the house. I was careful to steer the mower down the center of the path, half the mower in the long grass, the other half going over what I'd just cut to make sure I'd caught every blade.

Each pass allowed me a chance to look through the living room windows and study, without distraction and for the first time, the place where the murders had happened. The carpet, I could tell, was new, as was the sofa. The green plaid had been replaced by a caramel colored twill, taller and more plush than the old couch. Twin crimson pillows rested against each of the sofa's arms. Everything else looked as it once did: the television against the wall, the coffee table before the couch. Even the piano showcased its menagerie of photographs. At the back of the living room, the staircase led upstairs to Jeremy's and Bekki's rooms; to the right, the hallway led to Greg's room and the bathroom where Jeremy and I had shaved our arms and legs the night before the District Championships our freshman year. I'd spent so much time trying to recreate the living room in my memory and now here it was, on the other side of a pane of tinted glass, so similar to what I knew that I forgot why I was here, forgot the last two weeks entirely, and for a moment expected Jeremy to turn the corner from the hallway or slide on his socks down the carpeted stairs. But each time I passed the window I moved farther away until the glare from the sun turned the windows black.

I was near the back fence when Mrs. Woodley opened the kitchen door. I cut the engine. "Don't bother with the other side of the garage," she said. "We never go back there. And it's full of junk."

"Okay," I said and pulled the starter cord. Coach had said that integrity is who you are when no one's looking, and the definition seemed to apply here: Despite the fact that no one would ever see the far side of the garage, I needed to mow it. In fact, I needed to mow the far side of the garage *because* no one would ever see it, for only the far side of the garage could prove my integrity. I'd meant the things I'd promised.

I steered the mower along the fence behind the garage, back and forth in two short passes, and then I turned the corner. Dozens of flower arrangements lay in a heap, each dead bouquet laid perpendicular to the bouquet beneath it, like kindling for a pyre. The stems and petals had gone black and in the damp heat gave off a pungent, decaying odor. Behind the flowers, against the fence, was the Woodleys' old couch, now missing the seat cushions, and atop the couch, spilling over the sides and onto the grass, was the carpet from the living room. Unrolled, in a haphazard pile of misshapen hills, the carpet looked as though it had been dragged from the house and dumped in a hurry. Blood had saturated the fibers and had soaked through to the marbled padding, which had been bundled up and shoved to the side of the sofa. In some places, the blood was so thick and matted it looked like tar; elsewhere it fanned out into the crosshatching, a candy red the color of cough syrup.

I stopped mowing but left the engine running while I stared at the mound. This was as close as I had come to seeing the physical presence of death, and it was the nearest I had come to touching some essence of Jeremy after the murders. But rather than confirm his death, the bloody carpets only deepened the mystery of his absence. Death, in the abstract, was logical. Life comes to be, and at some point life ceases. In the particular, however, it was absurd. The more I tried to restore this carpet to its old place in the house, and to picture Jeremy kneeling upon it, all this blood spilling from his shattered head, the less plausible the whole thing became. I wondered if it was all a ruse: The death had been faked and Jeremy was hiding out with his father and brother in a mountain cabin. Or maybe, I thought, recalling my stepmother reading her Bible at the dining room table last summer—he'd been sucked up in a holy cyclone of wind and light, clean off the face of the earth.

The moment passed and I heard the lawn mower beside me, waiting for me to put it into gear. Chris and Mike and Curt Wood were on the other side of the fence, throwing Jeremy's basketball through the hoop above the garage, Curt yelling for Mike to pass it, Mike telling Chris to get his hand off his ass. I still had the front to mow, and on the way over my friends had been talking about going to a corn maze that night. I turned the mower around and pushed it away. I didn't promise Mrs. Woodley I'd be back next week, as I had planned to. I had no intention of coming back.

On Monday, we went back to school, back to swimming practice, back to life. I returned to my drivers education course, three afternoons a week in a sagging trailer at the far end of the student parking lot, and for the rest of October, I rode around with other sophomores in a gold Chevy Caprice while the instructor—a retired math teacher whose thinning hair had been dyed and permed so many times it had turned pink—stomped the auxiliary brake and refused to let us turn on the radio. I didn't know any of the other students in the car. They all claimed to have been friends with Jeremy.

The impunity the swim team was given the day after the murders I received for longer. I skipped class whenever I pleased, and no one said a word. One day in early November, when a fire drill emptied the school into the parking lot, I proposed to Vince, a teammate, and Carla, his girl-friend, that we take off. They hesitated, but I urged them on. I wanted to see what I could get away with. Sitting in school seemed pointless. In the car, however, none of us could think of any place we wanted to go. We drove to the mall. It was nearly empty at that time of day. An elderly cou-ple strode by in bulky white tennis shoes, and a gray-suited businessman talked on the pay phone while leafing through the pages of his day plan-ner. The security guard glared at us from across the food court. I regretted skipping school, and I wanted to go back, but I couldn't admit that. Vince said, "This blows. Let's go to my house and watch a movie."

We turned on *Ghost* and settled in on his brother's unmade bed. The sheets beneath us were musky and unwashed. Before Patrick Swayze ever got shot, Vince and Carla got up and went into the next room. I heard them having sex, and I sat and watched the rest of the movie with my arms looped around my knees. The sun through the plastic blinds was the color of mustard, and I could hear Carla squeaking and Vince grunting as the wooden headboard tapped against the wall—a rhythm out of sync with the second hand on my watch. Since the night of the murders, time had become a problem. It no longer moved in a straight line. I lost large gaps of it. Some mornings I arrived for swimming practice and couldn't recall putting in my contact lenses or getting into the car. I failed a his-tory exam after neglecting to fill out a single answer; the hour seemed to pass in an instant, and when the bell rang, I'd yet to write my name on the top of the sheet.

Other times, I felt as though I wasn't in the wrong place; I was just there at the wrong time. I shouldn't have been watching *Ghost* at one o'clock in the afternoon, just as I shouldn't have been watching the news at eleven o'clock at night back in September. I shouldn't have spoken with a detective inside a stranger's house at two o'clock in the afternoon. I shouldn't have been inside a church on a Monday. I shouldn't have been mowing Jeremy's lawn, looking through the rear windows of his house into the living room where the bodies were found. Everything was happening out of sequence.

When the movie ended, we went back to school. Vince and Carla were hauled into the principal's office and given three days' detention. I was called to the assistant principal's office a week later. Rising from my desk and walking to the front office, I thought, *Okay, now I'm going to face the music.* I was ready for whatever punishment they were going to hand out. I even looked forward to it. Jeremy had been dead for almost two months, and I understood no more about why he'd been murdered than I did the night it happened. The murders had occurred in a vacuum, a rift in the fabric of space and time that left no trace, no shred of evidence. I wanted confirmation that actions had consequences.

The assistant principal opened his office door and motioned me inside. He pointed to one of the chairs facing the desk. In the other chair sat a heavyset man clad in denim, both jacket and jeans, a gold badge clipped to his belt, a different man than I'd talked to at the neighbor's house. "You were friends with that boy," the principal said.

"Yes, sir," I said.

"It's been a hard couple of months." He bobbed his head, lightly.

"Yes, sir."

"This detective would like to ask you a few questions. That all right?"

"Yes, sir."

The detective shifted in the chair. He tried to look casual by leaning on an elbow. He asked me one question: "Was your friend Jeremy ever mixed up in any gangs?"

I laughed, though I didn't think the question was funny. The assistant principal laced his fingers together and stared down at his desk. The detective flipped through his notebook, turning the spiral-bound pages, searching for another question. The crime had appeared on the front page of the *Chronicle* for two days after it happened, but not once since. I'd heard, secondhand from my mother or the parent of a teammate—someone who knew someone who worked with Mr. Woodley or Greg—that the sheriff's department had searched both of their offices, seizing filing cabinets and removing the hard drives from their computers, and I knew that Mr. and Mrs. Woodley's companies had both put up money for a reward in exchange for information leading to an arrest. But in two months, nothing had been learned. The person who had arranged to buy the Woodleys' piano had only given a first name, left no phone number, and had never come forward. Investigators had dusted for fingerprints, but nothing had come of that either. And still, I'd held out hope that the sheriff's department had determined a motive and identified the suspects and had gone silent in order to build their case before making an arrest, and to possibly lure the killers into the open. Despite the feeling I had while staring at the bloody carpets behind the Woodleys' garage, that maybe Jeremy had been raptured from earth by God's own hand, I knew a crime had been committed. No matter how improbable the murders appeared, or how unlikely the victims, they had happened, and whoever was responsible remained in the world, waking up each morning with the knowledge of what he, or she, had done. Someone, somewhere, knew something.

Watching the assistant principal sign my hall pass so I could return to class, I saw that my delusions hadn't been wrong after all. Jeremy was simply *gone*. No one knew anything about the murders. Probably no one ever would.

December came, and with it the dark season. I arrived at the pool before sunrise and left it after the last of the light had drained from the sky. I went to visit my father and stepmother at Christmas, but I didn't talk about moving to California, and my father didn't ask me about it. Rather than refuse to come back, as I'd once planned, I went to the airport with my sister and boarded the plane and flew home.

The swimming team began to fall apart. Curt Wood locked himself in his car outside the pool and stayed there for hours. I knocked on the window, but he wouldn't let me in. Allen Swift wrecked his Honda CR-X twice before the collision that sent his girlfriend through the windshield. She went to prom with stitches crisscrossing her face, little railroad tracks from her eye to her jaw, and along the bone of her nose to her mouth. Trey Smith displaced his rage into hate and became a skinhead. He was an All-American with scholarship offers from the best swimming programs in the country, but now he wore ox-blood red Dr. Martens boots that rose above the curve of his calves and carried in his pocket a six-inch steel lag bolt, thick enough to join bridge girders, encased from top to bottom in chromed hexagonal nuts. It made his fist twice as large, ten times as heavy.

With Trey and Mike and Ted, I ventured into Houston's decaying inner-city wards, neighborhoods without streetlamps or lighted storefronts, neighborhoods with police cameras mounted to telephone poles. We went to poorly lit, spartanly furnished clubs, if clubs is the right word — cramped, boxy spaces without tables or chairs or windows, linoleum on the floor and walls, peopled by a mix of scalped young men and tattooed women, black men in groups of seven or eight, and grizzled gray-haired men you approached if you wanted a beer or a joint or a bump of acid. No one checked IDs at the door. I caught myself looking for Jeremy among the bizarre bodies and unfriendly faces. He seemed to show up in pieces, as though his body had been broken down and distributed to a thousand people. The bartender had received the back of Jeremy's head; the black-haired woman leaning over the balcony his pursed lips. The curious thing about memory, I discovered, was how much of it I had. I'd never consciously paid attention to the idiosyncrasies of Jeremy's body while he was alive, but here, surrounded by strangers, I could identify enough parts of him to fuse together a disjointed whole. It was, in its way, a pleasurable experience, and it kept me coming back.

The bands were all thrash-punk. The drummer pounded away with his eyes closed, the two guitarists leaned forward to crank the strings as though drop starting a chainsaw, the vocalist dripped sweat as he ran the length of the stage and screamed. There was a song that started out with a low, tempered riff on the bass and the singer whispering "Hi" into the microphone. He said "Hi" three times in a row — the first, a statement greeting the crowd the way musicians do, the second time louder, a question, and the third, a full-lunged, desperate wail. At that instant, the rest of the band launched into its electric protest, and the crowd began to brawl. In time I learned to recognize the band and the song, and I felt a flutter of anticipation whenever the singer mumbled the first "Hi." I lived in it in different ways. Sometimes I imagined Jeremy saying "Hi" when he opened the front door to the men who would end his life: his first "Hi" trusting and unassuming, his final "Hi" his plea to live as the revolver pressed against his skull. Other times I heard the band's words as my own, directed toward the killers, the singer's screams my screams when I let loose my fear and rage. I stood beside the woofer, the bass thumping in my face until my ears began to ring. I ground my teeth, banged my head.

The stage lights burned the rank air as they flashed from white to red to blue. Three security guards in yellow Windbreakers sat on the edge of the stage, pushing back the audience members who scrambled up to dive, backward, into the crowd. Some stood in place and punched at the air, others stomped in a circle, throwing their shoulders. Trey Smith fought the hardest and emerged from the pit with his knuckles and elbows streaked with blood, his eyes swollen. I liked the shoving and slugging, the anonymous slamming bodies, the armpits and sweat-drenched hair and bare backs, bodies hurtling from the stage, the atavistic urge to climb up from the swarming hive and crawl along the tops of heads and shoulders. I thought of the day the assistant principal had called me to his office to talk to the detective: After I left, I'd wandered the halls before returning to class. My high school had three thousand students, and more than two hundred teachers and coaches, but that day, I didn't see a single soul in the corridor. All the doors were closed, the lights in the ceiling dim. The entire school, and the world, felt vacant, as though Jeremy's death was the spark of an apocalypse, and soon everyone on earth, all the good people of the world, would begin to disappear. I took comfort in the claustrophobic heat, the beery sweat and body odor, the thump and strobe. Twice I took a fist in the eye, and after the second time, I grew cautious. Whatever period of good luck I'd been granted by the murders was over. I felt vulnerable and exposed, and I worried if the next awful thing was destined for me.

Once, on a long bus ride to a swimming meet on the southeast side of Houston, Jeremy had laid his *Sports Illustrated* against his chest and said to me, "I have an endless fascination with the female breast. I can't imagine ever getting tired of it." We laughed and held our hands cupped in front of our chests, imagining what such a thing might feel like. In Jeremy's absence now, my friends entered sex with the same violent abandon they entered drugs and music. They called it "fucking"—not "getting laid" or "going all the way" or "doing the nasty," but the baldest, hardest word they knew. They didn't want to have sex; they wanted to fuck. I wanted sex, too, and no less intensely than they did. I pondered girls' bras beneath their blouses, their cleavage when they wore tank tops or V-necks, the perfume Darcy Garbarek wore every day to geometry, the way she held her hair in her fist, exposing her slender neck whenever she took an exam. But the way my friends described *fucking* sounded to me like the opposite of eros; it sounded like two bodies feeding on one another, each trying to consume the other before they were themselves consumed. Since the murders, I'd felt as though I was detaching from the world, from other people, losing my capacity for human connection. I wanted confirmation that I was good, not permission to be bad.

It's possible my friends felt this way, too, and saw sex, however fleeting, as a way to hold on to another person. I'd see Mike Collins or Chris Mangold holding hands with a girl in the hallway, and the next week I'd see the same girl crying inside a huddle of her friends. I'd know without being told what had happened. I knew about, and had myself driven, the newly paved roads cut into the pines behind the McDonald's, the Safeway, and the Woodleys' church. The roads were for a new subdivision that hadn't yet gone under construction; without streetlamps, out of view from the constables who patrolled the neighborhood, the cul-de-sacs were the perfect places to park. Parties raged deep in the woods, hidden from the headlights of any passing car. Trey and Mike and Chris dropped acid in the woods and spent the night lying in the dirt, the stars falling through the pines. They took girls there more than any other place. Through their retellings, I learned the shape of a dozen girls' bodies: where they were fat and where they were lean, the colors of their underwear, the words they whispered when the boys wriggled and thrust.

In April, one morning after practice had ended and the rest of the team had gone on to school, I found Curt Wood in the locker room. He had his ex-girlfriend pinned against the wall. The vein in his bicep was pulsing, as thick as a shoelace. His ex-girlfriend's face was swollen, red, and wet with tears. "Get out of here!" he yelled to me. He held her by the neck with one hand and pointed at me with the other. "Get the hell out of here! This doesn't concern you." The girl, a tiny blond freshman, fourteen years old, yelped a weak little "help." It was the most terrified sound I'd ever heard.

I thought of Jeremy. Over the past months, his murder had come to feel like the source of every terror and sadness, his death a scene I imagined every time I saw someone crying in the school corridor, every time the phone rang late at night. Now in the locker room I saw the tendons in Curt's hand flex as he tightened his grip, and I thought of what Jeremy's last few minutes might have been like: the rope binding his ankle to his brother's, the deafening ring of the bullets piercing his brother's skull, the certain dread his own life was over. I wondered if he cried, and I saw his eyes squeezed shut, his trembling jaw, his chest heaving as he felt the barrel against the back of his head. Ten minutes before he'd been laughing on the phone with me.

I grabbed Curt's shoulder and pulled him back. I put myself between him and his ex-girlfriend, who quickly fled the locker room with her hands covering her face. Curt stumbled back a step, then spun around and pushed me. I pushed him back, the heels of my palms dead in his chest, as hard as I could. His back slapped against the lockers. His eyes widened, surprised. He was built more like a football player than a swimmer, with thick round arms and a solid chest. If he chose to fight me, I would lose. All the same, I was willing. I wanted to punch him, in fact. I wanted Curt to swing at me so I'd have a reason to ram my fist between his eyes. I'd never punched anyone in the face before, but now I squared up with Curt's face, aimed for the top of his nose.

He came toward me with both fists raised. I bit down to brace my jaw, expecting his punch to land there. Curt's arm sailed past my ear. He hooked his elbow around my neck and pulled my head until our ears were pressed together. I tightened my stomach and tried to duck out of his grip, but he held on tight. Then I heard him begin to sob. He let go of me and sat down in a puddle outside the showers. "She wouldn't listen," he said. "I only wanted to talk."

Curt wasn't a bad boy. None of my friends were. They were once loyal, generous, large-hearted boys. But one of us was missing, for unexplained and unfathomable reasons, and in his place the seeds of darkness had taken hold. Like a root in search of water, that darkness had snaked into the hearts of every person I knew, souring every good intention.

"I just wanted to talk," Curt said again. He shook his head, then looked up at me. I could tell he wanted me to stay with him. He was asking for my help. But my own good intentions had gone, too, and I left him there, sitting in the puddle, alone.

The Open Door

At the end of May, my mother and I struck a compromise. She'd allow me to spend the summer with my father, ten weeks instead of the regular three, so long as I promised to return with Devin after her short visit at the end of August. My mother agreed I needed a break from Houston.

Sitting beside her in the airport, I heard my name called over the public address system. My mother shrugged, surprised, and I went to the phone bank to answer. My stepfather was on the line. "I just wanted to tell you to have a good summer," he said. "Remember that your mom will be waiting for you to come home."

"I'm coming back," I said.

"I'm counting on you," he said.

When I returned to the gate, my mother was staring out the window and crying. A big-haired blond woman farmed through her purse for a tissue and offered it to her. "I promise I'll come back," I said. "It's not like last time. Things are different now."

"I believe you," she said. She pressed the tissue beneath her eyelashes, to keep from smudging her mascara. "But it's sad anyway."

My father and stepmother lived in Laguna Beach, in a little yellow bungalow hidden behind an overgrown hedge of oleander. The house was less than a third the size of our house in Houston, but it was only a few blocks from the beach and had a redwood deck overhanging a garden where he leaned three waterlogged surfboards, a brakeless bicycle for me to ride, and a rusted weight bench—all of which he'd rescued from trash piles.

My stepmother grew dill and mint in terra-cotta pots, brewed iced tea in glass jars along the railing. She prepared her Bible study notes in her bathing suit, the morning sun electric on her dome of curled blond hair. Her daughter, my stepsister Stacie, worked in a ladies' clothing shop in downtown Laguna Beach where the surfers slept in the backs of Volkswagen Buses or lay in the sand with their wet suits peeled to their waists.

An old hippie set up his easel in Heisler Park where he used the tip of his long beard to paint the coastline. Honeysuckle popped along the fences, and from my father's dining room we could see the wash of blue between the eucalyptus trees.

My father had always talked about living in a surfing town. He embraced the place as both the fulfillment of a dream and a release from the obligations of his old life. The trouble between him and my mother had started when the printing company he had worked for had shut down, five years earlier. My father had tried to strike out on his own; printing wasn't paying, so he worked to broker natural gas rights in Mexico. He and his business partner, Arturo, sat on the back patio with legal pads and the phone cord snaked through the open backdoor. Arturo's gold watch matched the chain-link bracelet he wore on the other wrist—symbols of his success to my father, but for my mother a reason to disapprove. In addition to gas, my father and Arturo also tried importing oranges and shrimp. It was a vague business. My father no longer left the house before dawn in a suit or carried a briefcase. He was now home when I got off the bus after school, sitting on the back patio in his undershirt and shorts. In an effort to get their shipments through customs, my father and Arturo drove all night to Nuevo Laredo or Brownsville, and afterward, turned around and drove straight back so they wouldn't have to spend money on a motel. Other times he and Arturo went farther, into the mountains near Guadalajara. He came home with stories of smoky cockfighting arenas and fan boats in the Centla Swamps, and with wooden spinners and puka shell necklaces for my sister and me, but no lasting business. The big petroleum companies controlled too many gas rights for him to get a foothold, and the oranges and shrimp rotted on the docks at the border.

Next he sold cheesecakes to local bakeries and catering companies. I remember the day he sat cross-legged on his bedroom floor in his shorts and undershirt, talking on the phone, doing his best to sound dispassionate and professional even though his cheeks were flushed. He hung up the phone, then clapped his hands, looked to the ceiling, and said, "Please work!" A month later, when the catering company couldn't come through with the order, he polished up a box of petrified redwood, one of those originless artifacts that had floated around the garage since the beginning of time, and sold the pieces as paperweights at the local flea market. He made $20 for the day.

My father accused my mother of spending money they didn't have. We were living off of savings, and she needed to make sacrifices. "Sacrifices?" my mother said, and pointed to the dining room, an empty space without a table or a single chair. Already she'd watched the Davidsons, our neighbors, bring home a boat, and the Accardos a new car, and said she'd be humiliated if Devin and I showed up to school in faded jeans or worn-out sneakers. She said working with Arturo was a dead end. He needed to find a real job so they could get back to normal.

My father met my stepmother when he gave in to my mother's demands and took a position as the Houston regional manager of a printing company based in Seal Beach, California. My stepmother was a saleswoman in his office. She'd come to Houston from Long Beach six years earlier, when she and her first husband had left their jobs as missionaries. A few months later, the Sunday before Labor Day, my father told my mother he'd fallen in love. I listened to my mother scream through the closed bedroom door for an entire afternoon. Once an hour, during commercials, I went to the door and stood before it. The door appeared to shake, as though waves were crashing against it. I pressed my hand to the wood but was afraid to knock and instead slipped back down the hallway to the tiled corridor, the other side of the house, the television. Devin and I raided the cupboards and waited. Hours later, when the door finally opened, my father was holding a duffel bag.

In California, my father was glad he no longer had a yard to mow or neighbors to compete with for stature. His immediate neighbors, in fact, were statureless. The painter next door shared his apartment with a man who cranked the parking meters for the city. In the studio apartments up and down the street lived a spate of divorced men who had by choice or circumstance left behind career ambitions and families to live near the beach. I knew them only by their first names, Ron and Andy and Bud, names already truncated, as though to suggest only the thinnest connections to the people they used to be.

My room was a five-by-eight closet off the dining room, barely wide enough for the collapsible love seat that doubled as my bed. My clothes hung from a bar on the back of the door. My stepmother said it had been a sewing room in the '30s, when the house was built, but it felt to me like a space an artist or a monk might inhabit, where the mind could be undistracted and free to roam the universe. I lay on my foam bed, my feet sticking out the bottom of the blankets, and watched the sunlight move across the wall and smelled the oleander and eucalyptus and salt water drift through the open window and remembered the landscapes I'd passed over during my flight, the dark Texas pines browning into mountains and canyons. As the plane began its descent, the ocean appeared, blue and infinite, my own destiny manifest. The flight had only taken three hours, and I'd done it so many times over the last few years I'd grown used to it, but this time I'd felt the miles stretch out below, the scale of the distance between the city I had left and the one where I was going.

I tried to think about Jeremy, but away from Houston I found it increasingly difficult to hold on to him. He'd skulked around my every thought for weeks after his death, walking across the stage in most of my dreams. In the curious way shock works, he'd been almost *more* present in death than in life. That shock had worn off, and a slower and less adrenaline-infused version had taken its place, one that looped back to the first days after the murders when all I did was drive around: in one beat-up old car or another, in my father's sterilized rental car, to the funeral service and the reception afterward. Or in Drivers Ed, where, whenever I wasn't practicing driving, I was sitting behind a fake steering wheel watching a simulator film and pretending to drive. The car in the film, like all the cars I rode in, never went anyplace specific. The more I returned to those hot, stark days, the more Jeremy's absence cemented itself inside me. He edged toward the periphery of my mind, which in turn made the reasons for his disappearance all the less knowable. Murder no longer seemed adherent to a particular set of circumstances, a thing one person did to another for a specific reason. It was just something that happened, and it could happen to anyone at anytime.

My stepmother had grown up in Hollywood, where her mother had been a stuntwoman in the 1950s. She watched old black-and-white movies and reruns of *I Love Lucy*, and pointed out the actresses her mother had stood in for, porcelain-faced women with dewy eyes in the camera's hot gaze. "It sounds like a more charmed life than it was," my stepmother said. In fact, it was anything but charmed. Riding a motorcycle off a cliff didn't exactly support three children. Some months they didn't have enough money for food, and my stepmother and her younger brother and sister had stood in line at the food bank. "I swore I'd never drink powdered milk again," she said.

On a Saturday trip to Los Angeles, she pointed out the iconic JESUS SAVES sign that once stood atop the Church of the Open Door. The original building was gone, but the sign had been rescued from a scrapyard and now topped the old United Artists Theater. "That's where I came to Christ," she announced. "Not there, but in the old building. But I'll never forget that sign." A couple in her neighborhood took her to a revival at the original Church of the Open Door, its amphitheater-like stage as grand as the Hollywood Bowl. She'd met her first husband there, when she was fourteen. They'd married when she was eighteen, and Stacie was born two months after she turned twenty-one. A year after they moved to Texas, her husband collapsed and died on the living room floor. He'd just turned thirty-five.

My stepmother's father had spent twenty years in prison, she hardly spoke to her brother or sister, and she'd raised her daughter mostly on her own. Now that she'd found my father she didn't want to let him go. She and my father shared a space on the couch big enough for one. She coiled her arms around his neck and put her head beneath his shirt to smooch his belly. "Honey," my father said. "The kids."

"This is where they should see it," she said. "In a healthy home."

"They do this every night," Stacie said, shaking her head.

My stepmother praised my father's every move, his every idea, laughed at every joke with her big raucous laugh—all things my father complained my mother had never done. My stepmother was intent on becoming the antithesis of the person she'd replaced. Because my mother had been a spendthrift, my stepmother was frugal. She bought her clothes at discount stores, remainder racks, even yard sales. My mother had been critical of my father's business failures in Houston, so my stepmother was endlessly adoring. She was this way, she said, because of Jesus. My family had been Catholic before the divorce, though hardly passionate and only occasionally regular. My father had attended out of obligation to his parents, who lived in Connecticut and whom we saw only every few years. Raised a non-observant Unitarian, my mother preferred to mouth the hymns rather than sing them aloud, and during the service she stared up into the rafters or gazed around the pews. My stepmother, in contrast, claimed her love for my father flowed directly from her love for Christ. She quoted Paul's letter to the Ephesians: "The husband is the head of the wife as Christ is the head of the church, his body, of which he is the Savior. Now as the church submits to Christ, so also wives should submit to their husbands in everything." "Do you know what that means?" she asked me one morning while we were eating breakfast on the deck.

"The man's the boss?" I said.

My father sat shirtless between us, his coffee mug steaming on the table. He lifted both arms and flexed his biceps. His sternum bounced the gold cross hanging around his neck. "Dad's the boss," he said.

My stepmother laughed, pressed her palm against his bare shoulder. "Yes," she said. "But there's more to it. Paul's saying that a wife should not just respect her husband, but *revere* him in the same way that the Church reveres Jesus. Do you know what 'revere' means?"

I knew what it meant, but given the context I wondered if "revere" meant something else. I said, "Worship? Wives should worship their husbands?"

"Not exactly," she said. "We only worship Jesus." She licked her index finger and turned the page in her Bible study workbook. "Another way of reading the verse is this way: 'Let the wife see that she respects and reverences her husband—that she notices him, regards him, honors him, prefers him, venerates, and esteems him; and that she defers to him, praises him, and loves and admires him exceedingly.'" She looked up and said the last word again: "*Exceedingly*. This is God's prescription for a happy marriage. If more wives lived by these words, divorce would become rare. Of course, too many women do exactly the opposite."

My father nodded in her direction, suggesting what she said was the truth, plain as day. Neither mentioned my mother, but they didn't have to.

My mother and father were separated for nine months before they finally filed for divorce, and for a while I was hopeful they'd get back together. My father brought my mother a dozen long-stemmed roses in a beveled green vase for her birthday. When he came over on Sundays for dinner, he and my mother walked together along the bayou and golf course and talked about buying a new car, possibly selling our house and moving to a new city. They sat together at the kitchen counter and penciled out a budget. They made plans. My father said he wanted to come home, but he had one condition: My mother had to agree to start going to church, and not back to the Catholic parish, but to a church where the people knew Jesus. Jesus was the one thing he would not give up. Going to church alone wasn't an option, he said. Christ needed to be the center of the family, of her life as well as his. My mother had never shown much concern for saving her soul, but she had no intention of giving it away. She refused to abide by a faith that proclaimed the supremacy of the traditional family even while its members tore our family apart. Her refusal, my father argued, was the reason he and my mother couldn't make the marriage work.

The evidence that my father's new life was better than his old—his life with me—was abundant. My mother and stepfather fought with each other as vehemently as ever, and as hard as my mother had once fought with my father, but in California whole weeks passed without a fight, without finding anything broken in the trash can the next morning. Friends dropped in unannounced and my stepmother demanded they stay for dinner. My father played the music he and my mother had once listened to together—Crosby, Stills, and Nash, Credence, and Buffalo Springfield—and sang along while he cracked ice into his vodka after coming up from the beach. I remembered him acting this way years before, when Devin was a baby and we lived in a smaller house in Houston, my mother laughing at his jokes, the two of them bumping hips while they sang together in the kitchen. It was as though my father had not only begun a new life but also had found a way to reach through time and reconnect with his old self, with the person he'd been before the economy tanked and my mother turned angry—long before divorce and murder had any place in my universe. For a while last spring, I grew obsessed with puzzling out how a single, spontaneous decision might have spared Jeremy's life. If I could have found a way to travel back in time, I would have had to nudge him out of his house for only twenty minutes in order to save him. As preposterous as the idea sounded, my stepmother claimed that for God, time travel was possible because God was not bound by time at all. My father, it seemed, was living proof of just such a possibility. He hadn't discovered his true self in California; he'd reclaimed it from the past.

My father stood up from the table and went to the deck railing. The sun through the marine layer glowed on his shoulders. He stepped up on the crossbeam and set both hands flat against his eyebrows. He looked through the eucalyptus trees, toward the ocean, and whistled. "I can see foam on the surface," he said. I could practically reach out and touch his excitement. "That means the surf is really big. This could be an epic day."

My stepmother's church was in the next town over, on the inland side of Laguna Canyon. The road there traveled through a bygone California, a mobile home park on one side of the highway, a chain of artists' studios and surfboard shapers on the other, then up through the orange groves, out of the cool coastal fog, and down into the sprawling suburban landscape of Lake Forest and Aliso Viejo, which from the crest of the hill resembled an enormous tic-tac-toe board, the streets laid out in grids, full of square houses beneath triangle roofs.

The church was adjacent to Leisure World, an enormous retirement village that occupied most of the city where the church was located. On Sunday mornings, the shuttle buses to and from the village ran every ninety minutes. Other congregants arrived in golf carts. But down the hill, the cities of Aliso Viejo and Lake Forest were exploding with young families. My stepmother said her ministry, and the church, were growing larger by the week.

Palm trees and recessed Malibu lights lined the walkway from the parking lot to the church campus—not a single structure, but a compound the size of a small college. The fountain in the central plaza flowed over a concrete terrace into a rectangular wading pool. I noticed the steps leading down into the water. "For baptisms," my stepmother said.

Instead of a choir draped in robes, a five-piece electric rock band led the congregation in "praise and worship." The lyrics of the songs were projected onto a JumboTron screen suspended from the ceiling. There wasn't a cross behind the pulpit, or even a pulpit to stand behind. The pastor paced the stage with a microphone clipped to his collar. The senior pastor wore a suit and tie, but the associate pastor—a young, tanned man with a shock of curly hair—preferred to preach in a golf shirt, the microphone receiver holstered on the waist of his khakis. "This isn't a church," he said, his hands on his hips. "We might look like one, but we're not. We're a community of Jesus followers. And here's another newsflash: No one in this room is religious. We're not here in service of some religion. If you're looking for religion, you've come to the wrong place. This is a relationship with God. We meet Jesus here. We get to know him." This brand of Christianity, the associate pastor explained, cut away every liturgical and canonical tradition, every division between denominations; it dispensed with every candle and vestment, every specter of religiosity, and instead interacted directly with Jesus. So true a form of religion it transcended the very word.

I knew my father's attraction to this place was connected to my stepmother, and to the fact that the church represented an about-face from Catholicism. But there was more to it than that. My father's life as a suburban Catholic had ended in disaster, and given a second chance, he was going to do things differently. He was going to swim in the ocean everyday, rain or shine. He was going to sleep with the windows open. Unlike the other men on his street who in their disillusionment with suburban life dropped out of it altogether, my father understood the church was suburban life idealized. The screen hanging from the ceiling was larger than any TV in any home, and the pastor wore his golf shirt like it was one of the perks of the job. Even the dramatic skits that preceded the sermon took place on an oversized orange sofa, as though the stage were a living room. Encased in a halo of light shining down from the ceiling, the air stirred by the faint tinkle of piano music piped in through the speakers hidden in the wall, the sofa looked like the Platonic form of sofas, the sofa from which all other sofas were copied. Immune from the decay of time, a shield against divorce and strife, heartache and despair, a home no evil could invade. The message was not lost on me. With Christ as the center of the family, the family became immutable. For those without families, those whose families had been blown apart, the fellowship of Jesus was there to take its place—more permanent and dependable than any family on earth. I wanted to walk up on stage and sit on that couch forever.

On Tuesday evening, my father and I drove to the rocky cove on the backside of the picnic area at Corona del Mar. A thousand people crowded the beach and the stairs leading up from the cove and sandstone outcroppings above it. Striped towels were spread out on the sand. A man in a white shirt and khaki shorts stood knee-deep in the rising tide, playing the guitar and singing. The crowd on the beach was singing, too, their palms spread open as though to press against the air, as though

God's spirit was *right there* and all you had to do was reach out and touch it. My father closed his eyes. He wasn't ordinarily given to acts of piety, but tonight it was hard to resist.

One by one, people walked out of the crowd and into the water. They crossed their arms over their chests, held their noses, and were dipped backward into the waves. They came up gulping and wiping the hair from their eyes. They took their time walking back to shore, trailing their fingers in the sea as though the water's chemistry had changed them and the ocean would be different the next time they saw it. Behind the guitar player the sky turned orange, and the stretched shoreline of Catalina Island emerged through the smog. A woman walked from the ocean with her wet T-shirt clinging to her stomach and breasts. She stood on the shore and flung her long hair forward and wrung out the seawater, working her fists from her scalp to the dripping ends. Behind her the sun slipped below the horizon and flashed green across the surface, a wink before departing. The sunlight caught in the water that fell from her hair. A man standing in the ocean lifted his hands, palms up, and closed his eyes. Another fell backward and disappeared beneath the waves.

My father and I swam in the ocean every night at dusk. If the swell was up we surfed—I was comfortable in the water and learned quickly—and if the waves were flat, we snorkeled around the reef until we couldn't see the bottom. My father said, "Here," and I kicked down into the frigid depths to grab a handful of sand, proof I'd touched the bottom. No matter how far down I had to swim, how black and cold, I had to touch the bottom. I'd learned to hold my breath when I was small by clinging to his shoulders while he dove toward the bottom of the diving well in our neighborhood pool, the shadowed grates to the pumps like a door in the earth's crust, a realm accessible only to him and to me. Now I felt I had to show my father I could go with him wherever he went, even to the bottom of the ocean. And I liked the sea floor, the pressure on my lungs, the rippled, untouched sand. Seeing the bottom emerge through the dark, I felt as though I was descending toward the surface of the moon. With fins and a good deep breath, I could dive thirty-five feet.

One warm night I slipped out of the house and walked down to the beach to watch the lobster hunters. They cracked glow-sticks and slid backward into the tide as their fins slapped the sand. The divers kicked along the bottom in groups of six and eight, pods of light trailing along the surface marking their position and direction. I swam out with my mask and snorkel and hovered in their green light, the phytoplankton illuminated in a whirl around my head, and circled down to the bottom to watch their sign language, their slow-motion reaching into the tight crags and cracks of the reef. When I waved to one of the divers, his eyes bulged inside his mask. I imagined him telling his companions about me: *Did you see the kid freediving with no wet suit?* and his friends jabbing his ribs with their elbows, *Sure, sure, a kid, out here, at eleven o'clock at night, maybe you should lay off the compressed air*, until the diver himself began to wonder if I'd been only a hallucination.

I surfaced and swam beyond the edge of the cove, into the open ocean. The waves out there were rolling, big and shapeless. The bottom was a long way down. The coastline was lit up—all the lights from the houses and restaurants and streetlamps and cars, all those lost souls, all broken, blended, and misbegotten, all ascending the hill like a gigantic wave pitching up to crash into the sea. All around me, phytoplankton glowed like stars in the moonlight. I felt like I had entered a world unhinged from the laws of physics, without a floor or ceiling or sides. It felt like the door through time I'd been looking for last spring; if I dove to the bottom and touched the sand I could return to last September and rescue Jeremy before it was too late. Except I didn't want to go back in time. I wanted to be right were I was—here in the ocean, away from all of it, offshore, unprotected, and alone.

I swam back across the lobster hunters' green pods of light, and when I reached the sand, I climbed up onto the lifeguard's chair. The wind off the ocean was cool and sharp. The tide advanced up the beach, erasing my footprints, until it began to lick at the camp the divers had left behind. A wave swept in and soaked a towel. The next carried off a flip-flop, the rubber sole a tiny raft on the water. A plastic eyeglasses case followed. I climbed down from the chair and considered gathering up the stuff to move to higher ground, but the wind had picked up and I'd grown cold. I didn't want to give up my fantasy that I was invisible, a phantom of the diver's imagination. I climbed the stairs to the street and walked home.

I awoke the next morning with my head full of mucus, my cheeks and jaw sore. My stepmother told me I shouldn't go to the beach that day.

Rain was forecast, and she said it would only make my cold worse. But the storm had kicked up the swell, my father and some friends were going surfing at Brooks Street, and I didn't want to miss it. The next day I had a deep, wheezing cough, and by evening I had a fever. "The rain washes the grime and bacteria from the streets into the ocean," my father said. "You probably should have stayed back."

"It was fun, though," I said. I lay beneath two blankets and an old quilt that smelled of the cardboard box in which it had been stored. I held my hands inside my knees, trying to get warm.

My father stood shirtless in my doorway, peeling an orange with his thumb. Juice burst from it each time he tore off a hunk of the rind. No fruit had ever looked sweeter. "You want one?" he asked me. "Packed with vitamin C."

"Sure," I said. "Maybe a glass of juice, too."

He peeled the orange for me and brought me a tall glass of apple juice. The orange burned my throat going down, but the tangy sweet that lingered in my mouth was worth it. An hour later, when I stood up to walk to the bathroom, the urge to vomit was too strong to resist. "Oh man," my father said as I crawled back to bed.

My father went for the sponge and my stepmother came in with the thermometer. "Oranges and apple juice probably weren't the best idea," she said. "Plain toast would have been smarter." She knelt down and brushed the hair away from my forehead, touched my cheeks with the back of her hand. "You're really hot," she said. She pinched the thermometer and held it at arm's length before zooming it right to the end of her nose. "105, holy cow! You need to get into the bathtub."

I crawled to the bathroom on my hands and knees. The water felt ice-cold when I stuck my hand in, but my stepmother told me it was the only way to get my fever down. She closed the door so I could get undressed. "Are you in?" she called.

"I'm in," I said. I was shivering. All the heat from my skin was leeching away. My stepmother opened the door and reached her arm around to toss a washcloth into the water. I covered myself and she pushed the door open and sat down on the toilet lid with her Bible. "Give me a sec," she said.

Her Bible had a burgundy vinyl case with handles for easy toting. Zipped shut, it looked like a square purse. Inside it my stepmother stuffed photographs, sermon notes, bookmarks calligraphied with scripture. She read from it every morning. Watching her eyes travel over the words, the slight movement in her lips as she recited the verses under her breath, I felt if I stared hard enough I'd see the spirit itself rise from the page. Not only did she read the Bible literally, to the words, their very arrangement and ordination, she ascribed mystical, even magical qualities. Spoken aloud, they had the power to heal. When her migraines attacked, she tapped her face and forehead with her index and middle fingers, chanting, "The Lord your God is with you, he is mighty to save. He will take great delight in you, he will quiet you with his love, he will rejoice over you with singing."

The tissue-thin pages crackled as she flipped them. She turned toward the end. "Here we go." She straightened her back and began to read. "'When Jesus came into Peter's house, he saw Peter's mother-in-law lying in bed with a fever. He touched her hand and the fever left her, and she got up and began to wait on him. When evening came, many who were demon-possessed were brought to him, and he drove out the spirits with a word and healed all the sick. This was to fulfill what was spoken through the prophet Isaiah: He took up our infirmities and carried our diseases.'"

She leaned over the tub, placed her hand on my forehead. "Lord, in your son's precious name, we ask you to bring David's fever down." She opened her eyes and looked down at me. "Feel any better?"

"Not yet," I said. I lifted my elbow from the water. The faint wave in the tub made me seasick. "I think I might barf some more."

She didn't move from the toilet. "Let's say some of these verses together. 'He took up our infirmities and carried our diseases.' Now you try it."

I lay back in the water, closed my eyes. "'He took up our infirmities and carried our diseases.'" I repeated.

"Any better now?" she asked.

I opened my eyes. My stepmother was leaning forward, her hands folded together, waiting for my answer.

I had a hard time finding a summer job, so I filled in as best I could. My stepmother hired me to paint the church's education building and to clean out the store closets in the classrooms. When that was finished, I rolled posters and shrink-wrapped lithograph prints for the artist who lived next door. I dug out a long strip of hardened cheatgrass from the backside of a carpenter's workshop. I went door-to-door with a bucket and sponge, offering to wash cars. I didn't have any friends, and I didn't mind. I spent every afternoon at the beach, and on my days off, I rode with my father to his sales calls. His territory ranged from Sherman Oaks, north of Los Angeles, to Oceanside, north of San Diego. I was happy to ride along wherever he went. I was happy just to be with him again.

Passing through the lobby of an office building, my father stepped back into his salesman's clothes, like Superman spinning through the revolving door in the opposite direction to return to his Clark Kent disguise. He was charming, quick with a joke, an ace at talking his way past the receptionist and administrative assistants. When he visited his vendors, he greeted the janitors by name, shook hands with the press operators and typesetters. He was neither brash nor flirtatious; he was friendly, easy to talk to. He swore when the situation called for it. As he had in Texas, he received no salary other than the commissions from his sales. He never entered a building without his tie crisp and straight, his breath rinsed with the peppermint oil he kept in the glove compartment.

In the car between calls, however, he listened to the AM talk station. For as long as I could remember, he'd liked talk shows, liked banter and argument, liked talk, though back in Texas the talk was mostly about strategies for selling and motivating corporate teams. Now the talk was about religion, and politics, and the imminent peril of the country. He listened to Rush Limbaugh and Dr. Laura and then punched over to the Christian station and listened to Chuck Smith and James Dobson. They all said more or less the same things: America had grown too liberal, and its traditional foundations were eroding. Soon the well of grace would run dry. Nations that turned away from God would be turned away by him. Wars would spark overnight. Planes would plummet from the sky.

My father's Honda Prelude sat so low to the ground I imagined him changing lanes by sliding the car beneath a semitrailer and emerging on the other side. The cars ahead of us dissolved into the rippling gas vapors. He kept the radio loud to drown out the traffic noise. Now and then my father said, "true," or he pointed to the radio dial and looked at me as if to say, "You hear that?," but most of the time he simply listened and nodded. In this way I was catechized into the Gemini worlds of evangelicalism and political conservatism, the two so tightly entwined I couldn't tell them apart. I assumed Rush Limbaugh was a Christian because he lined up with the people I was told represented true Christianity; likewise, I assumed it was Christian to laugh off evolution and scoff at the idea of chlorofluorocarbons from hair spray canisters having anything to do with the hole in the ozone layer. Or that there *even was* a hole in the ozone layer.

Listening to Dr. Laura's and Dr. Dobson's frothing tirades against promiscuity while my father nodded and pointed, I couldn't help noticing the irony. The voices promoted chastity and marital fidelity, no matter the circumstances, even though infidelity had catapulted my father from Texas to California and landed him in this car, on this freeway, listening to this show. My awareness of this irony had up till now worked as an antidote to my father's faith. I wore the silver cross I'd received the previous summer as jewelry, a totemic connection to my father, rather than as a declaration of my beliefs. Now I wore the cross on Jeremy's silver chain—his mother had given it to me, along with his Nike swim bag and all his caps and goggles—and I was beginning to think of my life as attached to forces other than ordinariness, to God's will rather than chance. Each afternoon when my father and I snorkeled through the reef and I watched the sunlight beam through the kelp and the garibaldi drift among the anemone, I wondered if everything—not only my parents splitting up but the murders, too—were part of a grand design I couldn't see.

Back in my tiny room, my hands folded behind my head, the more I thought about the things I'd heard in my father's car, the more sense they made to me. Rebellion, by definition, is a movement against established authorities or normative values, whatever they may be. It's always defined by its context. I couldn't think of anything that bucked the cultural tide more than if I vowed to preserve my virginity. It smacked of naiveté and brainwashing, of blindness to the realities of the modern world, but in the last year, I'd known too many realities. I'd seen more than I bargained for. I'd seen the bloody carpets upon which my friend and his father and brother were executed, and it stung me to recall how badly I'd failed to live up to my promise to mow the Woodleys' yard, the one other vow I'd made in Jeremy's name. Too much had been lost. I needed something to refuse. I needed something to save.

On Wednesday nights, the teenagers from my father and stepmother's church gathered for youth group at the beach, a few blocks south of our house. My father asked me if I wanted to go. I hadn't spent time with anyone my age in weeks, so I said okay. The other youth groupers were browned from the sun and knew how to surf. Some could surf so well that at fifteen and sixteen they had professional sponsors. They wore logo-screened sweatshirts, and the sun and salt had bleached their matted straw hair yellow-green. They'd packed their surfboards off to the most exotic beaches on the planet, including Fiji and Indonesia and the Galapagos Islands. I'd once fantasized about how moving here would transform me into a Californian like the boys in the youth group, granting me permission to wear clothes like theirs, to call my friends "barney" and "crusher," to shake my hand with my thumb and pinky extended. But that was last summer. Now, after the violence I had witnessed and the loss of my best friend, I wasn't sure who I was supposed to be, which words were permitted and which were earned. I sat cross-legged in the sand, listening to the conversations taking place around me, waiting for the pizza to arrive.

We ate around a four-foot teepee of flames. When the pizza was gone, one of the leaders, a student at the community college, played the guitar and we sang. *The name of the Lord is a strong tower,* the song went, *the righteous run into it, and they are saved.* I didn't know the words, but I sang along as best I could, and when the group prayed, I prayed along with them. Glowing embers drifted into the sky and disappeared, and the ocean crashed in the black night beyond the fire. The onshore breeze felt as though it had blown in from the other side of the globe. I was calm for the first time in almost a year. The leader spoke of the still, small voice of the Holy Spirit, the voice that spoke after the whirlwind, after the earthquake, after the fire, and I heard it. I heard it on the beach and again alone in my narrow room in my father's house, the sea fog pouring in through the open window. Filtered through the jasmine and mint, the voice sounded as though it belonged to this place, the quiet nights, the flaming pyre in the sand, the long car rides along the coast, my father's company: all things unavailable in Texas. With God's help, I might hold on to them a little longer. I might remain in California in spirit if not in body. A small comfort, but enough.

Stacie spent two weeks in July at a summer camp for college students in Colorado Springs where she analyzed "major worldviews" through the lens of Christianity. The afternoon of her return, she sat on the floor of her bedroom, cutting up her once-cherished cassettes with a pair of orange-handled kitchen scissors. She pulled the tape from the spools in long strokes, extending her arm toward the ceiling, as if she were curling ribbon. Her open suitcase sat on the bed, full of books about how Oliver North was a scapegoat in the Iran-Contra affair, how feminism derived from communism, and how bands like The Beatles and Prince and Quiet Riot were lascivious and Satanic. I picked up one of her cassettes. "I'll take these if you don't want them anymore," I said.

"That's not the point," she said. "They shouldn't be in the world. The music shouldn't even be heard."

"The devil's music," I said. I meant it as a joke.

"Exactly," Stacie said, pointing the scissors at me. "If only I'd known before."

That night we went to dinner at the Old Spaghetti Factory in Newport Beach as a welcome home for her. My father liked the restaurant because we could eat for $5 apiece, including salad and dessert. He ordered waters all around before anyone had a chance to ask for a Coke. When the waiter walked away, Stacie said, "I have something I want to say." She sat forward in her chair, her long blond hair falling straight down her back. Her boyfriend, Mike, set his hand between her shoulder blades. "The last two weeks helped me to wake up to the fact that my faith's been too passive. It's not enough to believe. Jesus calls us to work for his kingdom." I turned my eyes to my father. He sat with his arm on my stepmother's chair, a mirror of Mike and Stacie on the other side of the table. My stepmother was starting to cry. The family seated at the next table over looked our way. Could they hear what Stacie was saying? I wondered what they thought.

"I might do something with politics when I graduate," Stacie said. "Lord knows there aren't enough Christians in government. But maybe the most important thing the camp helped me to understand was the value of sexual purity. It's the first step in creating a healthy home." She turned to face Mike. "While I was there, I recommitted myself to keeping a pure body until my wedding night."

Mike nodded. "Me, too."

My stepmother's tears were streaming now. She stood up from her chair, circled the table, wrapped her arms around Stacie's head, and kissed her. My father smiled.

I smiled, too. It was a Saturday night, and beyond the restaurant's windows the sun was setting over the Newport pier and boardwalk and the blue horizon of the Pacific. The wind through the open doors smelled of salt and sunscreen. The valet attendants shouted as they shuffled the cars. We all ordered the same pasta dish, and when our plates were taken away, the waiter brought out silver cups of spumoni. It felt like family, even if my mother and Devin weren't a part of it. We were happy, and our happiness had been wrought by Jesus, the source of everything good and dependable.

After all the hours in my father's car, all the talk radio, all the sermons about the men and women turned into pillars of salt or struck dead for disobeying God's commandments, all the talk about how the leaders in Washington were leading the country toward the precipice of damnation, it was impossible for me to see a life *without* Jesus as anything other than a life of fear—a naked swim across a bottomless ocean where Leviathan himself lurked beneath the surface, waiting for me to cross his line of sight, waiting to pull me under, into hell. And not just the hell that follows death, but the hell of an unprotected life. The hell of murder. The hell of impermanent family. The hell of loneliness. Those hells were at bay, and my stepsister's cassettes were in the garbage. It seemed to me a fair trade.

I was being offered the same choice my father had given my mother a few years earlier: obedience to God in exchange for God's blessings, his protection from future calamity. My mother had been obstinate in her refusal, strong-willed and stubborn. Now the choice had been passed to me, and I didn't hesitate to promise God my entire life. I'd take up his cross and would deny my every want and desire in order to follow him. I'd remain celibate until my wedding night. I'd vote Republican in every election. Scraping the spoon against the side of my dish to catch the last of the ice cream, I felt safer than I had felt in months. Maybe longer. Maybe ever. I hummed the song I'd learned on the beach: "The name of the Lord is a strong tower. The righteous run into it, and they are saved." I had at last run into the tower. There was nothing on earth I wouldn't have traded to stay there.

The Fish Tank

The first week of freshman year: a baffling time when every new student who walks across a college campus emerges on the other side in love and involved, with a new credit card and a new long-distance calling plan. Wandering campus in search of the buildings on my course schedule, I'd been approached by the crew team, the Young Democrats, three fraternities, and a scout for a dating show on the prowl for male contestants. On Tuesday, wearing the Wells Fargo T-shirt I'd gotten with my MasterCard, I followed a freckled beach girl from Santa Cruz to a meeting of the campus fellowship.

The fellowship met in the student center, in a room with carpet on the walls and the floor and partitions that could be folded back to make larger rooms. Scattered among the chairs mingled the very Californians I'd come to live among. A guy in a chambray shirt with blond hair hanging past his shoulders stood talking with two girls in hibiscus-print tank tops, their bare arms and shoulders the color and texture of peanut butter. Against the windows leaned four dudes whose plaid shorts and sheepskin UGG boots looked like deliberate miscalculations, as though their clothes had been snatched at random from a pile in the sand as they ran from the ocean. That they managed to look cool while at the same time not caring how they looked heightened my desire to eavesdrop on their conversation.

"I'll introduce you," Annie said. She seemed to know everyone in the room, though she was a freshman, too, and had been on campus for only as long as I had. She waved to the guys tuning the guitars at the front, hugged a young woman as though they hadn't seen each other in months. She led me over to the blond in the chambray shirt, who stood checking his watch after the girls in the flowered tanks had turned to join a different conversation. "This is Brent," Annie said. "He's the emcee of the meeting."

Brent stuck out his hand. "Great to meet you," he said. "Really great." From across the room Brent had the bad-boy veneer of a singer in a metal band, but closer up he was softer, his cheeks and neck as pale as porcelain. His wire-framed glasses were square, like an engineer's, and his voice was lilting and rhythmic, on the verge of breaking into song. "I'm glad you could join us," he said.

Next Annie steered me toward the surfers, Dan, Paul, another Dan, and Jake. Jake was "on staff" with the campus ministry. "Where are you from?" he asked.

"Laguna Beach," I said. Being from Houston sounded so boring, so hot and flat, where there was little to do besides tip cows and throw horse- shoes and get pregnant. I'd imagined myself a Californian for so many years, and now that I was here for good I aimed to sever all ties with the past. What was Christianity—especially born-again Christianity—if not a platform for radical self-invention? I referred to my father and step- mother as my parents, as though I had no other, as though our common last names and their California address were proof I was a native, even though my room in my father and stepmother's new house doubled as their home office, and my clothes and books had spent the summer in the garage, waiting to be moved into the dorm. I didn't mention Jeremy's name at all, to anyone.

I'd made the mistake of telling the story of his murder to a girl in my dorm the second night after we'd moved in. We were lying on her bed after midnight, the saltwater fog just beginning to accumulate around the lampposts along the sidewalks beyond her open window. It was the kind of indulgent, star-crossed conversation I expected to take part in every night in college. She lay with her cheek on her flattened hands, her straight blond hair tucked behind her ear. We talked about our favorite books, the best concert we'd ever been to, whether or not we'd been in love. Then I told her about Jeremy. She looked at me first with incredulity and then with suspicion; it wasn't the story she suspected but my moti- vations for telling it. I hadn't known her long enough to need her sym- pathy or to explain away an eccentric behavior; the only other possibility was a cheap ploy for affection, possibly sex. "I'm not taking off my shirt," she said.

I left her room feeling ashamed and a little sick. She was right: I had wanted her affection—I wanted her to see me as infinitely worthy of her affection—and I'd used the darkest fact of myself in my effort to win it. If

I made a habit of telling Jeremy's story in this way, for this purpose, the story would quickly become a shtick, and as a shtick it would be predictable, boring. I realized that the story also worked against my new identity as a Californian because it tied me to Houston, to my past life. I vowed to keep Jeremy a secret, and like all secrets, it was an unseen source of tremendous power.

"Laguna Beach?" Jake said. "Do you surf?"

"Yeah," I said. I didn't dress like a surfer, but I owned a board. "Sure."

Jake nodded, crossed his arms. "Good to know."

Brent came to the microphone and asked everyone to find a chair. I settled in beside Annie. Brent closed his eyes. Without prompting, everyone else did the same. "Lord, thank you for this time of fellowship," he said, his mellifluous voice echoing through the speakers. "You say in Matthew that wherever two or three gather in your name, you'll be with us. We pray that you use us to further your kingdom and win hearts to your cause." When I opened my eyes, the guitarists stood up front with their instruments in their hands, as though the prayer had conjured them. An overhead projector flipped on, and the song lyrics filled the screen hanging from the ceiling. One of the singers shook a small colored egg, a gentle *swish, swish* behind the guitars. Some of the people in the room sang with their hands high in the air, their palms held open, as if to receive the nails and thorns—something I'd seen over the years in my stepmother's church but could never bring myself to do. Those fleeting moments when the spirit had filled me and I tried to raise my hands, the spell had broken instantly, and I looked around the room as if I'd taken off my clothes.

Annie clutched her hands to her heart and turned her shoulders in cadence with the music, like she was rocking a baby. She showcased her gleaming teeth when she smiled.

Between songs, I could hear singing coming from the other side of the wall. Twice, it was the song we'd just finished singing. Annie leaned in, "InterVarsity meets next door."

"Right," I said, though I hadn't a clue about what InterVarsity was.

The singing finished, and Brent returned to the microphone. "Everyone take off your left shoe and toss it over your shoulder. Now pick a shoe from the pile and try to find its rightful owner. See if you can learn a new name along the way."

On the other side of the windows, students processed along the sidewalk in the fading September twilight, their backpacks slung low over one shoulder. The lampposts leading into the campus park glowed like fire-flies as the glass became mirrored, my reflection following me as I crossed the room with a Converse All-Star in my hand. The shoe belonged to a woman with tiny silver studs along the arches of both of her ears. "I think this belongs to you," I said.

"I'd say so," she said. She stuck out her purple sock, hiked up an imaginary skirt.

"My white horse is parked out back," I said, kneeling, holding the shoe so she could slide her foot inside.

"That's good," she said. "My ride just turned into a pumpkin."

Twisting the lace around my thumb, I felt a presence looming over my shoulder, the eerie, unmistakable sense I was being watched. I turned to the window. Juxtaposed against the reflection of my humped back, my squinting stare, I could just make out the dark outline of a body, the brim of a baseball cap, the lump of an orange backpack. He stared at me in fascination while I tied the shoe.

I felt like an exhibition in a living history museum, where behind a pane of glass men and women in pioneer garb hammered horseshoes against an anvil or kneaded bread with their hands. A part of me wanted to open the door and explain to the onlooker that we were playing a mixer game, a get-to-know-you activity; it wasn't as odd as it looked. I remembered the meeting taking place on the other side of the carpeted partition, singing the same songs, as well as the signs for the other fellowship gatherings Annie and I had passed in the corridor on the way here. Some of the groups were ethnic-specific, like the Chinese Christian Coalition or the Coptic Orthodox Christian Club, but most were nondenominational, like ours, with names just as allusive and vague: The Navigators, The Mustard Seed, Alpha Omega, all meeting on Tuesday night, as though Tuesday had been designated for the communion of believers. Our meeting convened at the end of the hallway, so the student who peered in at us—at *me*—had passed rooms of glowing windows, like a row of aquariums at a pet store, each filled with students praying with their heads bowed or singing with their hands in the air.

On our way to the student center that night, Annie had warned me that there were two groups on campus named, simply and deceptively, Christian Students. One was legitimate and one was a cult. "How do you tell the difference?" I asked her.

"That's the thing," she said. "It can be hard to tell. The cult talks about Jesus, but they don't really follow him. They try to persuade people to leave other groups."

"What about the meeting we're going to?" I asked. "This fellowship?"

"What about it?" She stopped walking and turned to face me. "Obviously we're not a cult." She used the "we" proudly and in a way that included me. "We've been around the longest. We were the first in the country." At the start of the meeting, Brent announced that the ministry had been founded in 1951 at UCLA, only fifty miles up the 405 freeway, close enough to feel, as Annie's emphatic *we* suggested, that I had stumbled onto the epicenter of faith itself.

Except for the weeks when I visited California, my spiritual journey up to that point had been solitary. My mother and stepfather had joined a Methodist church in Houston, largely so the pastor would marry them. They'd attended only a few services since the wedding, but I went every Sunday, rising early to shower and eat breakfast while my mother and stepfather slept. Some weeks I persuaded Devin to come with me, but most Sundays I went alone, which I liked better anyway. I liked sitting in the back pews, behind the boys and girls my age who'd grown up in the church and held offices in the youth group and believed because they were raised to believe and accordingly believed whatever they were told. My faith, on the other hand, was my weapon of resistance against my mother's refusal to allow me to move in with my father in California—a transgression I wouldn't forgive even after I resigned myself to finishing high school in Houston. I liked it that my mother frowned when she found me reading the *Breakaway* magazines my stepmother sent me, even though I couldn't stand the magazines themselves and read them for no other reason than to mark myself as subject to influence beyond my mother's control. "Kurt Cobain's involvement in witchcraft explains his uncanny ability for coming up with alluring and seductive hooks that so frantically entice Nirvana's fans," one reviewer wrote. I still counted the night I rode in the back of a pickup truck, draped in a Hefty bag to stay dry in the rain, to see Nirvana play with The Smashing Pumpkins and The Red Hot Chili Peppers as one of the greatest nights of my life.

Such was the contradiction of my fledgling faith: Though California was the source of the magazines urging me to shun the music I listened to in Texas, my exile from California made my faith defiant. I'd entwined my ambiguous ideas about Christianity not only with the conservative social politics I heard in my father's car, but also with *being* a Californian and with everything the word implied: hardened surf wax beneath my fingernails, my hair streaked blond by the sunlight and salt water, mad skills with a skateboard and Frisbee—all of which added up to, in my mind, the epitome of cool. I could discern only two other categories of people in Laguna Beach: the migrant workers, mostly illegals, who drank coffee from small Styrofoam cups while they loitered beneath the magnolia tree at the Day Laborer Station, and the homosexuals who strolled among the art galleries in audaciously loud shirts and too-short shorts. My father's talk radio, my stepmother's church, and the friends who came to dinner all had plenty to say about the perils of membership in either group. My choices about the person I'd become once I moved to California were clear. If I could just get there, I thought, I could complete my transformation once and for all.

I swam fast enough my senior year of high school to earn a scholarship to the University of California at Irvine, an easy fifteen minutes from my father's house in Laguna Beach. More lucrative offers, or offers from more prestigious universities, couldn't compete. My path had been determined. It headed due west.

I might have ended up at any of the countless fellowship groups on campus, or just as easily, none of them. What I most wanted was a circle, a place to belong, and a means by which to codify my Californian citizenship. I had the swimming team, of course, but college athletics teams are by nature aggregations from different regions. I was one of three swimmers from Texas. Annie not only embodied the native status I wished to attain, but she was also was a diver on the team. When she'd invited me to the fellowship, I'd said yes, instantly, in thunder.

What I didn't know at the time was that the fellowship was the local chapter of the largest evangelical organization in the country, if not the world. I assumed it was a place for like-minded believers to gather and pray. I never guessed the ministry supported chapters at nearly every non-religious university and college in America, as well as countless domestic and international ministries, including ministries for the urban poor, athletes, the military, even for members of Congress and delegates to the United Nations. One ministry was solely devoted to showing a film about the life and work of Jesus in remote places, dubbed into dozens of obscure languages and projected onto a white bed sheet draped against a wall. Full-time campus staff members led Bible studies in which they trained and encouraged students to form their own Bible studies in which *they* trained and encouraged more students to form yet more Bible studies. It was a kind of pyramid structure for evangelizing a college campus, though such terminology was never used. At least a part of Annie's joyful smile during the singing was due to the fact that she'd done her part to fulfill the ministry's mission by bringing another soul into the fold. Only slowly did I come to understand that staff members weren't university employees, and years would pass before I learned of the ministry's roots in the evangelical revivals that followed World War II, its stake in the rift between Billy Graham's evangelicals and Bob Jones's fundamentalists, its fear of communism and resolve to weave together evangelism and military strength in the service of spreading Christianity and democracy around the globe.

Even more ironically, the ministry was the same one my stepmother had once worked for. Because she and her first husband had served the ministry together, she'd said very little about it, as if to erase the fact she'd been married to someone other than my father, just as I sought to erase the fact that she was not my mother. The few stories she told of her former life made the work sound like a cross between a political lobbyist and a sales representative, never a crusader for the soul of America. Since her time with the ministry had also occurred in Southern California, I never had cause to think the organization stretched any farther than the state border. I had arrived at college with an understanding of the ministry as amorphous as the body of the onlooker standing at the window.

When I stood up from tying the shoe, he was gone, dissolved into the autumn night that had spawned him. Brent was at the microphone, directing the crowd to return to their chairs. I circled back to Annie, happy to be reabsorbed into the crowd. Jake met me at the door after the meeting, shook my hand, and asked for my phone number so we could go surfing on Saturday. By the end of the fall, I'd signed up for a Bible study, and by the start of my sophomore year, I was writing the skits and mixer games. I was never pressured to join, never asked to give money. I could have left at any time. But I was committed, and stayed.

~~~

Despite his thinning hair and the faint, sun-deepened wrinkles around his eyes, Jake moved with the ease and posture of a student. He'd been on staff with the ministry for ten years, subsisting entirely on funding procured from private supporters who included him in their monthly tithing. It was a difficult way to make a living, and it meant a life of prolonged poverty. In his early-thirties, with an infant daughter and another on the way, he and his wife rented a tiny two-bedroom home in Costa Mesa and shared a well used, sadly abused 1977 Camaro. But he was dedicated to the work and had given up the chance to go to medical school to keep doing it. He'd since enrolled in a master's program in philosophy, and each week during my freshman year, when our Bible study met in a student center lounge, Jake arrived with a new theory by another great mind that pointed the way to Christ.

I'd fallen in love with philosophy my freshman year after taking a class from a charismatic professor who held discussion sessions on the white stucco steps between the two humanities buildings, a setting so idyllic it felt like the steps of Plato's Academy. I loved philosophy for the same reason I loved stories. I didn't want to escape the reality of life around me; I wanted the vocabulary to define it. Philosophy promised the testing of possibilities, the posing of questions that resulted in answers. Those answers almost always had something to do with metaphysics and ethics: whether a realm existed beyond our own and the delineations between right and wrong. The thornier the problem the better, for it offered the greater opportunity to triumph over unknowability, a crucible for revealing the secrets of existence. Philosophy was for me a tool for creating a world, a world not simply of my own making but vetted by the greatest minds of human thought, where Jeremy might still exist and where the men responsible for his death would be found out and held to account. In order for this place to exist, the conclusions had to apply absolutely. An afterlife had to exist whether or not we believed in it. Right and wrong had to be immutable. Evangelicalism, especially as Jake presented it, offered exactly such a system, and in a language I was fascinated with and was learning to speak for myself.

When I announced to my parents my plans to double major in English and philosophy, my stepmother had issued a caution: "Be careful with that stuff." Studying literature, in her mind, was bad enough, full of so-called heroes glamorizing sex and cursing at God, but philosophy was as dangerous to faith as witchcraft. "It tickles your intellect, and before you know it, you think you're too smart for Jesus," she said. In Jake's company, however, the intellect could be probed, flexed, stretched upon the table and pounded with a hammer, and still the conversation led toward the logical necessity of God, as though God could be expressed in a mathematical formula, which, according to Jake, he could be. Jake insisted philosophy was not a discipline to be refuted, but a tool for sharpening faith itself.

Bible studies, unlike the weekly fellowship gatherings, were small and separated by gender; six guys slouched on the couches in the corner of the lounge. The women had their own small groups. The other guys in my study, including Dave Durden and Rich Sarkisian, my roommates and teammates, studied engineering or math and had little interest in philosophy, nor did they feel any compulsion to defend their majors from the endless litany of questions about what they planned to do with their degrees. They enjoyed Bible study so long as we stuck to that week's verse and whatever "take home" lesson it contained. "Keep it simple, stupid," Durden liked to say. Whenever Jake started talking philosophy, the other men one by one would lean their heads against the back of the sofa and close their eyes. Jake would clap his hands to wake them up, but if he was on a roll, he'd let it go, and once the last head had nodded, he and I would be free to hash out Descartes' Cogito or Kierkegaard's *Either/Or*. It never felt like Christian apologetics in disguise; our discussions felt like genuine inquiry, a willingness to follow the argument wherever it led. That the inquiry led, improbably and recurrently, back to Christ only registered that my faith was as true, as *absolutely true*, as I'd been told. In his *Confessions*, Augustine recounts a conversation with his mother in which their thoughts "ranged over the whole compass of material things in their various degrees, up to the heavens themselves, from which the sun and the moon and the stars shine down upon the earth." Some nights I felt as though Jake and I were caught in just such an updraft, funneled toward the very center of the universe.

In Dante's *Divine Comedy*, the seven Christian virtues—humility, kindness, forgiveness, diligence, charity, temperance, and chastity—are ordered from the most important to the least, in antithesis to the seven deadly

sins—pride, envy, wrath, sloth, greed, gluttony, and lust. Humility is
the greatest virtue because pride is the deadliest sin. But each week, in
Bible study and campus fellowship meetings, I learned a different order
of virtue. I learned, in fact, precisely the *opposite* order. I learned that
lust, not pride, was the gravest of sins, and that nearly all the world's
social ills—teenage pregnancy, pornography, domestic violence, AIDS,
divorce—were produced by a culture that had devalued chastity. History
contained abundant examples of great men brought low by lust, men
who turned to greed and duplicity and rage in order to satisfy their sexual appetites. The chaste man, on the other hand, embodied every virtue.
He was tempered, charitable, diligent, forgiving, kind, and humble—all
because he'd sojourned through youth an enemy of temptation, an alien
to sex.

The algebraic logic of this schema appealed to me because it offered
a clear path toward righteousness. News of my former friends had begun
to reach me, and most of it wasn't good. Trey Smith had lost his full-ride
scholarship to Indiana University, tried to enlist in the Navy, but got hung
up during the physical evaluation when the doctor found a heart murmur that may or may not have been caused by drug use. Mike Collins had
married the girl he'd started sleeping with the summer before he left for
college, but the relationship was already on the rocks and appeared to be
headed south. Curt Wood had failed out of Stephen F. Austin State after a
single semester and was working at the used car lot next to the Kentucky
Fried Chicken. Chris Mangold had disappeared; no one knew where he'd
gone. I had managed to escape, and I viewed my liberation as both made
possible by my faith and conditioned upon it. More than I wanted to suc-
ceed, I wanted to not fail. The best way to insure against failure was—as
my stepmother said and now Jake and Annie, the two Dans, and everyone
else I met echoed in some form or another—"to walk closely with God."

Abstinence, though, was rarely ever couched as a protection against
the negative consequences of sex. It was an investment in the future; what
we gave up now would be returned in greater abundance later. God had
laid out a clear commandment for sex and adherence to it cut both ways.
Disobedience was a flirtation with disaster, but obedience guaranteed
blessings *in excelsis*: a passion-packed marriage to a woman who, knowing no other bodies, would find only my body erotic, and endlessly so; an
intimacy that never waned; a bond that could withstand any trial, great or

small. Arguments would become a curiosity observed only in other couples. Abstinence came to feel like a force field that would deliver me from every evil, and after the evils I'd already seen, I hoped for an easy life. Waiting for sex would result not only in an infrangible marriage, but also in financial stability, sound nights of sleep, healthy children down the road. I even came to believe—though I never confessed it aloud—that a faithful commitment to abstinence would result in better grades and victory in the pool. The only obstacles to attaining greatness were the desires of my body, but denying bodily desire I knew how to do, perhaps better than anything else. Every morning and every afternoon, one of my coaches stood above me on the pool deck, his eyes hidden behind his sunglasses, and called down a challenge to my body. Was I man enough to take the pain? Was I tough enough to resist the temptation to throw in the towel, give over to the quick way out? Could I keep going after everyone else had proved himself weak and incapable? Everyday I called up: *You bet your ass.*

When it came to sex, the same men who fell into narcoleptic trances at the mere utterance of the word "metaphysics" could philosophize all night long. The epistemology of marriage, the process of discerning the mate God intended for each of us, was cast into pseudo-scientific discourse, not unlike the predictive language used in meteorology. Love, like rain, was hard to forecast, but we understood the conditions in which it occurred. Ministry staff read passages from *The Five Love Languages* and *Preparing for Marriage God's Way* during the weekly meeting and encouraged us to make lists of our "negotiable" and "nonnegotiable" requirements for a spouse. We couldn't bumble along until we fell in love; emotions were untrustworthy. It was a page straight out of Plato's *Republic*: Reason governs courage, which governs appetite. If we allowed emotion to rule, we'd inevitably fall in love with a nonbeliever and would have to choose between forsaking that person and forsaking God—an evangelical's *Sophie's Choice*, a heartbreak either way. We needed to plan ahead.

Negotiables included movies and sports and our favorite authors; they'd be great to have in common, but they weren't the basis for a godly relationship. Nonnegotiables included a shared belief in Jesus, how a person becomes a Christian, how one remains a Christian, how Christ should be worshipped, and what the Bible teaches about financial responsibility, spiritual leadership in the home and church, and who should be the head of the household. Physical attraction was somewhere between the two: more important than movies, but not the ultimate factor. Sexual chemistry was a direct by-product of the nonnegotiables, God's wedding gift.

A couple who went on a date needed to have a DTR before going on a second, a conversation to (d)efine (t)he (r)elationship. If they disagreed on even a single nonnegotiable issue, they should discontinue seeing each other, posthaste. What was the point of dating if it didn't lead to marriage? If the DTR went well and all the nonnegotiables lined up, it was crucial to set clear physical boundaries. Any kissing below the neck was out. Kissing above the neck shouldn't be thought of as a free for all, either, especially if the tongue was involved. Holding hands and cuddling on the couch were okay, but it was not okay to touch other body parts, which was easy to do when you're alone at night, so it was probably wise not to do too much cuddling, either. Praying together was good, but we were warned that praying is a form of intimacy and could lead to something more, like kissing below the neck.

On Thursday afternoons, when my Bible study group gathered, the list of nonnegotiables shrank to only two: 1) Christian. 2) Smokin' hot. If our hypothetical brides-in-waiting met both requirements, and if we honored God by remaining celibate until our wedding nights, it was pretty much guaranteed that married life would be a nonstop sex carnival. It was its own kind of porn, imagining the splendors of married sex—the only sex sanctified by God, but, as a result of that sanctification, mind blowing. Tommy Baker cradled an invisible pair of hips between his hands, miming the thrust as he bit down on his bottom lip. "Oh yeah," he moaned. "That's the way, uh-huh, uh-huh, I like it."

"Oh Baby you . . . you got what I need," Durden echoed. Across the room, two women in Delta Gamma sweatshirts painted a poster for a spring party. Out of earshot of our conversation, they didn't notice us.

Tommy spun the hips in his hands, pretended to spank the bottom that wasn't there.

"Give it a rest," Jake said.

Tommy stopped and turned to Jake. His smile vanished and his face turned serious. "Let me ask you this," he said. "What does the Bible say about, you know, oral sex?"

"Before or after marriage?" Jake asked, growing impatient with the direction of the conversation.

"After, man," Tommy said. "Of course."

"It depends on the intent of the act," Jake said, hoping to shut down the conversation by injecting it with philosophy. "Thomas Nagel says sex is natural when each partner is aware of him or herself as the subject and object of their joint experience. Perversion occurs when mutual arousal is absent, when one is either wholly the subject or wholly the object."

The butcher paper crinkled as the DGs rolled up their poster and gathered their paints. The men on the couches shifted uncomfortably. "So, you're saying," Tommy said, "if you're married and she's into it, it's okay?"

"Something like that," Jake said.

"Nice," Durden said.

"I really hope that on my wedding night, my wife and I can pray together before we have sex," Tommy said, pulling at his fly. "I want it to be a holy experience."

"Sounds like you've got all the holies covered," I said.

Tommy shot me a serious stare. "You shouldn't pun on God's name."

"I didn't," I said. "I punned on the word 'holy.'"

"Which means God."

"Not exactly," I said. "Whatever."

I resisted the jargon, all the talk of DTRs and negotiables and non-negotiables, because it seemed drawn from the *Breakaway* magazines my stepmother had sent me when I was in high school or from the Christian living books that many of the women in the campus ministry carried in their backpacks—books with pastel covers lettered in wedding cursive, books depicting couples holding hands on the beach or releasing a rabble of butterflies in a park. Such language, I believed, could not describe me. My faith was rooted in Augustine and Dante. I was different. After the murders, I'd felt haloed by that eerie glow that often forms around the survivors of trauma, as though I represented a link between the banal, everyday world and the world of mayhem. That halo kept me from getting close to some people, but it also gave me a definition of myself as unique. My faith hadn't supplanted that definition, it had merely renamed it, and I didn't want to surrender it to the notion that my life could be so broadly and artlessly determined. I learned to make divisions at the campus fellowship meetings. I developed an eye for those who bought into the jargon and those who saw through it; those whose faiths were tied to a fear of the larger, messier world, and those who knew a thing or two about it. Never once did I consider myself a part of the former group. Never once.

But the camaraderie of the Bible study I loved. The evangelical argot largely disappeared there, and I loved the way conversations leapt from oral sex to philosophy to God, the Friday night poker games and Saturday morning surf sessions that began with protracted hunts for the beach where the waves were breaking perfectly and ended with six of us crammed into a booth at Denny's, the Frisbee golf tournaments and camping at San Onofre, the orphanage in northern Mexico we renovated over spring break, the debate we organized between an evolutionary biologist and creationist that drew a larger crowd to the events center than our hapless basketball team. I was, I believed, part of something momentous, something *real*—a friendship, a fellowship, a *family* that would remain long after college, after the drinking games and bong hits and sexual adventures had passed away.

Our sophomore year, the Bible study met in the off-campus apartment I shared with Durden and Rich. We met on Sunday evenings, the only day of the week we didn't swim. We gathered in the living room, slack-jawed, and slumped on the hand-me-down sofas that had once been in my parents' bedroom in Houston. My mother had given me the sofas when she and my stepfather moved to Austin the summer after my freshman year. It was strange to come home each night to such an old piece of my history. I could still catch the faint scent of my mother's perfume, and though he hadn't sat on it in years, my father's cologne. It was though a relic of my former life, despite my efforts to flee it, had followed me to college.

The same ambivalence crept in on Sunday nights. The knock on the door and the Bibles on the coffee table signaled the end of the weekend and the conclusion of my one-day furlough from the pool. Bible study was supposed to be a reprieve from all things competitive, the one night each week Durden and Rich and I set aside to commune with our better selves and draw strength from the fellowship of Christ. Bible study instead intensified our competitiveness, if only because it was one more thing requiring preparation and sacrifice, one more thing we did together.

We did everything together. We spent twenty hours a week in the water, four more in the weight room, and when we weren't swimming, we were eating, or showering in the big stalls in the basement of the athletic complex, or studying, or watching TV, or sleeping—all together. Since Durden and I were both named David, we were known as "the two Daves" or else "Big Dave" and "Little Dave." Durden wasn't little, but he was the thinner of the two of us, so I was Big Dave. He didn't comb his hair for a year, and in the chlorine and constant sunlight it turned transparent, stiff as straw, standing up from his head like an urchin's. Rich grew a beard so long and nappy he carried his breakfast crumbs around in it all day, his face a nest of maple bar chips and Frosted Flakes. He could do an impression of Gilbert Gottfried so dead-on that Jay Leno wouldn't know the difference.

We sang on the bus to our meets, and wrestled on the carpet of our apartment, and rode our bicycles to workout at five thirty in the morning when the rest of the campus was tucked inside an amber drowsiness. It seemed to me that every big thought and thunderous sentence ever spoken there belonged to us. Beneath all this wonder, however, lurked our unspoken, constant state of competition. Lying in bed at night, or reading, or sitting in class, I fantasized about Durden and Rich's gasping, asthmatic failures, their bewildered faces when they saw how far ahead I'd finished, their teary humiliations buried inside their towels. It wasn't enough to win. I wanted to eviscerate. I wanted to disembowel. I could remember the same emotion projected onto Jeremy, the ferocity with which I wanted to shame him by beating him in the pool and then shame him further by congratulating him on his time, on coming through with a solid performance, on not giving up after it became clear there was no way he'd get by me. I could recall this aspect of our friendship far more clearly than I could our more fraternal moments, all the times I felt I loved him and was made welcome in his home. I'd been made welcome in other homes since his death, and love seemed to me far more susceptible to the distortions of grief than hate. Hate was trustworthy. I could recall it in specific moments, in specific races, and know with certainty I felt it then. I felt closest to him in hatred because I knew without a doubt the memory was authentic.

Durden and Rich and I challenged each other at the things expected of young men on the cusp of manhood: who had the higher grades or the better-looking girlfriend, or a girlfriend at all, who could do the most pull-ups or bench the most weight. And each day an inordinate number of smaller, stranger contests: who could shower the longest in ice-cold water; who could withdraw cash the fastest from an ATM machine; who could ride a bicycle down the longest flight of stairs. Durden and I both wore contact lenses, and each morning before heading to the pool we stood in the bathroom, racing to see who could get his lenses in first. He and I overlapped in two swimming events, and Rich and I overlapped in every event but one, which meant that each time I stepped up to the blocks, I stepped up beside at least one person who shared my bathroom, whose snores and sneezes echoed against the wall of my bedroom, who pilfered my dresser when he ran out of clean clothes.

That brief time in the water—that harsh assembly of seconds and tenths of seconds and hundredths of seconds—between the starter's horn and the last lunge toward the wall felt, even more than Bible study, like the fulcrum of my existence. We'd come to college to compete, our abilities to compete paid for our tuition and books, and thus competition possessed us not only in the pool, but also in the courses we studied, the very words we read. Had we not been swimmers, we wouldn't have been friends. We wouldn't have known one another at all. Competition was the rule of our friendship, and we knew it going in. We were tired all the time; we wanted nothing more than to skip workout to sleep, and yet, as if we were driven by a compulsion that would one day land us in prison, we went, every morning from six until eight, every afternoon from three until five. Following the advice of a sport psychologist, we kept our goal times taped to the wall beside our beds. I fell asleep touching my times, while on the bottom bunk Durden fell asleep touching his. A win in the pool eclipsed everything, and no other victory in another part of our lives could surmount a loss there. And so often I lost, so often *I* was the one to finish gasping and asthmatic, so often I was the one to lift my head from the water to see Durden or Rich—or God help me, both of them—sitting with their goggles on their foreheads and their arms draped over the lane ropes. So many times I buried my hatred inside my heart as I climbed out of the water, slapped their backs, and followed them home for dinner.

For most of my freshman and sophomore years, I mounted the blocks with the undeniable awareness that no matter how hard I swam, I was going to get my ass kicked. Even Charlie, my coach, shook his head when I climbed out of the water. I could see him questioning his investment in me. To put in so much time and energy, so much of my ego, and have it amount to nothing began to take its toll. I came in dead last at a meet at USC in late January of my sophomore year, thirty humiliating seconds behind a swimmer I'd raced neck and neck with at the Texas State Champs in high school. After I climbed out of the water, I fled to the back of the locker room, found a pay phone, and called my father at home. "It's not fair," I blubbered into the receiver. "I've never been so embarrassed."

"It's the pressure," my father said. "You're making yourself miserable."

"It's not me," I said. My chest and legs were bright pink. I was trembling. "It's *it*." That I could not name what, exactly, *it* referred to was the crux of my problem. I went to bed early every night, I turned in all my homework, I hadn't skipped a workout in two years. I'd tried everything, and nothing was working. What was I doing wrong?

"Maybe God's trying to get your attention," my father said. "Maybe there's a sin in your life you need to deal with. Is there something you want to tell me?"

"I can't think of anything," I said. I hardly had time to date, let alone sin.

My stepmother got on the extension. "You're making swimming your idol," she said. "You've put all your self-worth into swimming, but swimming's of *this* life, not the next. Your real victory is in Jesus."

"What should I do?" I said. The air conditioner vent above my head dripped onto the back of my neck. The cold pulsed down my spine. I trembled harder.

"Maybe it's time to quit," my father said.

"Quit?"

"You've had two good years," my father said. "Nothing to be ashamed of."

"I've had two crappy years," I said.

"All the more reason," my stepmother said. "You can't keep going the way you are."

"But my scholarship."

"Don't worry about that," my father said. "It's more important to be happy."

"I'll be happy if I win," I said. "Just once. That's not too much to ask, is it?"

"You're still not getting it," my stepmother said. "Remember what Jesus says in Matthew. 'Be careful not to do your acts of righteousness in order to be seen by men. If you do, you'll have no reward from your Father in heaven.' Chew on that for a while."

I hung up the phone and returned to my team beside the pool. My races were finished, and I sat in my sweats and watched the sky, brown with smog, and the wrought-iron fence separating the campus from the sordid inner city that encased it. Had my father told me to quit because he'd sensed that, deep down, I really wanted to, or because, like my coach and teammates, he'd lost faith in me?

But quit? Hand in my parka and sweats, resign my scholarship, join the paintball club or start my own Bible study? I couldn't imagine it, largely because I couldn't imagine my life without competition, and the constant vigilance competition demands. How strange it is to turn a friend into an enemy, the focal point of your angst and anxiety and malice, only to realize you're the same thing to him, the bearer of faults you didn't intend and wrongs you didn't know you committed. Though competition can inspire excellence and move us beyond our limits, it's also narcissism's engine. Again and again it brings us to the mirror to evaluate ourselves, to hunt out our every imperfection before others hunt them out and exploit them. Every day presents the possibility of greatness, and in every day lurks the possibility of shame, the worry that the competition is, somehow, simply better. You glimpse it, shrug it off, and still it remains. You tell yourself your losses are the result of forces beyond your control. You talk yourself into the lie that you're kinder, or smarter, or happier, a winner at some other contest, until kindness and intelligence and happiness all come to feel like consolation prizes. In a final, desperate attempt to console yourself, you say you don't care, maybe even quit, and still there it is, after you like a shadow on a sidewalk: failure.

A life of perfect harmony and cooperation, despite all the times I'd told myself I wanted such a world to exist, in the end did not appeal to me. I wanted competition; I'd come to depend on it. I knew friendship, and so knew myself only by how I measured up against the wits and talents of others. Quitting would mean more than leaving the sport, more than losing the scholarship; it would require an entirely new definition of myself, one that didn't include Durden and Rich, didn't include all-you-can-eat lasagna at Pizza D'Oro on Sundays or long bus rides up the coast for away meets or the bullshit sessions on the bleachers between events, and worst of all, didn't include Jeremy.

Durden came back from swimming the two hundred butterfly. He stood in the January air, steam curling from his shoulders, his hands on his hips. He hadn't won his race, either, but his loss was more respectable than mine, the margin of his defeat half a second instead of a half a minute. His smile was a mixture of *chin up, sport,* and *who's your daddy?* and I saw that he measured himself against me as surely as I measured myself against him. That I was someone to be measured against made me feel a little better. I wasn't ready to quit, not yet.

Durden and Rich and I knew one another's every secret, and we knew one another's bodies the way only swimmers do. The body was the object of our constant attention. We weighed ourselves before and after every workout. Danny, the assistant coach, filmed our strokes with an underwater camera so we could study the position of our elbows, the rotation of our hips, whether our chin needed to ride an inch higher in the water or an inch lower. Even after four hours in the water, four thousand calories burned, I limited myself to one cookie for dessert while Donny Richmond, who needed to gain weight, strategically arranged his milk glasses around the perimeter of his tray so he could stack a second tray on top, as loaded with food as the one below it. For our championship meet at the end of the season, we stuffed ourselves into tiny triangles of Lycra several sizes too small. Our Speedos were as thin as a single sheet of paper and had the same unpliable, semi-coarse texture; they took fifteen agonizing minutes to shimmy above the thighs, and when they were finally in place, boy parts and butt cracks and unkempt pubic hair spilled from the seams. Whatever the suit didn't cover, we shaved, which meant we shaved nearly everything.

Young men spend so much time and energy cultivating their hair—nursing peach fuzz into wispy mustaches, moussing the three strands on their chests, stealing their sister's conditioner to fluff the curlies—that willingly shaving it off is tantamount to treason. Even my professors were surprised when I showed up to class with hairless arms and a bald head. The university newspaper ran an article about the swimming team the week before the Conference Championships, which focused exclusively on shaving—not on how removing body hair increased the distance per stroke, not the electric surge of power, the thrilling absence of friction a shaved swimmer felt when diving into the pool, not even on how the smallest reduction in time could make the difference between finishing first and finishing last. Instead the article quoted the swimmer who said the team held "shaving parties" before the final meet of the season. We sounded like a bunch of eleven-year-old girls at our first slumber party, taking the boyfriend quizzes in *Seventeen* magazine while we shaved our legs with pink Lady Bic razors.

Even worse, it was mostly true. We used pink Lady Bic razors because they were softer on our skin, and the night before the start of the meet, we'd spread towels on the floor of the hotel room, fill the ice buckets with warm water, and shave down as a group. Because our suits left so much skin exposed, shaving was a time-consuming, meticulous business. A woman who shaves her legs can get the job done in the shower before she runs out of hot water, but shaving an entire body takes time. It requires help. Fingers and toes, thighs and shoulders, necks and backs—we shaved it all.

Last to go was the hair on our heads. The big Wahl clippers would appear, the chromed handle like the handle of a gun, nickel-plated and gleaming beneath the lights of the bathroom vanity. We'd scowl into the mirror and whoop as the clippers traveled from our foreheads to our necks in a single, searing pass. Everyone got a stripe down the center to make sure there'd be no backing out. The shaving was a ceremony as steeped in mystery and fear as an ordination, the sink we leaned over the altar upon which we laid both ego and anonymity. Clumps of shorn hair mingled in the sink and on the countertop and floor. Slivers of shorn hair floated on the dust and steam, returning to us with every breath.

Once every head was reduced to stubble, we took turns lathering one another's skulls with Barbasol and shaving down to the flesh. The person being shaved sat in a chair before the mirror while the one doing the shaving stood behind him, the sink filled with the hottest water the faucet would dispense. In shaving our heads, we willingly became conspicuous and invited the stares and comments of every bus driver and waiter and classmate. But in going bald, we also declared our allegiance to one another. Shaving one another's scalps became a way of wishing the other person good luck, akin to the laying on of hands. We worked slowly, the music and television turned off, the razor gliding across the scalp as carefully as a surgeon cutting close to the carotid. We worked until every hair was stripped away, the blood was dammed, and the follicles beneath the scalp were allowed their first breaths of unobstructed oxygen. Exposed to the atmosphere for the first time, a newly shaved head emits a faint blue glow—the way a lightbulb continues to glow after it's been switched off—a look that says everything has been cast aside, all excesses have been discarded.

In moments like this, palming my polished dome, Jeremy would come back to me. He was the first person I'd ever shaved down with, the night before the District Champs our freshman year of high school. We used the tub in his brother's bathroom, not twenty feet from the spot where he'd be shot to death six months later. We listened to Nine Inch Nails and sang the lyrics we knew would prompt his mother to take the radio away if she heard them. At fourteen, neither he nor I had begun shaving our faces, so the prospect of shaving our bodies was terrifying and, like everything then, hilarious. We cut ourselves a lot. I pared off an eight-inch strip of skin from my shinbone, as though I was peeling a carrot. The more crimson the water turned, the harder we laughed, until at last his mother knocked on the door and told us to keep it down.

All the time I spent not talking about Jeremy sometimes allowed me to forget him. A few days, maybe as much as a week would pass without him coming to mind. But then I'd remember the time he wrote "Dave sux" in the dust on the bottom of the pool and left it for me to find the next afternoon, and for a few days I'd see his fingerprints show up on things, on car windows and the condensation that collected on the plastic sneeze shields above the salad bar in the dorms, until it seemed that he'd never fled my memory at all. And he always returned to me here, shaving down at the end of the season. Shaving was how I measured time relative to the murders, the hair and skin and blood swirling around the drain, sluicing through the pipes the symbolic stripping away of another year, a little farther away from him.

The last time I'd seen his mother or sister was at a swim meet a few weeks before I left for college. My sister Devin and Jeremy's sister Bekki were swimming, and his mother was volunteering as a timer. I'd come to watch Devin swim one last time before I left, and when I saw Mrs. Woodley standing behind the blocks, I walked over to say hello. At first, she acted like she didn't recognize me. She stepped back from the edge of the pool to make room for me, as though I had come over to cheer for the swimmer in her lane. She held the stopwatch in her hand, trigger finger on the stop button, and gazed intently at the tiled cross on the bottom of the pool. I wore a University of California T-shirt. I told her I'd been awarded a scholarship. "That's nice," she said. "Good for you."

I wanted Mrs. Woodley to see that I'd come through okay, I'd kept swimming, I was on my way to college. I wanted the blessing I might have received from her had her life stayed intact. It was a selfish expectation, and I understood as much as I remained trapped in the painful silence between us while around the pool the swimmers screamed and clanked cowbells and jumped up and down. Mrs. Woodley leaned over the water as the swimmer charged toward the wall. She pressed the button on top of the watch. When she looked at me, her eyes were liquefying; she was fighting not to cry.

"It was good to see you again," she said.

She stepped back from the coping and scribbled the time on the seeding card attached to the clipboard that was resting on the chair. She slid the card out of its clip and handed it to the runner, who ferried it to the scoring table. She reset her watch and backed out of the way so the next heat could come to the blocks. I waited for a moment to see if she'd say something more, even as I knew there was nothing more to say. Her son—both her sons, and her husband—were dead, and I was leaving for college. I walked back to the bleachers and sat down beside my mother. After a few minutes, I got up and said I was leaving. My mother moved to Austin the next summer, and I never saw Mrs. Woodley again.

The summer swimming season after my sophomore year of college finished up in early August, six weeks before fall classes began. I was thankful for the break from regular training and for the chance to let my hair grow back in. To stay in shape, I swam with the team at the local high school and at night ran along the shadowed, tree-lined streets into downtown Laguna Beach, past the art galleries and sidewalk cafés and icecream shops, working my way home along the boardwalk and deserted beaches. My father had installed a shower against the back wall of the house for rinsing off after coming up from the ocean, and I showered in it beneath the moonlight, exposed to anyone who looked over the back fence. The training, despite my disappointing times, was beginning to show in my body. My shoulders were sinewy and my stomach was flat, the muscles in my biceps as hard as river stones. I didn't wear a shirt all month.

One night Stacie and I were unloading the dishwasher, and when I bent over to remove the plates from the rack, I felt her hand on my back and a pinch. "You're growing hair on your back," she said. "Gross."

"Am I?" I said.

"It's all that shaving you do for swimming. You should have left well enough alone. Good luck getting a date in college."

I went to the mirror. It looked at first like a shadow, a trick of the light, but when I reached my hand around I felt the bristle on my fingers. My stomach flipped. *Oh no*, I thought. I'd been pudgy in junior high, leaner but unmuscled in high school, and right when I was getting strong and tan from swimming outdoors, I was turning into a werewolf.

A few weeks after school started, I arrived at the pool for afternoon practice. After changing into my suit, I found my teammates leaning against the door to the pool. The door was locked and our coach had left for the afternoon. "Are we swimming or what?" I asked.

"Danny's on his way," Rich said. "I saw him upstairs. He said to get started and he'll be down as soon as he can."

"So?" I said. "Who's got the keys?"

"The water polo team's in the weight room," Rich said. "You're the captain. Go get them."

The water polo team was the swimming team's arch rival, partly because we had to compete for pool time, and partly because the polo players thought the swimmers were jokers and the swimmers thought the polo players were a bunch of chest-pounding apes. The water polo team had won the NCAA Championships a few years before, and though none of the players who'd led the team to victory were still around, the team continued to swagger. They'd put several players onto the last Olympic Team, and their coach was the winningest coach in water polo history—a cranky old guy named Ted Newland who'd once lifted a referee off the ground by his throat. Newland had arthritic knees from forty years of running up and down the pool deck, and though he could walk fine, he preferred to push himself around in a hot-pink wheelchair. He also swore like a sailor reared by truckers with Tourette's syndrome. The backdoor of the weight room opened onto the stucco balcony overlooking the pool, and on the mornings when the swimming team lifted weights, the water polo team scrimmaged in the water below. The players swore every time they got into formation, or took a shot, but no one swore harder than Newland.

More than once I leaned over the balcony and listened to him call an eighteen-year-old freshman parts of the reproductive anatomy I never knew existed.

Climbing the stairs to the weight room, I could hear the weights clanking, a rhythmic metallic thud like a garbage truck hefting a dumpster, and I could hear the water polo players grunting and swearing. I realized I'd made a mistake. I should have gone to my locker and changed back into my clothes before going upstairs. I shouldn't have gone up in my Speedo. I walked into the weight room, and the clanking stopped immediately. Had there been a record player in the room, the needle would have scratched. Newland was at the rear of the weight room, near the door to the balcony, working the pull-down machine in tight bike shorts and a gray tank top, his ropy muscles twitching beneath his leathered skin. He was seventy-one years old and wore mirrored blade sunglasses even indoors. The water polo team stood between us. I had to walk by them all to get to the keys. Newland wasn't about to come to me. The taunting began before I had both feet inside the room:

"Sasquatch! Go back to the forest!"

"Quick, take a picture! We'll make a million dollars!"

"The full moon isn't until next week!"

"Hey McGlynn, the porno called . . . you're late for work!"

One player simply pointed his chin at the ceiling, arched his back, and howled, "*Ahooo . . . ow, ow, ow, ahooooo!*"

Newland didn't say a word when I asked for the keys, but he had a hard time hiding his smirk. He pointed to the floor where the keys lay atop his wallet. "Thanks a lot," I said.

"Anytime," he said.

That year, swimming taught me to swallow ridicule and to develop a sharper sense of sarcasm. Pat Keenan teased me for my hair, and I teased him for the scar on his balls from his hernia operation. John Spencer called me "Fozzie Bear" from *The Muppets*, and I dug into him for his flat-top haircut and for being Canadian. J.D. Nordberg yanked fistfuls of my chest hair, and I slapped the side of his head and needled him about wiping out on his skateboard—an injury that ended his season and forced him to walk with a cane for months. Nothing was sacred, no one was spared, everything was fodder. Everyone had something to pick on: pimples, pink shorts, an odd shaped head, yellow toenails, a mole where a mole shouldn't be.

I came to appreciate the taunts as an unexpected comfort. The exposure of my worst physical qualities, those malformed parts I was certain would prevent me from finding love, carried with it a measure of acceptance. That acceptance felt, in its way, unconditional, a cousin to the unconditional love that undergirded the campus fellowship, the Bible study, the worldwide body of Christ. The body's failings were turned into jokes, and insecurity had trouble taking root in such jovial company. The very place were my foibles were most on display, where I was literally stripped naked, became, paradoxically, the place where I was most comfortable in my own skin.

And yet, the feeling dogged me that I was turning weird. Each Tuesday night when I arrived at the student center for the campus fellowship meetings, I found an evermore inexplicable assortment of eccentrics lurking in the corners: a physics graduate student who combed only half his hair and wore mismatched shoes; a pudgy nineteen-year-old freshman who sported semi-tinted eyeglasses, as though he'd sprung from his mother's womb in the body of a middle-aged preacher; an Indian student who spent his summers "smashing idols" in his native country and refused to sit through any lesson taught by a woman.

One sunny day, during lunch, the Korean Christian Fellowship assembled in white T-shirts in the student center plaza, between the ATM machines and the coffee shop, and performed a sign-language routine set to music. It was somewhat like the videos I'd seen of Toyota employees doing calisthenics in the factory yard, except that this performance was choreographed to "My Heart's One Desire." Twenty men and women stood in a grid, in four rows of five, and sang with their eyes closed. They clapped their hands in unison and lifted them toward the sky. They pressed their index fingers into the center of their palms, beat at their chests.

I stopped and stood with the students who'd gathered in the plaza to watch. The singers occupied so much space, and were performing at the busiest time of the day, that other students had to weave between them in order to get to the food court. The students on the periphery wore the same white T-shirts as the singers and clapped along to the music, but deeper in the crowd, all around me, the onlookers laughed and shook their heads. A man in mirrored sunglasses stopped beside me. He leaned over and asked me, "What are they, Moonies?"

I shrugged. But I knew who they were. I recognized the song. I could even sing it.

"Someone should tell them to lay off the Kool-Aid," he said, shaking his head.

I stood and watched, hoping the singing would stop and someone in the group would announce that they'd been performing a traditional Korean dance. A traditional dance would have been benign, a celebration of diversity, a cultural lesson from a faraway land. Such dances were performed on campus all the time, in this exact spot, and the reaction was always positive. It wasn't their cultural difference that made the performance bizarre. It was their overt display of piety. They sang without a hint of self-consciousness, their faces lit up with smiles. There they stood, legs spread and arms waving, singing to my God, the same songs from my worship. My brothers and sisters in Christ—the great spiritual family to which I supposedly belonged. I wanted to feel their ecstatic joy; I wanted a faith so assured I could stand where they stood, in front of everyone, and shout and sing without feeling embarrassed. But standing in the corona of their devotion, I felt only embarrassment. I worried that if I got any closer, someone I knew might mistake me for one of them. More importantly, I worried that belonging to this faith would mean—regardless of how much I surfed or how much philosophy I read—a life on the fringe.

The week of the Conference Championships, I showed up at the pool when the water polo team was in the water. Morning workouts had been canceled for the week so we could rest up for the meet, but—such was my inability to give myself even a small break—I continued to swim twice a day. Newland was taking advantage of the open pool to get his players into shape for their spring season. The lane lines were in and the goal cages were under their tarps. Newland was making his players swim. He looked over the churning water from his pink wheelchair, his ankle crossed over his knee. His coffee cup hung from the arm of the chair like a pistol in a holster. The steam rising from the pool's surface was as dense as smoke, but still he wore his sunglasses. I asked if I could join the workout. Newland pointed to an outside lane.

I swam around until the warm-up was finished, and then Newland gave out the set: eight one hundreds, freestyle. "Fast as you can, you sons of bitches!" he yelled.

I'd held onto my scholarship by placing fourth and fifth in my events at the Conference Championships, respectable finishes that had earned me handshakes from the coaches and slaps on the back from my teammates. But I hadn't come to college to get fourth or fifth; I wanted to win, and the fact that I hadn't ate at me. I wasn't the college student I'd dreamed of becoming when I'd turned the pages of the campus view books that came in my recruiting packets back in high school, when I'd imagined California would unlock the greatness in me. My swimming career was washing out, my body seemed a thing of mystery and revulsion, and I worried my membership in the campus fellowship marked me as a freak. When I looked across the pool at the water polo players in the other lanes, I remembered their gibes in the weight room. I remembered Newland's trenchant appraisal of my body. I remembered Durden and Rich sitting with their arms draped over the lane ropes after handing me another embarrassing defeat.

"On the top!" Newland barked. "Sprint!"

One of the polo players turned and looked over his shoulder at me. He shot me a grin, a competitor's grin, like I was nothing, like he'd leave me in his wake and then forget I was ever there. Newland called out, "3, 2, 1!" The second hand on the clock swept toward the 60. I sucked in air, pushed off the wall.

I understood how little this set, like all swims, really, counted for in the world. How few people were here to see it, and how few would register its ever having occurred. When it was finished, the world would be no different than before. If no one else cared, then it was mine alone. It mattered because it was the task before me *now*, the thing I wanted *now*. Swimming was a constant choice between the now and the later: exhaustion now for the sake of fitness later, all those Friday nights in the pool in pursuit of an always-elusive goal. My whole life had become a battle between now and later, and later had won every time, my every desire deferred.

I tucked my chin, cleared my nose, and emptied my tanks. I came up charging, my legs driving, my hands slicing the water. The water polo players were strong, but their strokes were horsey and they were on my turf, swimming between lane lines rather than between goals. I beat every player on all eight one hundreds. I beat the wiry drivers who sprinted for the ball during the games. I beat the three players on the National Team. I even beat Omar the Orangutan, who'd put off enrolling in Harvard Medical School to train for a spot on the Olympic Team. No one could get by me. Newland's face screwed tighter each time I touched the wall ahead of the players. "Don't let that shaggy dog beat you!" he screamed. "You pussy wimps! You wipeholes!" But no matter how hard they pushed, how much steamy air they huffed, I finished first. If this was to be my victory, I wasn't going to let it pass. Not for all the riches in heaven.

No Man's Land

"You're either for me or against me," Tommy Baker said. He stood stiffly behind the black music stand at the front of the lecture hall, his back ramrod straight, his hands knotted together near his belt. He'd been looking forward to his senior address to the campus fellowship, but now his cheeks were turning puffy and splotching red. It wasn't a good sign. He'd talked for years about joining the ministry staff and eventually planting a church in a foreign country, but seeing him onstage made it hard to imagine him shepherding any congregation of believers. What he lacked in confidence he made up for with volume. He leaned so close to the microphone his teeth appeared to click against it. The speaker whined as it broadcast his warbling voice.

"You might say to yourself, 'I'm not against Jesus, I just haven't made up my mind,'" Tommy said, reaching to turn the page in his notes. "Oh yes, you have. To be undecided is to be decided. You can argue with me all you want, but I didn't say it. Jesus did."

I sat alone near the back of the room with my arms crossed, my bare ankles hanging over the seat back in front of me. My flip-flops were nested in a pair on the sloped concrete floor. I'd spent most of my college career in this lecture hall—I'd taken postwar fiction here, as well as literary theory and early modern philosophy and about a dozen other classes—and now, in the spring of my senior year, I attended the lectures given every Monday and Wednesday night by the internationally renowned philosopher Jacques Derrida. His lectures began at 7:00 PM, the same time that the campus fellowship met on Tuesdays, as though the two gatherings were alternating sections of the same class. I understood very little of what he said—Derrida's French accent was thick and he mumbled while he spoke—but I knew he'd rerouted the courses of literary criticism and philosophy, my two majors, and that I needed to make an effort to see him before I graduated. His topic that year, ironically, was the Book of Genesis.

Tommy slipped his hands into his pockets and leaned his weight on his right leg, an attempt at looking casual that he didn't quite pull off. "It's important to remember that being *for Jesus* doesn't stop with the decision to accept him as your Lord and Savior," he said. His voice kicked up a decibel. "Believing in Jesus is a commitment to live your entire life for him." Then Tommy moved from behind the music stand and paused at the edge of the stage. His eyes scanned the crowd, from the front row, where Jake sat, up to the back where I was. His eyes met mine. I smiled to encourage him, but he didn't smile back. He was down to business now. He leaned forward and said, "Here's a question to ask yourself: Am I honestly probing my involvement in the systems, institutions, and values of the world? Remember what John writes, 'If anyone loves the world, love for the Father is not in him.' We should be in the world, but not of it."

He was talking to me.

Two months till graduation, I was still *in* the campus fellowship, but I no longer felt like I was *of* it. For four years I'd attended fellowship meetings and remained involved with the Bible study. I'd spent three of my spring breaks rebuilding orphanages in Mexico. I'd even chimed in the new year at an annual gathering of all the campus ministry chapters in Southern California; we boogied to '70s hits until midnight, but rather than kiss when the ball dropped, more than a thousand of us dropped to our knees and sang "As the Deer Panteth for the Water." And yet, in a paradoxical reversal of John's maxim, the longer I was in the fellowship, less I felt like I belonged to it. The California attitudes and styles I'd once associated with the fellowship had been replaced by a conspicuous movement toward modesty, the men evermore straight-laced and buttoned-down, the women unwilling to wear a bathing suit to the beach for fear they'd cause their brothers in Christ to stumble into lust. And compared to Derrida's lectures, the lessons delivered at the weekly fellowship meetings sounded increasingly inane, and increasingly antagonistic toward the very subjects I was here to learn. I loved school — I'd discovered the endurance instilled in me through swimming also translated to studying — and I rejected the idea that academics and Christianity were somehow in opposition to each other, and that I needed to choose between the two.

Encouraged by my professors, I'd applied for fellowships to spend the next year studying overseas — a number in England, several more in Australia. The programs in England were more prestigious, but Australia was where I most wanted to go. I saw myself meandering though ancient cities, or modern cities built on ancient ground, drinking late in the pubs and coffee shops, recording everything I observed in the leather-bound journal that would become my first novel. But over the course of several rainy weeks in December and January, I received in the mail a series of featherweight envelopes, each containing a single-page form letter letting me know the awards had gone to someone else. I'd finished my senior season of swimming in March, and though I'd spent weeks counting down the days till I was paroled from waking up at five in the morning, from sacrificing my weekends and summers and Christmas holidays, when I climbed out of the water after my last race and shook my coach's hand, I felt strangely, suddenly, adrift. I'd been a swimmer a few minutes earlier, and now I was just a guy about to finish college, with no prospects on the horizon. The life of honor and adventure I'd once believed I was destined for, the life I felt Jeremy's death made me deserving of and that moving to California all but guaranteed, was evaporating. I had energy and ambition to burn, and I didn't know what to do next.

Nor did I know where to turn for answers. I'd occasionally see my teammates on campus. For a moment we'd stop and talk, but often we seemed not to recognize each other now that we were, officially, no longer on the team. Even Durden and Rich, my roommates, could slide by me unnoticed. While the campus fellowship was growing, my own Bible study had shrunk to only two participants. Jake had issued an ultimatum to the group the previous fall: We'd grown lazy, he said, and our Bible study had devolved into a weekly hangout instead of a forum for digging into the Word. We needed to recommit ourselves or else drop out. Everyone but Tommy Baker and I had dropped out. Tommy would need Jake's letter of recommendation for his application to join the campus ministry staff.

I considered calling it quits, too, but Jake and I still surfed together, and I knew he'd take it personally if I bailed out. He grew gloomy and withdrawn, and confessed that he was doubting whether he should stay in the ministry. He was having trouble raising the financial support, and mentoring two guys out of a campus of nearly twenty thousand no longer seemed like the best use of his time. Maybe he'd head back to medical school, he said, maybe a PhD program in philosophy, though with two young kids and a wife to support, either route would mean an even tighter budget than his current situation. He looked at me as though I was the linchpin in his decision. If I stayed in the Bible study, he could go on; if I bowed out, who knew what he'd do. I didn't want to let him down.

There was another factor to my discontent with the campus fellowship. That winter I'd fallen in love. Julianne worked in the scholarship office where I'd gone for help with my fellowship applications. She was feisty, irreverent, several years my senior—everything I'd been told to avoid, which made her irresistible. She wasn't a Christian, at least not by the evangelical definition. She had a degree in women's studies, and her three best friends were gay. Her last relationship had ended so badly, she said, so rife with unfaithfulness and bitterness that its annihilation had inspired her to buy her own condo in the hills above campus. The duplexes and homes were uniformly beige with white trim and long venetian blinds hanging behind the sliding glass doors to slant away the sun. Each year the university added another row higher up on the hill, the rolling green dotted with yellow poppies steadily receding upward, as though evaporating. By my senior year, the peaked brown roofs stretched all the way to the sky.

Julianne's condo was on a side street off the main road that curved to the top of the hill. Only faculty and staff were eligible to purchase there, and some nights I'd pass one of my professors returning to his office after dinner. He was an old gent who wore a herringbone jacket and a plaid ivy cap with wisps of thin gray hair bushed around his ears. The first time I passed him I froze as though I'd been caught trespassing, but he merely lifted his hand and kept on down the sidewalk, utterly uninterested in my destination or motivations for going there. He wasn't who I worried about finding me out.

Julianne waited for me at the bottom of her staircase, on the three-by-three tile square that served as her foyer. Stepping inside felt like entering a magician's cabinet; when the door closed, I vanished into thin air. At the top of the stairs, her living room looked like a floating city, the table lamps spreading their cones of light over the sofa and carpet. I resisted the urge to kiss her until we were at the top and I'd pulled my sweatshirt over my head, but I usually didn't make it much longer. She sometimes drank a beer before I got there, and I liked tasting it on her breath. On colder nights she'd light a Duraflame in her tiny fireplace and unfold an antique quilt that was as heavy as a lead vest in a dentist's office, so thick it made a tent we could hide beneath. Some nights we listened to music; other nights we watched TV. Every night we lay on her carpet kissing until midnight. For close to a month I slept for less than five hours a night, about the same amount of time I spent each day in the pool. But I didn't care. I wanted to be with her more than I wanted to sleep. I liked her voice, the scent of her body wash, the pressure of her head against my shoulder.

Only in her condo, sequestered from campus, could I forget about my unfathomable future now that I'd lost out on the fellowships: a job in one of the indistinguishable stucco office buildings surrounding the campus like a dust storm, consuming the orange groves from San Clemente to Fullerton. Most of my friends worked in such places. They'd transitioned from academic to corporate life without complaint, from the dorm to the cubicle as though the small rooms we shared at the university were preparing us for the tiny spaces we'd inhabit for the rest of our lives.

The night I got the bad news about the last of the fellowships, Julianne slid her hand inside my T-shirt, laid her warm palm against my back, and told me she was proud of the applications I'd put together. Every one of the scholarships was a long shot, and I shouldn't feel too bad about losing. "Maybe it's a good thing," she said. "Maybe you need a break from studying."

"That's the thing," I said. "Studying is what I like best."

"So studious," she said. She kissed me, lightly, on the forehead. "So serious, all the time. It's like you're trying to live up to something. Like you've got some standard that's been set for you, and if you don't hit it, you'll disappoint a lot more people than just yourself. Who's your famous sibling?"

"No one," I said. "That's not it at all." I interpreted her question only in terms of the present, the people I competed against or sought approval from: Durden and Rich, Jake, my father and stepmother. None of them had expectations that came close to those I imposed upon myself. I didn't think the real answer might reside farther down, that the phantom standards I needed to measure up to might have something to do with Jeremy. I came to her condo to escape my confined and pious life, not to interrogate it. Only now do I see how close she was to figuring me out.

"Then what?" she said. She withdrew her hand from my shirt and tapped her index finger against my chin. "What do you really want to do?"

"I want to travel," I said. "I want to go places. I never got the chance to study abroad because the swimming season never allowed for it. It seems like something I should have done."

"Can't you still?"

"That's what all the applications were for," I said. "You can't study abroad unless you're a student."

"There are other ways," she said. "You don't have to study to travel. You can just go."

I didn't have the money to support myself for more than a week or so, once I factored in a plane ticket, and I wasn't warm on the idea of spending months alone, making small talk with strangers, begging for company. Any one of the fellowships would have landed me in a university, provided immediate community.

"What about that Christian group you go to? Don't they do stuff overseas?"

"I don't know," I said. In truth, I wanted a break from my evangelical life. I didn't want out, I just wanted a vacation from it. I was tired of Bible study. I was tired of burning my spring breaks building retaining walls in Mexico. I was tired of being held accountable. I wanted to camp on the beach, and drink beer, and stay up late, just for a while. "I guess that's an option," I said.

"Or else you could stay right here," she said. "I'll keep you locked up in my house like Rapunzel. No one will even know you're here." She nestled her head against my clavicle, pressed her lips against my neck and held them there. A gust of warm beer rose from the nonspace between us. I breathed it in and held it until I felt my hands tingle from lack of oxygen, but also dizzy with the awareness that beneath my earnest promises to God lay a craving that no commitment to principle or Jesus or lost friends could satisfy. It was more than sex; it was the human connection that sex simultaneously sought and expressed, the very thing the fellowship's jargon wanted to block from blossoming too quickly or with the wrong person. I knew Julianne was the wrong person. I knew I disappeared inside her condo each night after swimming practice because I wanted to hide. I knew that what we were doing was somehow wrong, and that eventually one of us would wind up hurt, but the prospect of certain ruin, however chaste or extravagant, only made me want her more. And a small part of me believed that by staying awake into the black hours of the morning, I could elongate time and thereby slow it down. I could orbit in this anodyne fantasy forever.

I pressed my face against hers, let my mouth linger in the ionized charge between our lips, felt her exhale and then hold her breath, waiting for me to move the final millimeter, seal the gap. I felt her heart race. I said, "I like that plan best."

I thought about Julianne's body during my classes, her slender neck and birdlike shoulders, her slightly discolored teeth and her small warm hands. She was pretty in an unobvious way, and her hidden beauty, the fact that not everyone could see it, fueled my attraction to her. I counted down the hours until I'd see her again. But hiding places are only truly safe when you're inside. Pacing through my normal routines—the pool, the showers, the cafeteria, class, the library, the pool again—I felt want bump up against conscience. Was I foolish to think I could resist the temptation to sleep with Julianne? I'd already spent a night on the floor of her apartment; how long could I go on before one thing led to another?

At first, I kept Julianne a secret from my Bible study, afraid of what Jake and Tommy would say. The night I came clean, I tried to make it sound casual. Julianne and I were only spending time together, I argued. Enjoying each other's company. Surely there was no harm in that. Who knows, I said, maybe she'd come to know Jesus. Tommy Baker quoted, from memory, 2 Corinthians 6:14: "Do not be yoked together with unbelievers; for what partnership does righteousness have with lawlessness, or what fellowship has light with darkness?"

"I'm not yoking myself to her," I said. "I want to date her, not plow a field."

"You'll want to plow her soon enough," Tommy said. Jake slapped his knee and said, "Nice." When the laughter died down, we moved on with the Bible study. But the doubt had now been raised by a voice other than my own. Was I, as Tommy suggested, disregarding God's will?

That night before going to sleep, I read from the first book of Samuel, when God calls the boy prophet and tells him he is about to judge harshly the family of Samuel's teacher Eli for his sons' contemptible and unrestrained behavior. Eli knew God, but didn't obey him and would suffer as a result. I woke up at one in the morning out of breath, with the sensation that a hand was pressing down on my chest. I rolled to my side, hoping to make it stop, but the weight remained. Rich was snoring across the narrow aisle between our beds; I whispered his name, but he didn't stir. I sat up and pressed my hand to my chest. My pulse beat out of rhythm. A frightful awareness filled me, a sense that someone was near, beside, and above me, a presence without form or substance yet somehow able to invade me. The room had shrunk. I felt hot, gulping air. Afraid.

The next day, I rode my bike to Julianne's and told her my faith was too important to set aside. God was calling me, and I needed to obey.

"God told you not to date me?" she asked.

"Yes," I said. "In a way."

"I'm not good enough?" She narrowed her eyes and moved to stand behind her kitchen counter. Her black cat jumped up on the counter between us, like an omen.

"It's not that," I said.

"That's what it sounds like."

I didn't have a better explanation. "I'm sorry," I said.

"Fuck you," she said, and walked into the bathroom. The door slammed behind her. I waited to see if she'd come out and absolve me, tell me we could still be friends, tell me I was still the nice guy she thought I was. When an hour passed, I had no choice but to leave.

I prayed I would sleep better that night, now that I'd done the right thing, but instead I stopped sleeping altogether. Night after night, I lay awake listening to Rich snore, missing Julianne and our brief, scorched passion. The more I pondered the verse from 2 Corinthians, "Do not be yoked together with unbelievers," the more it made me angry, the idea that Julianne, unsaved, was "lawlessness" and "darkness." I watched the women file into the weekly campus fellowship meetings, their Bibles clasped against their chests, their overly modest clothes, and I hated them. I appraised their bodies, the shape of their breasts beneath their blouses, the way their pants hugged their hips. I didn't look with lust but with the hope that I would see something worth lusting after, a body that would stoke my desire now that the body I most wanted was no longer mine. I hated the guys for smiling all the time, for lifting their hands in the air during the praise songs, for inviting me to play Ultimate Frisbee on Friday night. I hated the ministry staff for wasting my time with their reductive sermons, for telling me to give up everything I wanted in service of an abstract purpose. But the truth was, I *had* given up the thing I wanted, I *had* chosen Jesus over Julianne, and the fact of having made that choice somehow led me to believe I was also bound to the campus fellowship, that I had no other option but to go back every Tuesday night.

By April, I spent most of my time hiding out in the basement of the library. There was a row of tables cloistered between a stack of reference volumes no one ever read and the windows onto the campus park. The time I'd once devoted to hiding in Julianne's condo I now passed here. I watched the squirrels stand on their hind legs to study their faces in the glass and the bicyclists glide along the shady paths. I listened to the low thumping of books against the tabletops, the pencils scratching, the whisper-faint swish of pages turning, like an ocean at low tide. In the books I read and the stories I wrote, desire had a freer range. What I could not have in my own life, I could at least read about, and I could voice my woes and wants through the voices of others. I withdrew the books from the shelf in my bedroom one at a time—Ford's *The Good Soldier*, Carver's *Cathedral*, Graham Greene's *The End of the Affair*, DeLillo's *The Names*—and read each one as slowly as a death row inmate consuming his final meal. I read all afternoon and into the night and stayed until the security guard came to tell me it was time to lock up. I went on Friday nights. On Saturday mornings, I feigned exasperation with a paper so my roommates wouldn't grow suspicious, and was waiting when the librarian opened the doors. The chair remembered my shape from the night before. I packed a lunch and stayed all day.

"Make a decision to feel better and then fake it until you make it," my father said. "If you can't sleep, try imagining something repetitive, like playing tennis or pitching baseballs." But I didn't play tennis or baseball. I swam, and swimming was over. My stepmother said I'd feel better when I got off my ass and found a job. Any job, just something to do. She was beginning to worry about my next move; more than once she commented about the amount of food I ate when I visited. Durden and Rich were also graduating, both dating women they intended to marry. Preoccupied with their own looming futures, they quietly withdrew.

Jake proclaimed a bolder hypothesis. "It's Satan," he told me. We were sitting in the campus pub after Tommy finished his senior speech at the fellowship meeting. A beer to celebrate Tommy's big night, except we all three drank soda instead of beer. Jake leaned back in his chair with his ankles crossed. He was in a good mood; he'd recommitted himself to the ministry and had landed a job as the staff director at Cal Poly in San Luis Obispo. The position included a hefty pay raise, a chance to buy a house. He was moving in August. "We don't like to talk about Satan, but he's real," Jake said. "He affects us. It's his goal to disrupt our connection to God."

"He's one bad mofo," Tommy said.

Billiard balls cracked and scrambled, and the music changed over to Nirvana. The fuzzed noise through the speakers sounded like it came from a dead channel. The pinball machine flashed in the mirrored windows. I was desperate for answers and desperate for good sleep. My angst had grown larger than Julianne, larger than the usual graduation anxiety. Julianne had turned prickly and churlish, cold whenever we ran into each other on campus. I felt caught between two worlds, unable to heave off the yoking of my faith, yet unable to fully believe that God's plan was something I wanted a part in. The limbo was worse than either extreme. I needed to make a choice, one way or another. Something needed to be done. "You think I need an exorcism?" I said.

"Don't be silly," Jake said. "Just prayer."

We left the pub, and Jake gave Tommy and me a lift back to my apartment. They followed me upstairs to my bedroom. Jake sat on my bed and Tommy sat on Rich's bed, across from us. Rich came in and said he'd like to pray with us, too. Jake was wearing a sweatshirt from the swimming team, as if he were here to cheer me on. We bowed our heads and closed our eyes. Jake laid his hand on my pillow, the floodplain of my disquieting dreams, and prayed for Satan to leave me alone. He prayed for God to triumph over the Enemy.

We walked back downstairs and Jake and I stood together on the narrow concrete patio between the sliding glass door and the parking lot. Marine fog settled over the strips of lawn between the apartment buildings while a wrecker slowly hoisted an illegally parked car, a sleek, silver Acura. Jake checked to make sure his car was still in the lot. We watched the wrecker winch the front wheels off the ground, and then Jake put his arm around my shoulder. We'd spent a lot of time together in the ocean, from Pismo Beach to Rosarito, Mexico, and we'd had our share of good long talks. I loved him, he was the only one who never told me to snap out of it, and I wanted to tell him my sadness owed a little something to the fact that he was moving to the central California coast, four-and-half hours north. The job in San Luis Obispo was a good opportunity for him, but it meant our friendship would be yet another casualty in this season of endings. I said, "Thanks for praying for me."

"I hope it helps," he said. "I don't like seeing you so down."

"Me, too," I said.

Jake lifted his sneaker to scratch his bare calf. He said, "Your thing with that woman hit you pretty hard. Harder than I would've expected. I need to ask you, did anything bad happen?"

Besides the awful way we parted, the empty days afterward when I felt ready to give up my faith to run back to her? But I knew what Jake meant: Did I have sex with her. "Nothing bad," I said. "We kissed a lot, that's all. Everything else was in my head."

"I have to ask," he said. "It's my job to hold you accountable."

"I promise nothing happened. A momentary lapse of reason."

"There's one other thing," he said. "Try sharing your faith. Satan wants to prevent you from working for God's kingdom. Don't let him."

I was no good at sharing my faith. Whenever students from the campus ministry set out in search of new souls to save, I came up with an excuse as to why I couldn't go along. Jake had tried to teach me how, one spring day near the end of my sophomore year. We'd spent an afternoon working the lunch tables at the student center, but walking up to people I didn't know and asking to tell them about God, why my God was the One and Only True God, felt like an invasion of their private space. I stumbled nervously through the booklet we used and felt calm only when I was finished. Jake, too, was calmer. "It feels good to obey, doesn't it?" he said. But he didn't ask me to share my faith again.

A few weeks earlier, a man had come down to the library basement. He turned the corner from the elevators, and right away I could tell he didn't belong. His T-shirt was yellowed from being sweated up and slept in; the plastic grocery sack slung over his wrist crinkled and slapped against his thigh. He walked right up to the woman at the first table in the row, who was reading with her cheek propped on her fist, and set his hand on the corner of her table. He leaned so far forward he appeared to balance his hulking frame on that one hand. He dropped his mouth to within a foot of her ear. The woman recoiled, her shoulder flinching toward her chin, and she moved her hand to cover her open purse. She shook her head frantically. The man withdrew a magazine from his plastic sack and set it beside her before moving on. I sat at the last table and watched him work the row, whispering and withdrawing magazines from the sack. When he approached me, I planted my eyes on my book and didn't lift them until he set his hand on my table and whispered, "Excuse me." I hoped he'd see I was busy and leave me alone, though everyone else was busy, too, and he'd approached them all the same. When I turned to him, a rainbow of beaded moisture arched across his upper lip, and his eyes floated unhinged in their sockets. One eye did not follow the other. "Excuse me," he whispered again, "are you interested in joining a Bible study?"

"No," I said. I didn't tell him I was already in a Bible study. Inviting him to identify with me, or for the others in the room to identify me with him, was exactly what I didn't want to do. I wanted him to go away.

"Well, thanks anyway," he said. His shoulders rose and fell, and he extracted a magazine from the sack and set it on my table. "I'll leave this with you, if that's all right," he said. Before I could say no, he turned around and walked away.

The magazine, of course, wasn't a magazine, but a tract inviting me to begin a personal relationship with Jesus. The cover pictured a globe on which was superimposed a "We Are the World" montage: a hairless African boy with yellowed eyes; a prepubescent Indian girl adorned in a bridal sari, complete with a gold chain linking her nose and ear; a wrinkled Asian man in a furry ushanka hat, the kind Russian soldiers wear. Along the bottom was The Great Commission, Jesus' exhortation in the Gospel of Matthew: "Go, therefore, and make disciples of all nations, baptizing them in the name of the Father and of the Son and of the Holy Spirit." I swept the tract into the trash. The woman at the front table turned in her chair and peered back over each row, as if to check for victims. She rolled her eyes and laughed. I shrugged, but didn't laugh. I didn't see the man as an oddity but as a vision of my own terrible alternative future, the zealot I might one day become.

~~~

At the fellowship meeting the following Tuesday, a slide projector sat on a wheeled cart at the edge of the stage, and the screen had been pulled down from the ceiling. One meeting each spring was devoted to stories from the mission field, to testimonials from students who spent their summers in foreign cities or in stateside vacation spots living with members of the organization from other campuses, working and reaching out in the world for Christ. The summer excursions were officially termed "Summer Mission Projects," but most students simply called them "projects." It was easier to tell your nonreligious friends you were spending the summer on a project rather than on a mission. "Project" also made evangelism sound like a kind of extracurricular homework, an activity to fill the doldrums of the hot months.

The first testimony was from a tall guy who lumbered to the front with his hands in the pockets of his jeans. He'd spent the summer in Newport Beach, five miles from campus, living in an apartment a block from the sand. The proximity was the appeal. He had a good job in Irvine, and the project allowed him to keep working and "do ministry" at the same time. He tapped a new white sneaker against the carpet, as if he had his spiel timed. The pictures that spun through the slide projector were of places I recognized—the beach, the taco stand, Balboa Pier—but were filled with people I did not. He was followed by a small orange-haired woman who'd spent the summer in inner-city Los Angeles, directing plays and activities for children in a homeless shelter. She'd collected food and clothing donations for the men and women holed up in the cardboard boxes along Skid Row. Her soft soprano voice had an aggressive edge to it. "Christians shouldn't be complacent about the poor," she said. "We should do better." Her slides were of chain-link fences and barred windows and industrial all-metal kitchens where she and other students in plastic yellow aprons smiled for the camera while spreading mustard on an assembly line of bread slices.

The next slide was of a mountain peak, a loose gravel scree dropping into a run-off lake with water as blue as a gas flame and covered by a paper-thin sheet of cracked ice. It could have been anywhere, the Sierras or the mountains bordering Death Valley. Kevin, Jimmy, and Darin came forward, friends I'd known since freshman year. Darin was one of the few members of the fellowship I still counted as a friend; we got together every now and then to play Ping-Pong in the rec room of his apartment complex. So I knew the image was not of California, nor of any place in America. The regional chapter of the ministry had committed to sending summer project teams and missionaries to Kyrgyzstan and Kazakhstan for yearlong "stints," an acronym for "short-term international service." Now that communism had fallen and the Soviet Union had splintered, a window of opportunity had opened. Millions were waiting to hear the good news of Christ.

The team had spent the summer in Osh, in the Tian Shan Mountains in southern Kyrgyzstan. The Kyrgyz, Kevin explained, were historically a nomadic people, Muslim for nearly a thousand years, and hard to win over. On the screen flicked exotic images I couldn't quite decipher: Silk Road children in bright woolen caps with their arms around long-eared goats, Lenin's vandalized statue still recognizable in the city square, oddly labeled soda cans on the kitchen table of the team's apartment, a sink that had fallen from the wall and shattered into a thousand white cinders against the hard cement floor.

The slide carousel clicked and lurched, and Darin was standing in front of his own image. On the screen he wore a short-sleeved shirt with an open collar, a tuft of hair sprouting from the neck. He looked like he was trying to hold in a laugh, his standard mug. Beside him, a young Kyrgyz man was dressed in wrinkled gray pants and a brightly striped sweater, his black hair hanging in an uneven fringe across his forehead. "This is Rhuslan," Darin said. "He was our translator and guide for the summer. He became a Christian right before we got there, and we helped him start a Bible study. If his family found out he'd accepted Christ, they'd disown him for sure."

Darin paused, and an ethereal silence descended over the room, as if a curtain had dropped from a stage rafter. Above the fan noise of the slide projector I could hear the hum of the fluorescent lights in the ceiling, the particles of electrified mercury zipping through the tubing. It was an instant that passed in an instant, a room filled with college students in love with Jesus, hearing about a summer spent sowing the seeds of Christ among the ruins of communism. The electric instant was over, Darin was talking about the challenges of the trip and the team's layover on the way home in Izmir, Turkey, the historical Ephesus. Everyone was nodding along.

I was still studying the slide, my friend turned into a holograph, blown up to twice his normal size. Darin was tan and fit from the altitude and the exotic diet that kept him lean; he possessed a radius of understanding that exceeded my comprehension. Darin had been to one of the most remote corners of the world and now belonged to that other world. He looked otherworldly. It was a look I'd seen in other people who'd trekked around the world, a knowledge that remains embedded in the face, not fully communicable in words; a knowledge gained only by traveling to a distant place and surviving there and making it back home. That Darin had gained this enlightenment in the service of his faith seemed to me a revelation. I could have it too, if I was willing to accept the one option still available to me, the option that had in fact been available to me since the night I first attended a campus fellowship meeting in September of my freshman year. I could take up my cross and follow Jesus. I could double down on my faith.

The vision crystallized in my mind. I saw myself humping my backpack through a foreign airport with a missionary team, good guys like Darin and Kevin, unpacking our clothes in an apartment perched above a busy street, molting from our tourist's skin as we became citizens in an alien land and dialed into the city's idiosyncrasies, its cheap eats and good bookstores, righting the misdirections of lost tourists—all the things I'd dreamed about last fall when I applied for the overseas fellowships, now returning to me. I couldn't name the exact city, but I felt I already knew it, that I recognized myself there. I felt as though I'd once again gone through the open door I'd found when I swam in the ocean at night. This time the passageway led through space rather than time, to the other side of the world. It felt right. It felt like God's will.

With Jake's help, I found a last-minute spot on a summer project team going to Brisbane, Australia. The summer was a warm-up; if the project went well, I'd have the opportunity to return for a yearlong stint, maybe even longer. I raised the $3,500 for the trip by writing to my stepmother's church friends and citing in my letter statistics about the decline of Christianity in Australia. The country was quickly becoming "post-Christian," and, if something didn't change, it would soon be as secular as France or the Netherlands. At the end of the letter, I wrote the verse from Matthew, the same verse from the tract given to me in the library: "Go, therefore, and make disciples of all nations." I thought only briefly about the tract I'd received in the library, or the man who gave it to me. I saw myself as an antidote to people like him. The idea that we were in any way similar was unthinkable.

Graduation weekend delayed my departure a few days, so rather than meet the team in Los Angeles to fly with them to Brisbane, I arranged to fly to Australia on my own. My father and stepmother threw a graduation party for me. My mother and stepfather attended, chugging mimosas as they sweated through their dressy clothes. My stepfather tugged at his tie. My stepmother waited until all the guests had arrived—a few teammates from the swimming team, my coach, my boss from my on-campus job—before presenting me with a framed collage of photographs she'd culled from the last ten years. A lot of beach pictures. On the back was an inscription from Psalm 112, "For he shall never be moved; the righteous shall be in everlasting remembrance." "Of all the ways I'm proud of you," she said, "I'm most proud that you were unmoved in your commitment to stay sexually pure." She raised her champagne flute and toasted my virginity. My mother's eyebrows collapsed and her mouth narrowed to a point. I gulped my champagne and asked my father to fill me up.

A few days later, my stepmother drove me to the airport. "If you find it's not for you, try to hang in there," she said. "Being a missionary isn't for everyone."

"I want to live my faith," I said.

"That's the right frame of mind," she said. "When Jesus sets your hand to the plow, you can't look back." She got out of the car to kiss me goodbye. The circle at LAX was crowded with cars and buses. My stepmother waved the bus fumes away from her face before opening her arms. "We're praying for you," she said. She patted my backpack and got back in the car. I moved toward the sliding terminal doors. I looked back to wave goodbye one more time before going inside, but she was already gone.

After seventeen hours on the plane, a taxi ride from the airport to a downtown hostel, and breakfast the next morning in the tiny lobby café, I realized it had been two days since I'd had a conversation that didn't involve an exchange of money. I walked around Brisbane's city center after breakfast. The government buildings were made of blocks of humid gray stone—colonial, cold-weather buildings plopped down on tropical soil, flanked by palm trees. It was a colorless morning, and my body, fifteen hours off schedule, didn't know whether to wake up or shut down. *No one knows I'm here*, I thought. *No one knows where I am at this very minute.* The people who passed by in the square didn't know me; if I disappeared and my picture showed up on the news, none of them would remember seeing me. My ministry team wouldn't recognize me, either. I walked over to the bus station, much farther on foot than the map suggested, and when I slumped off my backpack, I saw that I had sweated through my T-shirt. The cotton sucked against my back and in twin stripes down my shoulders. I got in line for the ticket counter.

The team was staying at a camp on the Sunshine Coast, an hour and a half north of Brisbane, planning the summer's activities and getting to know each other. Two other backpackers with masks and snorkels clipped to the outside of their packs stood in line ahead of me. They bought tickets to Cairns, the launching point for excursions to the Great Barrier Reef. The woman between us bought a ticket to Grafton, in the other direction. The backpackers stepped aside to shuffle their change back into their wallets, and as I approached the counter, they eyed me with a mixture of curiosity and expectation, as if waiting for me to join them. I looked like a backpacker, but I wasn't. I looked like I was free to meander my way around this bat-shaped continent, to go where I pleased, but I wasn't. For a second, I considered buying a ticket to the Reef. I had $3,500 in my pocket, money I was supposed to turn over to the team leader upon my arrival. It would be close to $6,000 Australian if I exchanged it, enough to travel on for a while. The solitude and small talk that had once daunted me no longer did. The clerk tapped his fingernails on the metal counter behind the glass, and I bought my ticket to meet the team. I nodded at the backpackers and climbed on board.

The sun popped out as soon as we left the city, and before long, I was watching the South Pacific flash and recede between the high-rise condominium towers and trees, the road sweeping against and away from the coast. Green hills leapt up from the sea, and the trees looked upside down, their winter branches tangled up like roots. My backpack on the seat beside me fell against my shoulder or the window with every turn, and my emotions began to pitch back and forth: I was ready for company, but the team had been together for five days without me. Several of the members attended UC Santa Barbara, so they knew one another already. I wondered if my stepmother, trying to reassure me in the car on the way to the airport, had issued a prophecy. But when the bus pulled to my stop—nothing more than a metal bench and a flag beside the

highway—the sky was windswept blue, and everyone on the team, all fifteen of them, stood shoulder to shoulder, holding up a twelve-foot strip
of butcher paper that read, G'DAY DAVE!

I made my way toward the front of the bus. The driver asked, "Are you
Dave?"

"Yes."

"Well, then," he said. "G'day."

The team cheered when I stepped down from the bus. The bus pulled
away, and we stood in the road, shaking hands and exchanging names:
Eric and Lisa, the leaders, and Pat and Joanie and Steve and Amber and
Rusty and Annie and Jeff and Kathy and Ben and Tanya and Josh and
Emily and Hannah. "David," I said, over and over, until my hand was slick
and tight. "Or Dave," I said, looking again at the sign. "Dave is fine. Either
way. It doesn't matter."

"You're finally here!" Joanie said. She wore dark sunglasses, a hooded
sweatshirt. Ben, beside her, wore a sweatshirt that said, THAT'S RIGHT: I'M
A JESUS FREAK.

"We're all together now," Eric said, lean, tan, and shirtless. Pat took my
pack to carry it, and we headed toward the beach.

After two days on the coast, we moved down to Toowong, fifteen minutes
by bus from central Brisbane. We headquartered in an old holiday lodge:
two little apartments upstairs and a larger one, with a good-sized living
room and kitchen, downstairs. During the summer months, the place
probably exuded a certain tropical charm, the green-and-brown plaidwork
in the wallpaper faintly reminiscent of Pacific Island teakwood, the elongated conical light fixture hanging from the ceiling like an enormous bee-
hive. In the winter, when the beaches were deserted and the pool behind
the lodge was too cold for swimming, the compound felt antiquated, the
jacaranda in the courtyard untended, the oven and refrigerator rusty and
unreliable, the clothes washer nothing more than a basin with a hose.
But we had the place to ourselves, and after a day or two, we grew fond
of the décor and began to bestow adjectives upon it. "Discoteca," Tanya
said. "Groovy."

"Pimp," Jeff said. "Totally pimp."

Eric and Lisa lived in the upstairs studio, next door to the women's apartment, a big one-bedroom with a narrow sitting area at the front. The women's beds were arranged barracks-style in the big room, their twin mattresses lined up on the floor in two parallel rows and decorated with pillowcases brought from home, pink or purple or flowered. Porcelain cups from the kitchen tea set were commandeered to hold necklaces and earring backings, the bric-a-brac of hair spray canisters and lotion bottles and nail polish. In the mornings I woke to the sound of water running above me as the first of the women rose to shower. They descended the stairs still steaming and flushed, their wet hair soaking through the shoulders of their T-shirts. Through the damp cotton suctioned to their skin, I glimpsed the knobs of their shoulders, the shape of their breasts, the hook and sweep of their collarbones.

We sat around the table and drank coffee and ate Weetabix heaped with sugar. Some sat quietly and read the Bible while others wrote letters to the boyfriends or girlfriends they left behind. I had no one to write, and I was one of the exceptions. Despite the tethers to home, several team members had discovered a romantic chemistry and paired off into couples. Maybe it had something to do with the hemispheric switch, or our singleness of purpose, or simply our close quarters. We were seven unmarried men living with seven unmarried women, and though we'd all vowed to remain virginal until marriage, desire, like a river, wound its way though our cautions either by channel or fissure. In the city during the day, one of the men would spy an attractive woman and issue a warning not to look in her direction, lest we fill our hearts with lust, but at home there was room for a gentler flirting. Sitting in the same room with a woman blow-drying her hair was a kind of intimacy, even if it wasn't explicitly sexual. Carrying two coffee cups to the table—this too could be intimate. But we stayed out of one another's bedrooms. Everything took place in the common areas, in plain view. Just two people cooking together, rubbing each other's shoulders, sharing a magazine on the couch.

I'd arrived too late for couplehood, so it was easy for me to avoid the physical contacts that led some of the team members to whisper that "Annie and Ben spent too much time by themselves," or that "Rusty and Kathy shouldn't fall asleep against each other." But I was an odd fit anyway. I read Rilke's *Duino Elegies* at the kitchen table. My T-shirts weren't

screened with Quicksilver or Billabong logos; my jeans were regular-fit
Levi's. I was sarcastic and had a tendency to swear. A sip of coffee that
burned my mouth: "fuck." The slab of purple beetroot that came standard
on every Australian cheeseburger: "get this shit off." The city bus driver
who made fun of our "Yank" accents: "what an asshole." The words spilled
out of my mouth before I could catch them, and I'd receive a piercing
stare of reproach from someone on the team, sometimes a look of frank,
contemptuous astonishment. "Sorry," I'd say, and rap my knuckles against
my skull. I blamed my swim team for its bad influence, but in truth, I
loved the power contained in those words, their defiance of decorum,
their acrid, economical protests.

In private, Steve confessed: "When I surf, I cuss up a storm. In my
book, the rules don't apply at sea." So I worked to hold my tongue unless
I was in the water.

Our surfer culture helped mask our missionary purpose. We called
Bible study "small group" and the weekly meeting "The Gathering." The
Australian branch of the ministry organization was called Life Ministries,
short for "Lay Institute for Evangelism," and the tables we erected at the
universities displayed signs that simply read STUDENT LIFE. An unsus-
pecting first-year could approach us thinking we were a desk for campus activities, and we hoped for precisely such a mistake. Such a bending
of language was the manifestation of the larger evangelical impulse to
make Christianity more contemporary and appealing, unafraid of lingo
and rock music and computers, embracing the forms of modern culture while simultaneously dissenting from its values. We operated on the
premise that, though some people knew nothing about Jesus, most knew
enough to have developed preconceptions about what it meant to be a
Christian, and to be scared off by the presence of missionaries, by the
idea of answering the door to a person holding a Bible in his hands. If we
could lead them past their prejudices, to an encounter with the *real* Jesus,
they'd naturally see the true benefits of the Christian life. So we moved in
secret, festooned in our emblazoned surfer wear, jamming to mainstream
music, our hair sculpted with gel, convinced we were here to be cool, to
be attractive, to infiltrate and affect.

Unlike many Christian groups in foreign countries, we weren't there
to build homes or clothe and shelter the weak. We were there to spread
the Word. Our second night in Toowong, Eric passed around the tract we

would use on campus. It was the Australian version of the tract the ministry organization used in America, titled "Knowing God Personally." In our addiction to acronyms and coded language, we promptly took to calling it the KGP.

Four pages long and small enough to hide inside a breast pocket, each page contained a single verse from the Bible and a diagram illustrating mankind's separation from God and Christ's atonement for human sin. At the end, a six-sentence prayer invited Jesus to sit on the throne of our hearts. The founder of the organization and the author of the tract, now in his late seventies, famously could move from page one to the prayer in thirty seconds. I'd always resisted the tract, just as I'd resisted sharing my faith. I'd told myself that *my* relationship to Jesus didn't come from a tract and therefore couldn't be summarized by one. The real reason for my resistance, though, was that tracts were the calling cards of the wild-eyed street-corner proselytizers, of protesters lying in the street to block the entrance to women's clinics, of disheveled men stalking the basements of university libraries. The appearance of the tract marked the boundary between an informal conversation and an official act of proselytism, and no exchange was more awkward than a tract passing between a proselytizer and a person who'd rather not receive it. But the KGP was what we'd been given to use and what I would teach other students to use when I returned for the yearlong mission. I committed myself to overcoming my misgivings and learning how to use it.

We were divided into three teams and dispatched to campuses in different sections of Brisbane. While the other two teams went to the satellite campuses in the remote suburbs, I was relieved to be on the team assigned to the flagship campus of the Queensland University of Technology (QUT), nested on the south end of downtown against the Brisbane River. Each morning, Steve, Amber, Hannah, Josh, and I set out for campus with our pockets and backpacks stuffed with KGPs rubber-banded together in stacks of fifty. We rode the bus into the city, climbed the stairs from the underground depot, and emerged onto the Queen Street Arcade, cobblestoned and quiet, populated with locals and tourists, T-shirt shops and fancy boutiques, noodle stands, a big Billabong store from which wafted the aroma of rubber and surf wax. Some days an Aboriginal man in Levi's striped his face and chest with whitewash and sat cross-legged humming into a six-foot, hand-carved didgeridoo. After Queen Street, we crossed into the angular grid of financial towers and either cut across the lawns of the Botanic Gardens or headed down George Street past the Parliament House. Outside the campus gates was a deconsecrated Anglican church now operating as a pancake restaurant. I snapped a photograph of the vinyl banner suspended from the red brick façade to use in the support letter I'd need to write to earn money so I could return full-time. It was evidence Christianity in Australia was in stark decline. Churches were turning into storefronts rather than the other way around.

Once we'd erected our table on the patio outside the Student Centre, we divided ourselves yet again. Two stayed at the table and three fanned out to walk the campus. In addition to the KGPs, we were armed with a brief survey of spiritual beliefs to use as a conversation starter. QUT was like a compact city of sleek, modern buildings, all steel and glass, organized into alphabetical blocks. The campus map resembled a children's primer for learning shapes and letters. *A is for Acute Triangle . . . D is for Decagon.* I searched for students eating lunch alone, students who might welcome a little conversation, students with their heads bent over a book. I told myself people didn't mind getting interrupted. Who wouldn't rather talk than study? I thought, purposefully forgetting that I'd rather study than do almost anything else as well as the looks my own classmates gave to the man who visited my college library.

Steve and Josh and Hannah walked up to people as though it was second nature to them, but I stood on the edge of my messianic destiny as if I were standing beside a swimming pool before a race. My mouth was dry, and I yawned to settle my pounding heart. I approached someone, a KGP tucked beneath a stack of surveys, a pen squeezed between my fingers. I said I was polling students about their spiritual beliefs and the influence of religion on campus—would they mind answering a few questions? In my sunglasses and backpack, I looked like a student, so most people said okay. My questions were brief and open-ended: "What is your religious background?"; "What is your conception of heaven?"; "If you died today, do you know what would happen?" I glanced around the terrace at the other students filing toward the Student Centre for lunch. I told myself we were just two people sitting in the sun having a conversation. We looked normal. This conversation was normal. Evangelism was normal.

The questions were designed to provoke shrugs and shakes of the head, my opening for sliding the KGP to the top of my stack and asking to share it. "It will only take a minute," I said. Some were surprised by the KGP and realized the survey was a gimmick, but most shrugged and told me to go ahead. They listened to what I had to say, and they followed along as I turned the pages. At the end I asked if I could leave the KGP with them. I didn't corner them into praying; I handed it over and asked them to think about it. I walked away relieved and exhilarated to have made it through the pitch one more time. No one screamed at me, no one told me to get lost, but no one prayed with me, either. I distributed dozens of KGPs and filled out dozens of surveys. I got my testimony down cold.

Reunited in Toowong at the end of the day, we cooked spaghetti in a cauldron-sized pot and sat around the table or on the couch with our plates balanced on our knees. After dinner, we prayed and sang. Rusty and Jeff were our lead guitarists, and Pat played a little too. They played the same praise songs we sang during my weekly campus fellowship meetings, which I could sing along with, and Christian rock songs I didn't know and had to sit and listen to in silence. Then the devotional was finished, the guitars were back in their cases, the lights were turned up, and for the rest of the night we played Mao and Hearts and told stories. We talked about the people we'd dated (I said nothing about Julianne), the Bible studies we'd formed and led (for me, none), the other projects we'd participated in (also, none). The longer these stories went on, the more I felt like a different animal, an interloper among the apostles. Emily asked me, "How did you go all four years of college without leading a Bible study?"

I shrugged. "I was busy," I said. "I swam four hours a day. I studied a lot." She frowned. "That's too bad."

One evening Eric passed around sheets of construction paper and a sack of markers and asked each of us to draw a timeline of our spiritual lives, how we came to God and the paths by which God had led us to Australia. I sat on the living room floor, my Rilke book beneath the paper so my marker wouldn't punch through. Some of the markers were scented, and as ink bled into the soft paper the room began to smell like bubble gum and acetone. I considered making a crack about getting high on Christ, but thankfully, I thought better of it.

For a long time I stared at my blank sheet. It occurred to me that I could, if I chose, make my life sound as devout as anyone in the room:

My stepmother had been on the ministry staff and was now a pastor; my stepsister had attended a Christian college and even volunteered with the Family Research Council in Washington D.C. I drew a line across the page and began to write these things down, but as I did, they began to look false. I didn't believe them myself; surely no one else would either, and this sharing exercise would only push me farther apart from them. Eric already seemed to doubt my sincerity, and I knew it was his job to evaluate whether or not I should come back for the stint.

"Okay, McGlynn," Eric said. He sat on the sofa, his bronzed arms folded behind his head. "Your turn."

"When I was fifteen, my best friend was murdered," I said. Hannah, beside me, made a small noise, but everyone else was quiet, stunned. I continued, "I talked to him, like, twenty minutes before it happened. His mother had gone to pick up his little sister and my little sister from swimming practice, and when they got back home, they found Jeremy and his older brother and father on the living room floor. They'd all been shot in the back of the head, execution-style." The phrase "execution-style" surprised even me; I hadn't heard it since the days immediately following the murders, when the news repeated it every time it reported on the crime. I now understood its value: It removed ambiguity. "It was a professional hit," I said.

"My God," Amber said. Her mouth hung open.

"Who did it?" Hannah asked. "Why?"

"No one knows," I said. "The crime's never been solved."

"Never?" Hannah said. Her cheeks, spotted with freckles, were plum colored.

"Never," I said. I told how I talked to the detective in the neighbors' living room the day after the murders, and the other detective in the assistant principal's office a few months later. I told about the bloody carpets behind the garage, Trey Smith and Mike Collins dropping acid in the woods, Curt Wood's hand around his girlfriend's neck. The only parts of the story I left out were the moments I couldn't explain: zooming in and out of time in front of the TV, and at Vince's house, and later, in California, the door in the ocean. Every face I looked into stared back with rapt attention, their eyes on me and nowhere else.

Hannah leaned on her arm and set her hand so close to mine that I could have hooked my pinky around hers and no one would have seen me do it. I'd known the power of this story for a long time, the kind of sympathy and forgiveness it could generate, and I'd sworn never to use it in this way. But the more I talked, the more the details came back to me, and the more the story seemed to swell. I felt myself swelling along with it, gaining the team's esteem, at last winning their love. "For me, evil wasn't evidence against God," I said. "It was a reason to believe. After Jeremy died, I saw how much I needed Jesus in my life."

"That's quite a testimony," Eric said.

"It's the truth," I said. The high the story had created was deflated the moment I heard myself say these words, as fast as a needle in a balloon. The fact that I needed to defend the truth of the story, to make sure the team knew I wasn't making it up, showed me that I was a fraud. No one else heard it this way; I was still haloed in their saintly regard. My stomach dropped. I stared down at my hands.

Rusty and Jeff approached me afterward to tell me they were moved by my story. Pat asked me if I wanted to walk down to the Toowong Shopping Plaza for coffee. I wanted to run outside and jump in the swimming pool with my clothes on, a frigid plunge to cleanse me of my sin. But the lure of friendship was strong, a temptation too great to resist, and I followed Pat out the door.

After that night, I began to gravitate toward Josh, the other misfit on the team. Josh was an oddball, an art student from Chicago, one of the two on the team not from California. His hair was so blond and short that from a distance he looked bald; his head bobbed around atop his elongated neck as though he was missing vertebrae. He laughed in a way I imagined a horse laughing, all teeth and gums, and washing dishes in the kitchen or waiting for the bus, he showcased a series of dance moves, all pantomimes of working-class jobs: the bus driver, the dishwasher, the yardman, and several more made up on the spot: the meat packer, the chimney sweep. Each one was a variation on the same axial principle: loose hips and a big dopey grin so you knew it was his joke from start to finish. His dark navy workpants and matching jacket looked more like a sanitation worker's than an art student's or a missionary's. Like me, he resisted the KGP. Unlike me, he shared his faith with everyone he met.

Josh kept an eye out for anyone riding the bus alone. For me, the fifteen-minute descent into Brisbane was a time to talk, a chance to dream. I studied the bus's wavy reflection in the storefronts' mirrored windows, the shops' wide awnings trimmed with wrought iron, their cumbersome eight-digit phone numbers. I tried to convert the price of gasoline from Australian to American dollars, and from liters to gallons, but I lost track of the numbers when my attention floated to the Union Jack hanging in the chemist's window or the brightly colored office buildings that looked made of Legos or the palm trees shushing in the tropical wind. I practiced pronouncing the vowel-heavy Aboriginal words. Baroona, Mount Coot Tha, Warrawee. Meanwhile, Josh strode up to any solitary rider and asked to sit down, even if the rest of the bus was vacant. We climbed aboard one morning and saw a woman, heavyset and plain, sitting with her ear and temple against the window, a few rows from the rear. Threads of brown hair clung to her cheek. The bus was otherwise empty. Josh pretended not to know the rest of us as he shoved his hands into his jacket pockets and stomped to the last row. I sat near the front with my back to the window where I could look back without appearing to watch. Each time the bus stopped, Josh moved one seat forward. When I glanced back again, he was in the seat behind the woman, with his elbows hanging over her seat. His head undulated in cadence with the bus. One more stop, and he swung around to sit beside her, the KGP in his palm. He hadn't exactly come around to the tract, but he'd promised Eric he'd use it. The woman leaned her head toward his, and from the front, they looked like a couple gazing down together at a map of the city. Josh's eyes pendulated from his lap to the woman's ear. His lips almost brushed her lobe. She nodded along as he talked.

Two stops before Queen Street, the woman pulled the cord. She stood and squeezed past Josh's knees, her stomach pressed against the seat back. Josh stood to let her pass and then followed her off, not even a sideways glance toward the rest of us. None of us followed him, and a second later the bus was in motion. Hannah pulled the cord and we scrambled off at the next stop and hurried down the sidewalk. Josh was on the corner beneath the blinking DON'T WALK hand, face-to-face with the woman, right where we'd left him. The woman had her back to the building. A red Australia Post truck rambled past, emitting an oily black cloud of diesel exhaust. The woman stepped toward the corner, and Josh took hold of her sleeve. Hannah gasped. Josh's hand on the woman's arm changed the rules of the game. She now had the right to scream for help. "Should we do something?" I asked.

Steve, Hannah, and Amber shrugged. None of us had been in this situation before.

Josh was shaking his free hand, his palm upturned and open, as though measuring the weight of a melon. He was pleading, and despite his fervor and zealousness, he didn't look menacing; he looked earnest. Evangelism wasn't an abstract exercise for him. When Josh shared his faith timeline, he'd confessed to worrying that before he accepted Christ, he'd committed the unforgiveable sin—blasphemy against the Holy Spirit—and now, no matter what he did, the blemish remained, indelible and varicose. He shared his faith with the urgency of a man who believed his time was short. His arm fell to his side and he and the woman stood immobilized. She didn't run away. Josh pressed the tract into her hand, extracted a pen from his jacket pocket, and wrote on the cover. He left her standing there and walked toward us. The woman slipped around the corner, disappeared.

Josh restrained his smile until he reached us. By then he couldn't resist.

"You're kidding," Steve said. "She said yes?"

Josh nodded.

"Prayed the prayer and everything?"

Josh nodded again, his big bobble-headed nod. "I gave her our phone number in case she wants to talk. I hope Eric won't mind."

"No way," Hannah said. She kicked the toe of her flip-flop against the sidewalk. "Amazing."

"God did it," Josh said. "Not me."

God worked through Josh more times than I could count. It happened more than once on the bus, and larking along Queen Street in the late afternoon, and in the Thomas Cook where we cashed our traveler's checks. I'd stop before a shop window, and when I turned around, Josh would have struck up a conversation with a stranger and was already on page two of the KGP. He wasn't the only one. Each night when the team gathered for prayer, the other members recounted the students they'd led to decisions to follow Christ. The Gathering grew and grew. Each week more students crowded into the house of the local staff member where the meeting was held. Six women sardined together on a couch built for three; dozens more sat on the floor and stood against the walls and bookcases and in the hallway leading to the toilet and in the front entryway, the door hanging open to let in the winter air, the windows fogged with moisture. My teammates stood with the students they invited, over-whelmed and eager young men and women in DKNY sweatshirts and cardigan sweaters. I helped mix the punch into pitchers and carried the plates of Anzac biscuits to the living room. I mingled among the new-comers and introduced myself. No one was here because of me. Summer was half over, and despite the dozens of times I'd shared my testimony, I had yet to save a single soul.

Friday night the guys dressed in khakis and collared shirts, the women in glittered makeup and strapless dresses, and we rode the bus into the city. Eric and Lisa stayed behind. Eric had spent the last two days seques-tered upstairs with the flu; our going out was a favor to them—a few hours without the murmur of conversation and guitar strings vibrating through the floor. The bus's long descent into the sparkling city felt like a rollercoaster on a nosedive, the steep plunge you have to ratchet up to reach. Were we not missionaries, the night would have felt charged with sex, electrified with that crackling, corpuscular pop of expectation. Joanie pulled a black Vivitar from her purse, and we leaned into the aisle to pose then leapt up to pretend we were going to jump through the windows. The driver shouted for us to bloody sit down, and when we settled back into the seats, Hannah leaned against my shoulder. Joanie snapped the shutter. For an instant, Hannah felt like my girlfriend. It was a night when I was eager to be leaned against.

Queen Street and the Myer Centre were by now no longer tantalizing, and when we hopped down from the bus, we hurried away into the dark. We didn't have a destination. A few blocks south, we arrived at the river. The water held the skyline like a mirror. The water taxi sat moored to the dock, white and blue like a police cutter. It was part of the city transit sys-tem, and our bus passes entitled us to ride for free. We scrambled aboard and leaned against the railing. The boat floated loose, caught the current, and the engine below the deck rumbled to life. I felt the floor rise up into my knees, then quickly fall away. A little distance from the shore, the sky-line came into panoramic view. The windows in the middle of the finan-cial towers still glowed, and the few lighted windows on the upper floors stair-stepped into the clouds. The warning lights atop the towers dif-fused their crimson flashes across the sky's wide canopy. We bounced our knees as the boat cut the chop. Steve and Josh walked in big steps across the deck, from port to starboard, their hands spread out as though walking on the moon. The boat plowed over a wake field, and we shook and stumbled and called out, "Whoa!" Kathy, dirty blond and broad-shouldered, shook her solid hips and pumped her butt up and down. Tanya and Joanie joined in, and the three women bumped hips in a triangle, in sync with the boat's rise and fall. A sudden dip pitched Tanya into Joanie. Their breasts smashed together; they were close enough to kiss. Steve called out, "Oh yeah! Get your freak on!"

"Hey now!" Jeff said, and clapped out a beat. The women gyrated in rhythm. The others joined in, even Emily, and though I clapped along, I couldn't help thinking that I was on furlough in a country I'd wanted to visit for years, and this is what my adventure amounted to: phantom touches, toying with innuendos we pretended didn't point to sex.

With wobbly knees, we stepped from the boat and walked into the silent grid of the financial district. We were alone on the street, in groups of two and three strung out over the length of the block. We moved like a school of fish. Amber at the front made a turn, and the rest of us followed. On Caxton Street we passed by an Irish bar, Kitty O'Shea's, the windows covered with a black film thick enough to mute the neon beer signs and stage lights. Music pounded through the windows and the heavy oak door. The bouncer pulled open the door's brass handle, and music screamed out like a wild animal let out of a cage, a gust of funk and smoke. We passed through the door as if this was our intended destination all along.

The bar was decorated to simulate old-world Ireland—Guinness' and Murphy's streetlamps above the bar, the cash register of tarnished brass, distressed road signs measuring the distance to Kilkenny and Wexford and Galway, as though it wasn't so far, as though we weren't two oceans away. But it still felt like Australia: Men in T-shirts and oxfords stood on both sides of narrow counters only wide enough for a pint and an elbow, facing each other as if they were squaring off to arm wrestle. A squadron of taps lined the bar rail. The bartenders worked the levers as if they were playing a cathedral organ, a practiced yet hurried rhythm, and along the rail sudsy foam, XXXX and Power's and Guinness, cascaded down the curves of the pints, leaving oily haloes on the counter and puddles on the floor.

The team had decided not to drink for the summer. They made the decision before my arrival, but I'd agreed to abide by it. Tonight, though, I wanted a beer. I wanted to lift a pint from the bar and raise it to my mouth. I wanted to feel the glass clink against my teeth. It wasn't the alcohol I wanted, it was the feeling that would come from drinking beer in a faraway land, in the Southern Hemisphere, on a Friday night. If I could have a beer, I could pretend I'd made it across an ocean for a reason other than saving souls. I wanted to lose contact with my old self, the self who had spent his college years in Bible studies and campus fellowship meetings, the self who had balked at love and shut himself off from someone who'd taken his breath away. I wanted a break from that guy, for just a night. I wanted to be—I winced at the word, but there it was—*normal*.

The band was into something fast, the fiddler running ahead of the other players, who held their instruments at their sides. The singer, the lone woman among the quartet of men in black jeans and unbuttoned vests, stood with her eyes closed, her hand gripping the microphone. She bounced one tall black boot and kept the beat with her free hand against her hip. Her skirt was wrinkled, paisley, and pleated, separated from her T-shirt enough to reveal a sliver of her milk-white belly. Her red hair hung past her elbow in a heat-crimped curl. Beneath the stage lights it was the color of an apple.

Her name was Fiona. When the band broke and she stepped down from the stage and pressed through the dance floor on her way to the bar, Josh asked her her name. He leaned on an elbow against the bar and talked with her for longer than I expected, long enough for her to enjoy the conversation. She waved at the bartender. The stage lights dimmed over the drum set, and radio music came over the speakers. Though it was U2, an Irish band in a simulated Irish bar, it sounded out of place. With the music lower, the conversation kicked up a few notches, and soon the room was all clamor and clanking, "With or Without You" droning in the background.

A red-cheeked man spun from the bar with a pint in each hand and bumped against my shoulder. I now had beer on my shirt and neck, close enough to taste, but I didn't give in. I watched Fiona make her way toward the stage with a pint in her hand and a bottle of water tucked under her arm. I followed her onto the dance floor, and when the band reassembled and started up with a slow song that I could tell was going to break and run, and the crowd began to move, I moved with it. I swayed to the right and back to the left. Amber and Joanie and Kathy came onto the floor, and then Pat and Steve and Jeff and Hannah, and soon we were all dancing, all except Josh. The song hopped up to an electric jig, and the crowd began to leap. Fiona punished a tambourine against her hip and belted out a wail. I linked elbows with Jeff and Joanie, and we and spun and kicked. I was at the center of the gyroscope, lost in the whirl, and a sensation like abandon swept through me. I felt myself forgetting, I felt my manners and buttonholes trailing away like the rippling vapor from a jet engine. This was the closest I had come to otherworldliness.

I reached for Hannah's hands and we spun around. She slid closer, put her right hand in my left and her arm around my back. Her cheeks were bright red, and for a second I considered kissing her—a kiss to celebrate the moment, the kissing I'd missed on New Year's Eve when I was on my knees in a hotel ballroom. Closed up in this hot little bar we found by chance, we were free to indulge in the present, protected from the rest of the world, even from God's own watchful eye. I had lost time to make up for.

I spun her until our arms were outstretched. I pulled to reel her back, but Kathy hooked her elbow and swung her away. Hannah's moist palm slid from mine as she twirled off. Bodies closed in between us. Rather than chase her down, pin her against the wall, and plant one on her before she could object, I worked my way in the other direction, toward Josh. He leaned against a pillar at the end of one of the long, chest-high tables. His eyes were fixed on the stage, and he bounced a leg not quite in time with the beat. I wiped the sweat from my forehead and leaned into his ear. "Come dance," I said. "This is fun music to dance to. You can do your crazy moves."

"I can't."

"What's the matter?"

"Fiona," he said. "There's something about her."

Fiona's legs were spread for balance, and her red, red lips worked the black orb of the microphone. Josh was studying the exposed crescent of her stomach, the sway of her hips. I could feel him want her. "I know," I said. "There *is* something about her."

"She has this, like, glow," Josh said. "An aura. It's like her spirit is talking to me."

"She's a singer. She's got a Stevie Nicks thing going on. The aura is part of it."

"It's not like that. It's different. I need to talk to her when she's done singing. I've got to see if I can get her alone for a minute."

"For what?" I asked.

"I need to share Christ with her," he said. "I feel like God's pulling on my heart."

He turned to me, his eyes full of resolve, though his resolve didn't look like zeal for Christ. It looked like loneliness, like the same frustration that pulsed through me, longing squeezed into a different container and labeled with a different name. I recalled Josh's hand on the arm of the woman from the bus, his released and airy smile as he floated back to us, and for a moment I entertained the idea of an erotic component to proselytizing. Wasn't this what we'd been told? That saving a soul led to a deeper gratification than sex? Could it produce a pleasure felt in the body? Such a pleasure, if it existed, seemed at best a substitute. A booby prize.

"Come on," I said. "Not tonight. We're in a bar. We're dancing. Let's have fun for a little while and then go home."

"We're here," he said. "We found this place out of the blue. You think that was an accident?" He pushed his shoulder away from the pillar, stepped onto the dance floor, and pinballed his way through the crowd to the stage. Fiona smiled without missing a note. Josh was not the first guy to cross a crowded dance floor to get a second whiff of her aura. He stood with his arms at his sides, his hands open, waiting to catch her when she jumped.

The band was still playing when we headed back to Queen Street to catch the last bus to Toowong. Josh wanted to stay, said he was willing to stay alone, but we didn't let him. On the street he lagged behind the group, his fists in his jacket pockets, his eyes on his shoes. In the shadows between the streetlamps he dissolved into the dark. The top of his head, burred and blond and disembodied, floated along like a searchlight on the bow of a fishing trawler. Pat and I dropped back to make sure he was okay, but he shuffled his feet and stared away. I was angry with him for trying to ruin the night, for taking my one flimsy brush with wantonness and turning it into an opportunity to evangelize. When he didn't answer me, I walked ahead of him and let him be. He sat alone on the bus, and when we at last opened the door to the house, he walked immediately into the room he shared with Pat and Steve and went to bed without brushing his teeth.

Before going to sleep, I opened the door and looked in on him. He was turned toward the wall, the blanket up over his shoulder, his jacket and shoes in a heap beside the mattress. There was something about him I couldn't quite figure, a cavern in his heart that was frightening to behold. Even in his most joyful moments he seemed on the verge of desperation; being around him was like watching a gambler on a cold streak lay his last dollar on the table. It was a feeling I knew myself, and watching him sleep, I remembered my own nights of despair. Was this because of Fiona? Because of a singer in a bar? He had to know he never had a chance with her—but then again, my own short-lived affair with Julianne had come to little more than six weeks of rolling around on her living room floor, and still I emerged from it feeling amputated. I winced, recalling my room-mates' efforts to help and their frustration when they could not.

Josh stayed in bed until after three the next afternoon. Through-out the day we checked on him, offering plates of eggs and cups of tea, but he didn't respond. By eleven AM he was awake but still in his sheets, his Bible open beside him on the pillow. When he finally emerged, the daylight had turned golden in the windows, the winter slant illuminat-ing the billions of dust particles atomizing the air. Josh's undershirt was wrinkled and damp in the chest and armpits. The stitching of the pil-lowcase had imprinted a bumpy road from his temple to his neck. With the light behind him, he looked translucent and ethereal, all smoke and wind. Seeing Josh standing in the doorway, I remembered the man who'd approached me in the library—his soiled shirt, his unreined eye—and it frightened me to realize how little separated that man from my friend.

Josh stood on his toes and leaned forward, poised to make an announce-ment, but he didn't speak. "Josh?" I said. "You okay?"

"The bathroom free?" he asked and drifted down the hallway. I heard the toilet flush and the shower turn on. Thirty minutes later he emerged wide-eyed and smelling of soap, his signature smirk curling the corners of his mouth. The tempest apparently was over. He flopped down in one of the wingback chairs to listen to Jeff play the guitar.

Later that night, I felt a hand on my shoulder. Lisa's straight blond hair fell over the back of my chair. She leaned in and whispered, "My hus-band would like to see you upstairs." She smiled like she was joking. The door to their apartment was ajar, an arrow of lamplight slicing the balcony. I knocked and pushed it open. Eric was sitting on the edge of the bed, a frayed beige blanket wrapped like a shawl around his head and shoulders. The sheets and quilt were in a twist at the foot of the bed. His legs looked thin inside his sweatpants.

"How're you feeling?" I asked.

"Horrible," he said. He was shivering so hard he could barely speak. His teeth were chattering. "This bug really got me hard. Some kind of a tropical fever."

"Can I get you anything?" For a moment, I thought he'd summoned me because he needed my help, some physical act his wife wasn't strong enough to do on her own.

"I'm okay," he said. "Have a seat."

The room's only chair had been turned around to face the bed. I sat in it. Eric's surfboards—he'd brought two—leaned against the wall, wrapped in padded polyester sleeves. "Things going okay over at QUT?"

"Good," I said. "We're making a lot of good connections."

"You're all doing good work," he said. "I'm glad you're a part of the team this summer. Your testimony about your friend's murder totally blew my mind. You could really have an impact on people's lives if you told it more often. It would be a great honor to your friend if his death could lead people to Christ."

"Yes," I said, and for a moment I thought that this was why he'd summoned me. He wanted to ask me to tell Jeremy's story at whatever church we visited tomorrow, or else at The Gathering on Tuesday. He wanted me to make it part of my pitch when I roamed campus with tracts in my pocket.

Eric paused and nodded, a movement intended for him, not for me. He cinched the blanket tighter and said, "Listen, we need to talk about something. Some of the things you say, especially around the women, aren't so . . . appropriate."

"I know," I said. "Sometimes my mouth gets away from me."

"Well, Paul says in Ephesians 4:29: 'Do not let any unwholesome talk come out of your mouths, but only what is helpful for building others up according to their needs, that it may benefit those who listen.' I know you're still weighing coming back for the stint next year. If you do, you'll spend a lot of time on your own. You'll be the whole show at QUT, not to mention an ambassador of Christ. You'll have to keep after yourself."

It was the rebuke I'd been waiting for, and even though I'd invited it and knew it was coming, I felt my face and neck flush with shame. I was twenty-two years old, getting my mouth washed out with soap. I could have insisted I wasn't the only one with a wayward tongue, but that would be even more sophomoric, and I was too embarrassed to consider anyone else's failures. I nodded, repentantly. "You're right," I said.

"Do you think you want to come back? Has God led you to a decision?"

"Not yet," I said. "The jury's still out."

Eric shook his head, lifted his fist and coughed into it. "There's no jury," he said. "There's only Jesus. What do you think's holding you back?"

"I don't know," I said. "I like it here. I could see coming back."

"That's fine, but liking it here isn't really the point, is it? I don't think the missionaries in Nigeria or Kazakhstan are there because they like the place. It's whether or not you're called. Maybe God's hit the pause button until you get these issues worked out."

I nodded again. "That's probably true."

"Saying you're a Christian doesn't amount to much if you don't live it," he said. "In fact, it's worse than that. It's hypocritical. You might not think of it that way, but that's how people will see you. You've got to walk the walk."

I'd wanted Eric's respect so badly I'd sold out Jeremy's memory in order to get it, and I'd still come up short. He saw through my pretensions as easily as Tommy Baker had, and Tommy had known all about the nights I slept over at Julianne's condo and how close I came to leaving the campus fellowship. The problem, I understood, went deeper than my recalcitrant language. I was six weeks into my career as a missionary, and had lived for all that time within a community of devoted believers, without touching so much as a drop of alcohol, and yet, though I was among them, I was still not yet one of them. "I'm sorry," I said. "I'll try harder."

"Give it over to God," Eric said. "Trust him to help you. His kingdom needs you." He lay back on the bed and worked his socks beneath the covers. I helped him unravel the twisted sheets and pulled them up to his chest. Eric pulled everything to his chin, the beige blanket still wrapped around his head. He couldn't get warm enough. "Thanks," he said, wriggling further down inside the covers. "I meant what I said earlier. You have the power to do a lot of good, to make a real impact. The team wouldn't be the same if you weren't here." His encouragement only sounded like an attempt to ballast his reproach. I needed to prove myself, and we both knew it.

Back downstairs, I stood in the courtyard beside the jacaranda, its few remaining leaves black on the stems. I moved in darkness around the back of the house, past the shed housing the washer and clothesline, and toward the pool. I planned to sit there awhile, but found it already occupied. Josh and Tanya sat together on the steps descending to the concrete patio, the rectangle of water in the center a lacquered plain beneath the sliver of moon. Josh hugged his knees, and Tanya had her chin in her palm. I could tell she was deep into their conversation. She was treading over deep water. She had a boyfriend back in Santa Barbara whom she talked to once a week; a photograph by her bed showed them together, her long chestnut hair tied in a ponytail, on a skateboard, beside a tall young man whose long blond hair blew in the breeze. The team members from Tanya's campus teased her with kissy noises and ooey-gooey voices. Here she was, leaning into Josh. The oddball. The star evangelist.

In the last weeks, Josh had become the center of the missionary team, while I'd remained its outlier, because he didn't fear being alienated or isolated or spit upon or mocked or called a freak. He wasn't afraid to stand alone and cry out in the wilderness. Lack of fear was the first ingredient of greatness, and Josh effused enough of it that we all leaned toward him in the hope of catching a little ourselves.

My embarrassment receded and in its place crashed a new, sharper tide of reproach, pushing back my anger. I'd spent the summer pretending to be a missionary, but all along, I'd kept my distance from the very message I'd proclaimed, even while praying for the courage to proclaim it. Up until now, I'd felt certain that because I could locate the origins of my faith in Jeremy's murder, because belief had been born in blood, that I'd been set apart from the regular tides of Christianity. I hadn't been converted with a tract while munching down a peanut butter sandwich; I'd been thrust into the fold of Christ by the wheels of the universe; my faith had been determined during The Big Bang. Yet, despite what I saw as my ongoing sacrifices in the name of Christ—my daily public embarrassment, my strained relationship with my mother and her brothers and parents, my incessant denial of so much bodily desire—I was the last person on the team fitted to become a missionary because I knew I lacked the discipline to live a Biblical life. I'd held my fear of the world's judgment so close that judgment became the lens through which I now viewed everyone else—judging those who rejected our message as close-minded and selfish, and, more ashamedly, those who accepted it as malleable and weak. Whenever I was asked what I was doing in Australia, I said, "I'm here to work with college students," not "I'm here to spread the good news of Jesus Christ." If my faith was a pretense then very likely my reasons for faith were pretenses as well.

It was an awful thought, and I stepped into the laundry shed and flicked on the light to escape it. Josh and Tanya's heads spun around. I waved, then shut off the light and walked back toward the street.

I resolved to make myself a freak. On Monday, I approached three men in Ray-Bans sharing lunch at a table. One of the three was holding forth with his hands in the air, and I didn't wait for him to finish. I passed out KGPs like a casino dealer. I didn't lower my voice to conceal the message. I told the table, "This is the most important decision you'll ever make," and then waited for an answer. One of the men bit into his sandwich, and the man I'd interrupted flicked back the KGP and said, "No thanks, mate." I moved on to the next table, wishing the lunch break would last a little longer. I walked up to men changing in the locker room at the recreation center. I left no bystander unaccosted. I needed to win one heart for Christ, just one before we left. If I could win one, I could win another. I could make it as a missionary. I could come back.

Josh and I were sharing a seat on the bus, two weeks before the end of the mission, when he leaned over and told me he'd fallen in love with Tanya. Not fallen in love like Romeo and Juliet; rather, God had revealed his plans and they included Tanya. "I had a vision," he said.

"Really? Not a dream?"

"I know when it's from God and when it's not. I didn't expect it myself. And I was awake when it happened." He looked down at his knees, as though his clothes held the secret about what to do next. Steve and Amber had taken him to the Billabong store on Queen Street and talked him into replacing his Dickies pants and mechanic's jacket with cargo pants and baggy jeans, his woolen beanie with a ball cap, and a half-dozen logoed T-shirts and sweaters—Billabong and Quicksilver, Rip Curl and Hurley. He looked enough like a surfer almost to pass for one. "You think I'm nuts?" he asked.

It did sound a little crazy, but I also saw the appeal: God pointing out, in no uncertain terms, the life we were destined for and the people we were destined to share it with. I'd wanted the same thing. I was on this bus, on the far side of the world, because I'd wanted *exactly* the same thing. I slapped Josh's knee and said, "No man, I don't think you're nuts. God's spoken to me before, too. At least I thought so at the time."

"That makes me feel better," he said.

"You and Tanya look good together," I said.

"Thanks for saying that," he said.

"What are you going to do about her boyfriend?"

He shrugged and sank lower in the seat. The bus pulled to a stop, and an old woman with a clear plastic rain bonnet tied beneath her chin hobbled off, into the drizzle. "I don't know," he said. "Maybe God is right now revealing to him that he's supposed to be with someone else. Maybe he's writing Tanya a letter as we speak."

I pulled up my sleeve to check my watch. It was 6:00 PM in California. "Could be."

"Wouldn't that be nice?" Josh said. "Make everything so much easier."

A few days later, Josh told Tanya about his vision. It was my night to do the dishes, and from the rear kitchen window I could see them sitting beside the pool, their two humped backs dimly lit by the bulb above the clothes washer. By the time the last plate was dried and stacked in the cupboard, Josh had left Tanya sitting alone and had come inside. He didn't say a word, but his face revealed everything. He went to his bedroom, closed the door.

For the remainder of the week we moved beneath the dome of an impending disaster. An offer was in the open, and Tanya had to deliberate over whose heart she would break. She and Josh acted like they hardly knew each other; they didn't sit together, and they didn't talk. After the evening prayer, Tanya retreated to the pool or down the hill to the coffee shop to read her Bible and write in her journal. Josh worked on the sermon Eric had asked him to deliver that weekend at our farewell retreat in Noosa Heads. Jeff and Rusty rehearsed a batch of songs. Amber, Pat, and Hannah went over the devotionals. I called to check on the bus schedule and hotel. Each night was busy with preparation. Tanya later told us how, on one of those nights, alone by the pool, she heard a clear and audible voice tell her Josh was the one. It fell from the sky like an echo from an airplane, only closer, smack in her face. The voice told her to say nothing until the retreat in Noosa Heads. There, God's plan would be made manifest. There, all would be revealed.

Noosa Heads is a postcard surfing village two hours north of Brisbane. Two small rivers wind out of the rainforest and disperse over polliwogs of white kidney-shaped islands as they empty into the Pacific, carving out a wetland reserve, a harbor, and long strips of squeaky white sand. The main street, Hastings, has a promenade lined with boutiques and bistros and eucalyptus trees, idyllic enough to rival any California tourist town. We occupied ten rooms in a one-star hotel at the far end of the promenade, in walking distance from the beach. We spent the day playing in the shore break and throwing Frisbees, and at night built a bonfire to cook hot dogs and sit around, talking and singing.

The hotel rooms were uncarpeted and the furniture slid easily over the linoleum. On the second night, we pushed the beds in one of the rooms out of the way and sat on the bare floor with our knees tucked beneath our chins, forty people in a room meant for four. Jeff and Rusty sang "Arms of Love," and then it was time for Josh's sermon. We pressed closer together to open the floor so Josh could pace. He held his Bible in his palm. He'd decided to speak about Paul's encounter with Jesus on the road to Damascus. He tapped Pat on the shoulder and asked him to get on his hands and knees, and then straddled Pat like a horse. Pat blushed and let his head sink toward the floor. The room chortled in concert, but Pat didn't mind; he was a bit of a ham. Josh's new red Billabong cap rode high on his forehead, high enough for the light from the table lamp to shine on his nose and mouth.

"So Paul's riding along, minding his own business, when suddenly Jesus appears in the sky," Josh said, scanning his eyes over the room. "It's like a bomb going off. *Kaboom*. Paul's knocked from his horse and struck blind." Just in case someone wasn't paying attention, Josh launched himself backward from Pat's spine. He was airborne for an instant, his feet above his waist, his hands in the air. The Bible landed with a flap and flutter a second before Josh's back smacked against the linoleum. It was the kind of physical goofiness we'd seen from him all summer, his ability to tumble and fall, but this fall was so integrated with the message that the room was struck dumb. Josh lay with his eyes closed, long enough for us to wonder if he was acting or hurt, or whether in an uncanny confluence of mimicry and divine intervention, he too had seen Jesus. The instant the question changed from dramatic to disconcerting, Josh leaped to his feet and scooped up the Bible. He held his arms stretched out, the big black Bible like a barbell at the end of his long right arm. He was breathing hard and his head and back eclipsed the light from the table lamp. He appeared to have doubled in size. "Sometimes God speaks in silence," he said. The room had yet to exhale; I could feel the pressure of forty held breaths. Josh slapped his palm against the Bible's back cover. "Other times he speaks in thunder. Make sure you're listening. Make sure you're listening as hard as you can."

He looked over at Tanya and winked.

The devotional finished, we headed back to the beach to watch the moon over the waves and to rebuild the bonfire. Tanya walked to a pharmacy on Hastings Street where she bought an extended-rate phone card and placed a call to her boyfriend in Santa Barbara. An hour later she appeared in the firelight. Her eyes were swollen, and in the flickering orange light, she looked afraid.

Tanya circled the fire to where Josh sat with his legs crossed. She touched his arm, he stood, and they walked down the beach together. I turned around and saw they'd wandered about a hundred feet. Farther down the beach were the outdoor seating areas of the Hastings Street bistros. The tables and chairs were sheltered from the onshore winds by clear plastic tarps suspended from a metal frame. The tarps rippled in the wind, capturing and dispersing the candlelight from the tables and the larger floodlights beneath the awnings. In the heavier gusts, the tarp filled with a flash of light, and in the flash I could see Tanya and Josh standing face-to-face. Josh had his hands in his pockets, and Tanya's hands hung at her sides. I couldn't hear what they were saying or see their faces, but Tanya worked her foot into the sand as though she was talking, and Josh nodded his head as though he was listening. When they separated and returned to the fire, there was no embrace, no long impassioned kiss. The moon sparkling over the South Pacific, the candles, and the starlight couldn't have been more romantic, and what they shared wasn't romance, not yet, but the terror of having heard God's voice. They shared the awe and burden of the sound.

~~~

A cloudy Brisbane morning, Hannah and I went for breakfast in the youth hostel where I'd eaten the morning of my arrival. It was our last day on campus, and I wanted the summer to end where it began. Fried eggs and bacon, and a grilled tomato I vowed to eat at every meal the rest of my life. Afterward, Hannah and I walked across the Botanic Gardens toward the QUT campus. The grass was heavy with dew, and when we stepped onto the footpath, my shoes and socks were soaked through. Water squished beneath the arches of my feet. Sweat beaded in the creases of my elbows and knees.

Although I'd thought of the last months as summer, a gap between semesters, they'd taken place in a different season. I'd left California in the late spring and would return at the beginning of autumn. I'd missed the whole summer, just as I missed a Tuesday during my flight from Los Angeles to Brisbane, and it was sad to think that in a few days, we'd re-enter our old lives and breathe its familiar air. The outer-space surrealism of this summer would begin to feel as crepuscular as a dream. I was already longing for what I was about to lose—our cheap big-pot dinners, our nights with the guitar, the courage to share my faith that I had only recently begun to find—and that longing had allowed me to announce to Eric that morning that I'd made a decision: God was calling me back, and I intended to listen. I'd be returning to Australia as soon as I could raise the support—the first of the year if God willed it, the end of January at the latest. I was going to live my faith once and for all, and this time I'd do it right. Eric had greeted my declaration a little warily, at first only scratching his chin and nodding, but even if my motivations were false, it was better to err on the side of Christ. "I'm glad," Eric said. "Australia needs you." And yet, I took in everything we passed by, from the church-turned-pancake house, to the street signs, to the swollen, urn-shaped trunks of the bottle trees with a photographer's eye, half aware that I'd never see any of it again.

Hannah slipped off her flip-flops and walked barefoot until her feet dried on the warm sidewalk. Her small footprints grew fainter with each step, and soon she left no trace behind. I was grateful to spend this last day with her, grateful she and I had been given the task of shutting down our operation here, and grateful for her company. We'd developed a sweet platonic friendship that was harder to come by than romance. Her parents and her older brother were ministry staff members, and though she'd always believed she'd follow a different path, she now felt the lure of a longer trip. I told her to come back to Australia with me. If we came back together, I could handle it. "We'd have a lot of fun," I said.

"Oh, sure," she said, giggling, a more definitive "no" than the word itself.

We crossed through the windswept corridors between the buildings, not really going anywhere. If we made it to Z block, we'd go inside and check our emails before wandering back to the Student Centre to take down the table. The team had boosted the ministries on three campuses, and it was now up to the Australian students to keep it going.

We rounded the corner into an empty courtyard, gray light and faint shadows and a few metal benches. A little chain link and a basketball hoop and it would have felt like a prison yard. It was deserted except for a young Asian woman sitting on one of the benches. She lifted her head and smiled. Her face was washed with a glassy and departed mask of loneliness, as if she'd just gotten the worst news of her life.

We asked the woman if we could sit down. We told her our names, and she said her name was Jiao. She was from Taiwan, and was in Brisbane studying marketing and English. English was harder than she had expected. In a voice barely above a whisper, she spoke in short spurts and colloquial phrases. "Australia is pleasant," she said. "I miss home."

"How long are you here?" I asked.

"One year." The way she said it, it sounded like all the time left on the planet.

"Have you made any friends?" I asked.

"Few," Jiao said. "I get here in July. I don't know many." With so many Taiwanese students on campus, it seemed impossible that a dozen friends weren't waiting to take her in. But not everyone makes friends so easily, I reminded myself, nor is loneliness always remedied by company.

"What about church?" I asked. "Do you go to church?"

Jiao shook her head. "In Taiwan I'm Buddhist, but not . . . observant. I see churches here and I think about going. Sometimes."

"The church outside the campus gate sells pancakes," I said. "We're with a campus ministry. We know people who'd love to talk to you."

"I'd like to talk to you right now," Hannah said. She leaned to the side and slid her hand inside her back pocket, from which she withdrew a KGP. It was molded to the shape of her hip. Faceup, it made a bowl in her palm. "Can I share this with you?" she asked.

Jiao nodded, and Hannah slid her thumbnail inside the front cover. She spoke slowly, her voice soft, her painted fingernail landing on each word as she pronounced it. It was an English lesson as much as a sharing of faith. Jiao nodded along. Hannah paused to make sure Jiao understood, and Jiao turned her head and smiled. Hannah turned to the prayer on the final page. "Is this prayer something you might want to say?"

"Yes," Jiao said. "Okay."

"Do you feel ready to pray with me now?" Hannah asked.

"I think I am."

Hannah reached for Jiao's hand, and Jiao allowed her hand to be held. The women leaned their heads together. I set my hand on Hannah's shoulder to strengthen her prayer with my own, to channel God's power and might from me to her to Jiao. "Just say what I say," Hannah said.

Hannah's prayer was simple and bold. Jiao's repetition sounded like an echo down a long hallway, fractured and reticent. The wind carried her voice away. "Don't worry," Hannah said. "There's no wrong thing to say."

Class was finished, and people were starting to pass through the courtyard. I could feel their eyes upon us as they walked by. Jiao's hand trembled inside Hannah's. Jiao's loneliness was a skin, and we were piercing through it. I felt relief fill the center of the circle our three bodies made, relief and surrender. Or was it the Holy Spirit descending into Jiao's heretofore unredeemed soul, the windy mass of salvation? Either way, I could claim to be a part of it. When we returned to the house, we'd tell the team we shared Christ with a young exchange student from Taiwan, and she accepted, right there, on the spot. We saw her sitting alone, and we shared our faith with her. Hannah would shake her head while telling it, and every time she would use the first-person plural: *we* and *our*. We found Jiao, *we* shared *our* faiths. It was a lie, but it was as close to success as I was going to come, the only story I had to tell.

The Ancient Shoreline

California changed overnight. I'd been gone for only three months, but the 405 freeway felt different driving home from the airport. More crowded, faster than I remembered, full of cars I'd never seen before. As he piloted the Honda through the thickening traffic flowing south from LAX, my father pointed out the new Volkswagen Beetle, a silver dome that looked, as we whizzed past it, like one of the pods from Space Mountain had been mounted on a set of Goodyears. My father drove like he was behind the controls of a dogfighter, working the brake and accelerator with different feet, racing up behind cars so fast I pressed my feet into the floor mat to brace myself, only to avert disaster at the last minute by sliding into the adjoining lane. Half past three o'clock, he had thirty minutes to make it to our exit before rush hour hit and the freeway transformed from a racetrack to a parking lot.

"Ease off," I said, as he darted into the carpool lane, changed his mind, and raced back out. "You're making me sick." I pressed my hand against my stomach and leaned my head against the rest. The sky above the freeway was vast and indifferent, scrubbed bare by the Santa Ana winds that had kicked the temperature into the mid-nineties and given the air a gritty, metallic taste. The foothills of the San Gabriel Mountains bulged on the horizon east of the sprawl, the grass gone the color of burlap, more foreign to me now than the first time I'd visited California a decade earlier, the Thanksgiving I was twelve, three weeks after my father had backed down the driveway of our house in my stepmother's car, away from Devin and me, away from Texas forever.

"Yeah, really," my stepmother called out from the backseat. "Slow down. It's not *actually* a race."

"You'll thank me when we're home," my father said. Hearing the word "home," I felt my stomach clench a second time—a turn of the screw in my intestines, the result not of travel but of travel's end. I didn't know whether to consider my return to California a true homecoming or merely a layover. Raising the money to return to Australia would involve an activity far more harrowing than passing out tracts to strangers: I'd have to make face-to-face appointments with potential supporters and ask them to contribute to my mission on an ongoing monthly basis. Their donations, and their donations alone, would fund my travel and housing, my extremely small salary, even my food. Missionaries sponsored by the campus ministry didn't spend a dime that they didn't procure themselves, from people they interacted with personally. The transaction of a soul wasn't easy, but at least it was free; a single year in Australia would cost $40,000. I figured I'd write to some of the people who'd mailed me small checks toward my summer mission, but I also knew I'd have to ask my father for the names of some of his business contacts and my stepmother for the wealthier congregants from her church. Eric told me I needed to treat each support meeting like a job interview. My conviction had to be airtight, my motivations for rescuing the Australians from perdition more convincing than even my testimony. The prospect of calling people I hardly knew and asking them for money in order to spend a year doing something I had little talent for produced an anxiety I felt in the tips of my fingers.

I decided to try out my pitch on my father and stepmother that night over dinner. We ate on the back patio, at the big glass table. My father grilled chicken marinated in balsamic vinegar and corn wrapped in aluminum foil, and my stepmother peeled cucumbers for a salad. Through the juniper hedges at the back of the yard, I could see people milling about the elevated deck attached to the neighbor's house. The windows of the houses ascending the hill were mirrored gold against the setting sun, and the sky was turning orange and green. I anticipated a celebration similar to our dinner at the Old Spaghetti Factory the night Stacie returned from the Summit Ministries Camp in Colorado, for my father and stepmother to hang on my every word about my summer, and for my stepmother to cry with pride at my courageous service to Christ. Their questions were far more ordinary. My father asked me what movie I saw on the plane, and my stepmother wanted to know if I'd tried Vegemite. "It's kind of salty," I said. "Good on crackers. I tried ostrich meat once. I totally expected it to taste like chicken, but it was a lot closer to steak."

"Interesting," she said.

"What else?" my father asked. "What else was cool?"

I told them the story of Hannah and me leading Jiao to a decision to follow Christ, just two days before we returned home. "God swept in and saved her soul in the nick of time," I said. I told myself I meant it, that my joy in her salvation was unlike any joy I'd known. I said, aloud, my heart was for the Australians. From my Rilke book, I produced a photograph of Josh sharing the KGP with a kangaroo, handed it to my father. "The harvest is plenty, but the workers are few," I said. I meant it as a joke, but my father and stepmother glanced at each other, warily. My father passed the picture across the candle in the table's center to my stepmother. She stared at it intently and asked, "How long do you think you'll be staying here?"

"The fall semester at QUT starts in February. I'd like to go back a few weeks before then, so I can get settled before classes start."

My stepmother counted the months on her fingers. "Four months? Maybe five? You'll live here that whole time?"

"Sounds to me like you'll be paying rent," my father said.

"How much?" I asked. My car, an old Volkswagen Fox I'd bought from a guy in east Anaheim who turned out to be a drug dealer and skipped town without signing off on the title, had broken down last spring. I'd cashed in $800 worth of savings bonds from my grandparents, some of which I'd had since I was eight years old, in order to fix it. I had only three hundred left in my savings account.

"We can work it out," he said. "But the gravy train's tracks don't run too far."

My stepmother looked at me squarely. Her chin glowed orange, lit by the candle in the center of the table. "You're a college graduate now. An adult. You should be on your own." Then she softened, and for a moment her eyes turned glassy, twinkly in the candlelight. She reached across the table and took hold of my hand. "I'm proud of you," she said. She leaned an inch closer. "Well done, good and faithful servant."

My stepmother had left her job at the church, and now my room, which had always doubled as her home office, overflowed with the jetsam from ten years of pastoring. The desk took up half the room and was covered with Sunday School curricula in fat three-ring binders, a teetering tower of video cassettes, piles of photographs and handwritten letters and crayoned pictures on construction paper. The other half of the room was occupied by an enormous oak-framed bunk bed, so large it completely blocked one of the room's two windows. The top bunk had been cleared off so I could sleep there, as had a square of floor space behind the bedroom door where the rest of my stuff from my college apartment sat piled in boxes and laundry baskets. That night I lay in bed, jet-lagged and exhausted, but unable to sleep. I listened to the traffic slash by on PCH. The birds in the avocado tree sounded as though they spoke Spanish, trilling *treinta, treinta, treinta*, as the night began to fade toward dawn. It felt strange to sleep alone after a summer of sharing a room with Rusty and Steve that was so small I could reach out and touch them both from my bed without lifting my head. The last time I had slept had been in that room in Toowong, more than forty hours earlier, a time and place so far away I could hardly comprehend it. Nor could I comprehend the prospect of boarding a plane and crossing the Pacific again. But how could I get up in the morning and tell my father and stepmother my missionary life was over? To do so would be to confess my faith was weak. That I never belonged on the team in the first place. Eric had been right about me all along: Jesus could make no use of me.

For the first few weeks, I told everyone I talked to that my return to Australia was imminent, ordained, hoping that if I convinced enough people I was destined to return, I'd also convince myself. I'd fake it until I made it, as my father had advised. I wrote thank you letters to the people who had supported my summer mission wherein I announced I'd soon be contacting them to set up appointments to talk about making a longer commitment. I even landed a job with the admissions office at UC Irvine—a temporary position that expired with the application deadline at the end of November—on the premise that I wouldn't be sticking around much after that anyway.

Josh called from Chicago. "Have you talked to anyone from the team yet?" he asked. He sounded upset.

"Not yet," I said. I listened to the silence on the line for a moment. "What's the matter?"

"I'm embarrassed to say," he said. But he told me what had happened. The day after he'd returned home, Josh had withdrawn from art school, emptied his savings account, and boarded the next flight back to California. He took a bus from LAX to Santa Barbara and showed up, unannounced, at Tanya's door. He planned to find a job, spend a semester at Santa Barbara City College, and eventually transfer to UCSB. Steve and Jeff had offered him a place to stay, and he figured he'd couch surf there until he found his own place. He and Tanya could get married when they were ready. But by the time Josh arrived in California, Tanya had reconciled with her boyfriend. Steve and Jeff had girlfriends and their own lives on campus; they let Josh crash for a few nights, but he'd need to find another place after that. Out of money and with no place to live, Josh had no choice but to call his parents and beg for plane fare home. "I was sure I was doing the right thing," he said. I heard him begin to cry, a thin wren-like whimpering he tried to suppress. "The whole way there, on the plane, I never had a single doubt."

"What did Tanya say? What about the voice she heard beside the pool and all that?"

"She said she wasn't sure it had really happened. She said she lost her courage." He set down the phone and blew his nose. "I don't blame her," he said. "It's not her fault."

"Whose fault is it then?" I'd never doubted the purity of his intentions, or the intensity with which he pursed them. I felt awful for him, but also secretly glad. I'd been skeptical about Josh's love for Tanya, at least its supernatural source, but over the summer, Josh had come to define for me what it meant to be an evangelist for the cause of Christ. I'd worried that returning to Australia would obligate me to somehow turn into him. Now I had a reason to doubt whether his vision had been anything more than infatuation scrambled with fervor. He was as prone to want as anyone else, no longer a different species and thus no longer a model for who I needed to become.

"It's no one's fault," he said. "Maybe it's America's fault. It's *being* home. I think I belong in the mission field. Everything is so much clearer there. I know my job, and I know how to do it. Are you still planning on going back? Maybe I'll come with you."

I tried to picture Josh and me reuniting in Los Angeles, the two of us hashing out a game plan as we flew into the night. Josh could be the evangelist; I could manage the organizational end of things. My efforts would free Josh to spread the Word, and free me from having to share my faith at all. "I'm still praying about it," I said.

"When you make up your mind, let me know," he said. "If you're in, I'm in."

I asked my father what he thought the next day over lunch at Taco Bell. We sat together on a wooden bench overlooking the Cleo Street beach, the surfers lined up in their wet suits like seals in the tide. "Josh can lead a horse to water *and* make him drink," I said, unfolding my taco from its paper wrapping. "You ought to see him in action. He's a rainmaker."

"What about you?" he asked. "What do you want to do?"

"God's set my hand to the plow," I said—and realized I was quoting my stepmother. I heard its shallowness even as I said it, how completely I did not believe it.

"Hand to the plow?" my father said. He cocked one eyebrow as he squirted salsa on his burrito. I'd never been able to lie to him. To other people, yes, but never to him. He knew my truest self and where it had come from. With him I could swear without worrying he'd rebuke me with a quote from Ephesians. "You don't have to be a missionary to serve God," he said. "There are lots of other ways."

"I know that," I said.

"So, what do you really want to do?" he asked.

"Go back to school," I said. "Study. Write." What I did not say, though I believe I could have and my father might have understood what I meant, was: *I want a normal life, a life that isn't always defined by reaping and sowing, spreading the Word, growing the kingdom.*

"Your own place to live?"

"Absolutely," I said.

"There's your answer," he said.

Seagulls circled in the clear sky, squawking for crumbs. A pelican dive-bombed into the ocean and flapped away with a fish in its mouth. The sun was warm on my face, and that warmth took hold of my body, a limb at a time, loosening each joint and muscle as it moved down my spine—a warmth I knew immediately was relief.

My father pointed the bitten end of his burrito at my Volkswagen. The gearbox was held together with wire, the dashboard lights were shot, and the windshield leaked in the rain. "Set your hand to *that* plow," he said, chewing, "and push that piece of junk off a cliff."

I rented a room in the back of a two-story house in the heart of the Newport peninsula, a skinny finger of sand and tumbledown cottages squeezed between Pacific Coast Highway and the mouth of Newport Harbor. Only a narrow alleyway, four or five feet wide, separated the walls of the houses. The drunk hippie who owned the place lived downstairs. He was so cheap, he cleaned his windows with a homemade concoction of vinegar and iodine and rented out the other bed in his own room. I knew no one else in the house, and spent as little time with my roommates as possible.

My room was a nine-by-eleven rectangle wide enough only for my bed and desk, a stack of books in the corner. My surfboard leaned against the wall at an angle because the ceiling was too low to stand it upright. Besides the small reading lamp clipped to my headboard and another on my desk, the window was my only source of light. It looked directly into the window of the room across the alley: a big room large enough for a queen-sized bed and a couch, a private bathroom.

One night I came home after dark and found the light from the window across the alley flooding my room, a bright orange square projected onto the wall above my bed like a film on a screen. In the window I saw my neighbor, a young woman in her early twenties, leaning into her bathroom mirror to brush mascara onto her eyelashes. Her red hair hung in wet ropes down the center of her naked back. Her towel lay piled at her feet.

I froze, unsure of what to do. Flick my lights on and off, so she'd know I was there? Nonchalantly dial my blinds closed? Either would have been more respectable than what I did, which was to stand in the dark and study her body as intently as a criminal witness studies a police lineup. I studied the pear-shaped curves of her bare hips, the small butterfly tattoo at the flattened tail of her spine, and in the mirror, a frontal view that revealed her nipples, the petal of hair between her legs. The allure was the utter lack of sexual staging, the absence of silk sheets and strings of pearls clenched in her teeth; she was merely a woman applying makeup in the nude. The lust that surged through me was incontrovertible, as narcotic as a drug. It kept me from turning away even when I told myself, aloud, to do so.

Until I saw her there, I hadn't realized just how lonely I was. I spent most of my days driving my rusty Volkswagen up and down the California coastline, staffing booths at college fairs and giving presentations to students at every fourth high school between San Diego and San Francisco. When the job took me out of town, I avoided the late-night pornography on the hotel cable channels, and I kept my distance from the business men I saw in the airport, shuffling their skin rags inside their folded copies of *The Wall Street Journal*. Now a naked woman stood inside my bedroom window, so close that if she were to turn around and reach out her hand I could take hold of it, and I felt in my body what the businessmen found in their magazines: the mitigation and confirmation of loneliness's power to rewire the brain. Too much time without touch makes us untouchable. I was a college graduate, I'd lived for a summer in Australia, I had a car and a full-time job, and yet I'd never touched a female body, at least not in the way that mattered.

The next day, I saw her sitting with her friends at the plastic patio table in front of her house. Behind her sunglasses and veil of cigarette smoke, she didn't recognize me. It made me think of the afternoon I watched *Ghost* at my friend Vince's house while he had sex with his girlfriend in the next room. At the time I'd identified with Demi Moore, the one left behind to grieve while forces she couldn't see conspired both to kill her and avenge the murders. Now I saw myself more like Patrick Swayze — a witness to life in a body but deprived of that life myself, my hand whooshing through flesh each time I tried to reach out.

I drove from school to school in a shirt and tie and wrinkled khakis, my elbow on the open window frame, the radio turned all the way up so I could hear it over the wind. Between appointments, I wrote stories in local libraries and in the plastic booths at Del Taco and filled out applications for graduate school. After work, I swam in the ocean.

I lived on 33rd Street, but I liked to ride my bike down to 14th, where the peninsula turned south and an elementary school took up most of the block. The schoolhouse had a belfry with a bronze spire, and its playground and basketball courts stretched far into the beach, almost to the water. The perimeter of the blacktop disappeared beneath the sand. The school was a dividing line: The board surfers stayed well to the north of it, typically above the Newport Pier, while the body surfers moved south, toward Balboa Pier and farther on, the Wedge, where big storms sometimes sent thirty-foot waves crashing into one neck-breaking foot of water. Necks got broken there. The lifeguards policed who got to go into the water, and a lot of the bodysurfers who braved it wore Speedos. They'd learned the hard way that the Wedge could rip their board shorts clean off their legs.

Fourteenth Street got big, but not that big, and the beach in front of the school was almost always empty. I locked my bike to the fence and folded my shorts and sweatshirt into rectangles and set them atop my shoes at the edge of the blacktop. I left my wallet at home; my house key I tied to the drawstring of my trunks or stashed in the pocket inside the zipper of my wet suit. The water grew greener with the changing seasons so that by winter's onset, it was the color of a pine tree, a layer of foam as thick as a cappuccino. I didn't like to wear my wet suit until the water temperature fell below sixty degrees because the suit was secondhand and didn't fit me well and because I liked to feel my skin against the sand and then in the water. I lay belly-down in the sand, and when my back grew hot from the sun, I stood and walked into the water. I stood with only my ankles submerged, letting my toes go numb in the cold. I watched the waves roll in, counted the interval between them and the length of the lull as my father taught me to do, years earlier. He'd taught me how to read the ocean's movements, to swim toward the largest waves rather than away from them, to let my body go slack if I got caught in the break. I could not enter an ocean without having him with me.

When I could no longer feel the sand beneath my feet, I waded out to my waist and then dove in. I swam out as far as I could, until the needle-like antenna atop the belfry spire was the only thing I could see over the rolling waves, a slim black disruption on the otherwise blue horizon. In the other direction, the Pacific stretched on and on, forever. On the clearest days, the long shore of Catalina Island stood on the horizon.

In the ocean, I was not afraid, though I had plenty of reason to be. The water was dark and cold, the waves could swell to enormous heights, and no one knew where I was. I didn't want anyone to know where I was. I wanted to edge away from myself. I'd left everything I owned on shore, and feeling the cold water work its way into the creases of skin beneath my arms and behind my knees, I was reduced to the raw dimensions of my anatomy, all body, no spirit, and so free from the burdens my spirit demanded. It was the same solace I'd felt—the first solace I'd felt in a long time—when I swam with my father in the cove near his house, the summer after Jeremy's death. The ocean was the first place I was able to forget about the murders. Now, swimming alone a half-mile out to sea on a bright November afternoon, I imagined the life I might find in graduate school: wilder and yet more sophisticated. Less constrained.

I forbid myself from admitting it, but deep down I understood that my faith had been the price of admission into my father's life, and into the family he made with my stepmother and stepsister. Ten years after the divorce and five years after I'd moved to California, I still relished every second of my time with him and came away feeling like it wasn't enough. He could express no ire, reveal no ugly side that would cause me to prefer his absence to his presence. He was simultaneously the source of all I believed and the direction in which that belief pointed. I knew he loved me, and I believed he'd love me no matter what, but I also knew that a relationship with him meant a relationship with Jesus. It was the choice he'd given my mother. Without Jesus, a gulf would separate us, just as a gulf separated him from my sister Devin. She hadn't professed the faith, and whenever she visited California, she spent most of her time reading in her room. The idea of not being a Christian, or even a Christian by a name other than evangelical, was impossible.

But my father had come to Jesus through a relationship, through my stepmother. He'd found a loophole around loneliness. I'd given my life to the faith as a teenager, before my life was truly my own to give away. I'd pledged my allegiance to evangelicalism's elaborate denials because I didn't know what they cost. I knew that cost better now; the glass separating me from my neighbor's naked body felt like a symbol of my stunted development. I wasn't yet part of the human race. If I wanted to break free of the strange mold into which I'd been cast, I'd have to leave my father again, and likely leave California. I tried to picture myself in new cities as I stroked back and forth in the ocean: loitering in downtown bookstores, sipping wine at literary readings, hanging out in the hole-in-the-wall bars adorned year round with Christmas lights. The clichés of becoming a writer adhered to such places; in my mind they comprised the Gulf Stream of humanity. I'd become part of it simply by walking through the door.

I swam until my hands grew so cold I could no longer make a fist, and then paddled back to shore and wriggled back into my sweatshirt and stood in the sand watching the sun work the horizon through the color spectrum. Eventually the lights of Avalon, Catalina's port town, would show up as tiny white dots against the otherwise black shape of the island. The prospect of leaving this place was at once thrilling and deeply saddening.

~~~

Durden and Rich had moved to the high desert, forty-five minutes away from the ocean but closer to their jobs. I saw them when I could, which wasn't very often. However, after a few months in Newport, I learned that a few women from my freshman dorm lived two streets over from me, and three of my ex-teammates from the swimming team shared a house at the peninsula's far northern end. I ran into them at the grocery store or jogging along the boardwalk, and the coincidence of our encounter always felt like good fortune, an opportunity not to be wasted. A lot of parties formed this way.

The party I went to at the end of February took place in a house with heavy oak paneling on the cabinets and walls and brown shag carpet. The room was dark even with all the lights on. Six or seven guys in baseball caps sat in lawn chairs beyond the sliding glass door, staring intently into the bell of a glass bong. Every face kindled with a goofy, expectant hopefulness. I half expected a genie to appear in the cloud.

I pumped a beer from the keg and then held the tap for a woman wearing a black cardigan sweater buttoned across her silk blouse. Her name was Veronica; she was an office manager for a car dealership in Fountain Valley. She asked me what I did, and I told her, and I told her I was hoping to go to graduate school to become a writer. She shuffled back a half step and looked me up and down. "You'll need some Clark Kent glasses," she said. "And a corduroy jacket with patches on the elbows." She nodded and smiled. "I can see it. Very literary."

She didn't wear much makeup or jewelry, only a pewter charm bracelet dangling a chorus of winged cherubim. Her friends waved her into the living room where they had gathered on the carpet. She asked if I wanted to sit down. I followed her out of the kitchen, a beer in my hand. If I could make the conversation last, I'd ask for her phone number.

After several failed attempts to find a topic the group could discuss, a freckled guy in the circle proposed playing a game called "I have, I have never." The rules are simple: You confess a secret, and anyone in the circle who's made the same mistake cops a plea by taking a drink. Freckles lifted his cup and said he'd had sex in the driveway of his parents' house. Everyone in the circle drank, everyone but Veronica and me. The next guy said he'd done it in his parents' bed. His head was shaved on the sides, a spiked mohawk down the center. He slapped my knee. "Your go, bro."

I hefted my cup and said, "I've streaked the beach in Mexico." I didn't mention that the streaking occurred during my spring break with the campus fellowship. The circle drank, glug, glug, glug.

The Mohawk piped up again, out of turn, "Oh yeah? I've *done it* on the beach in Mexico." Now I was the only one who kept the cup in his lap.

"Damn, dude. What are you, a virgin?" Freckles asked. He meant it as a shallow taunt—the same way he'd call a straight man a fag—but I felt it as an accusation.

"Leave him alone," Veronica said. She let her sweater slide off her shoulders and fall to the floor. Her sleeveless blouse was opalescent in the dim light, her arms the color of milk. "He's a gentleman," she said. She hugged my neck. Her hair smelled like coconut, her neck like vanilla.

"Your turn," the Mohawk told her. Veronica straightened her back and raised the cup to hide her mouth. "I did it with my boss," she said, covering her lips with her fingers, as if to suppress an embarrassed giggle. She'd confessed the act as if it was a mistake, but her smile lacked any discernible remorse. She swallowed and added, "On a pool table."

"Damn!" said Freckles.

"Boo-yeah!" said the Mohawk.

Talking to Veronica in the kitchen earlier and sitting beside her on the carpet, I'd glimpsed the normalcy I imagined for myself when I swam in the ocean: I was a person who could go to a party, drink a beer from a keg, and meet a woman. I was not so unlike the other partygoers; the distance between my life and theirs wasn't so great. My faith and my abstentions hadn't permanently cast me out, and by one path or another, circumstances had led us all here, to this house, this circle on the carpet. Now I saw how completely I didn't belong.

I sat, hardly drinking. But as the game wore on, and the circle waited to see whether or not I'd lift my cup, I began drinking no matter what was said. Freckles and the Mohawk stopped heckling me, which made me worry they'd begun to suspect the truth about me. Soon they were drunk and forgot all about me.

I was almost relieved when the woman seated beside Veronica drooped her head and vomited into her own lap. Veronica leaped to her feet and helped the other woman stand. "Let's go outside for some air," she said. I at last had an excuse to quit the game, and I stood to open the front door. A gentleman. I took a clean cup from the stack beside the keg, filled it with water from the sink, and carried it outside. Veronica took it and said, "I've got it from here." Her friend leaned over the huckleberry bushes, and Veronica pulled the woman's hair away from her face, stroked her back with her palm. "Let it out," she said. "You'll feel better if you get it out of your system."

I unlocked my bike and rode home.

When I stepped inside my room, my neighbor stood before her bathroom vanity in nothing but a white thong. The only light came from the panel above her mirror, and in it I could see her face, her pale breasts, and the darkened window behind her. The window in the mirror looked like a black well into nothing. She wet her hands in the sink and ran her fingers through the sides of her hair. A naked man walked up behind her, wrapped his arms around her waist, and began kissing her neck. She reached around and held the back of his head. The bathroom light flicked off, and the room was swallowed away. I lay down on my bed, dizzy with wanting, more lonely than ever. I tried to picture the future I'd imagined for myself in the ocean, but found I could not.

I applied to graduate schools in every major city in the Pacific Northwest and along the Eastern seaboard, from Washington D.C. to Boston. One by one, I got denied to all of them. All but one: the University of Utah, in Salt Lake City. It was the last place I'd applied, and for the most irrational of reasons. Utah's basketball team had played UC Irvine the winter of my senior year on their way to the Final Four, and had won so profoundly, their players so fluid and deliberate with the ball, that I translated their prowess on the court to the university and its location. My maternal grandparents had also grown up in Utah in the 1930s and '40s and told stories of trolleys clanking through the city streets and dancing at the Saltair Palace on the shores of the Great Salt Lake. Neither of them were Mormon, and they'd lived all over the world, in London and Boston and for a brief time in Africa, and still they spoke of Utah with an affection the other cities couldn't match.

Still, when I visited Salt Lake City, I had to trick myself into seeing the place for more than it was. They'd host the Olympic Games in a few years, so that was something to look forward to. I'd been awarded a teaching fellowship that came with a tuition waiver, which meant I could go for free.

My father's company had an office in Salt Lake. "It's a nice place to live," he said. "Real family oriented. Our guys there are great to work with. Very salt of the earth."

"It's in the water," I said. "The salt."

"Just don't buy into any of that Mormon nonsense," my stepmother said. I could tell she didn't want me to go, though I didn't yet understand why. I thought she saw more schooling as frivolous, a further delay in my getting a real job.

I moved in August. I hadn't seen my mother since my graduation from college, a few days before I left for Australia. She hadn't wanted me to go. She'd disliked the prospect of my asking people for money and refused to give me the addresses of her friends in Texas, even those who probably would have contributed. She saw Australia, like my evangelical faith, as another step in my becoming my father's son, my stepmother's son, no longer hers. Now that I was moving to neutral territory, she asked if she could visit. She and my stepfather flew out the week I arrived.

Twenty years after her last visit, my mother knew her way around better than any of us. Riding in the passenger seat of the rented Buick, she pecked the window with her fingernail, remembering the little café where her grandfather used to take her for lunch, which was still standing, and the drugstore where they went for ice cream, which was long gone. She directed my stepfather past the cemetery where three generations of my ancestors lay, then to the house where her mother was born, a brick Tudor with dark windows and a steeple roof set beside a wooded ravine. My stepfather shifted in his seat and leaned over the steering wheel to stare into the sky through the windshield, half-shouting for my mother to give him more warning before he had to turn. He muttered under his breath before gunning the accelerator through a yellow light.

Even after ten years, their marriage continued to teeter on the brink of collapse. A few years earlier, when I was still in college, my stepfather went out of town on business, as he usually did, but didn't come home at the end of the week. One week turned into two, then into a month, then into the whole of autumn. My mother didn't know where he was. She left him voice messages, but he didn't return them. My mother was sad on the phone when she called me at school. Full of self-righteousness, I told her, "You reap what you sow." I meant that she had shunned my father's faith and now was paying the price for it. I told her I'd pray for her. "I should get going," she said. "Your sister needs help with her homework."

One night, when my mother was driving home from work on the freeway, a drunk driver hit her from behind. He was going over one hundred miles per hour. She tried to swerve, but she couldn't get out of his way fast enough, nor could she hold on to the wheel when he rammed her bumper. The passenger side windows shattered against the guardrail, and the slim metal bar framing the rear window on the driver's side shot forward. It hit her skull at an angle, which stopped it from piercing the bone. A passing motorist with a car phone called 911, and the ambulance arrived before my mother lost consciousness or went into shock, though both happened soon after.

That was the night my stepfather chose to return my mother's calls. He hadn't called in three months. Devin told him what had happened, and he drove to the hospital from Dallas. I didn't hear about any of it until my mother called to tell me she and my stepfather were back together. Injury had reunited them yet again.

Neither of them talked about my mother's accident or my stepfather's unexplained absences. No one said a word about the uncompleted tax forms, the maxed-out credit cards, the fact that my stepfather kept a storage unit and owned an "investment property" on the south side of Austin. Instead they went on in silence, biding time until the next business trip or the next accident. My own reconciliation with my mother relied on similar evasions. Not once did I mention, and not once did she ask, about my summer in Australia proclaiming the news of Christ.

The car accident had occurred at the height of the semiconductor boom, when new tech companies were moving into Texas. My stepfather's business was thriving. He traveled often to Europe and Asia, returning with tchotchkes from street bazaars, playing cards in foreign languages, stories of strange customs and stranger food, and most importantly, a sense of importance. He was someone who received phone calls in the middle of the night. His expertise was in demand. As the boom waned, he traveled less, earned less. He switched companies, switched again, got passed over for a promotion, and now had a boss who was twenty years his junior. My stepfather craved authority more than ever, especially now that he no longer had it. Whenever he landed in a new city, he read every historical marker and hotel brochure and poured over the local newspapers in search of the one inscrutable detail to carry him across the threshold from visitor to local. Every day during his visit to Utah, he told me a different factoid about my new home state: Utah was home to the nation's first department store; Butch Cassidy, the outlaw, and Philo T. Farnsworth, the inventor of the television, were both from Beaver, a small town in the center of the state; the cemetery we'd visited on our first day had been created by Ulysses S. Grant.

At our last dinner together, my stepfather asked my mother if she knew about Lake Bonneville. When she said she'd never heard of it, he set his elbows on the table and told us all about it. The lake once covered the valley. "All the way to Nevada and Idaho," he said, excited by the opportunity to impart knowledge. "You can still see the old shoreline in the foothills." Some people maintained that the salinity of the lake, five times that of the ocean, was proof of Noah's flood.

I knew enough about Utah to know the Mormons saw the Salt Lake Valley, really the whole state, as a holy land, a kind of Jerusalem West. They didn't see the insects that had threatened the early settlers' crops as a consequence of irrigating and farming arid land, but rather as a plague, a testing of faith, analogous to the locusts Moses rained down on Pharaoh. The gulls that gobbled up the bugs were a miracle, faith's reward, which they commemorated with a statue in Temple Square. So it was no surprise that someone, somewhere, saw the Great Salt Lake as a diluvian leftover. We all wanted a sign we'd chosen the right path, landed in the right place, including my stepfather. Including me.

Every once in a while, when my guard was down, one of my stepfather's factoids slipped through my defenses. Weeks after he and my mother returned to Texas, I found myself thinking about Lake Bonneville. The old shoreline traversed the russet foothills above the city and the university, and was now a popular running and biking trail. It was a short hike uphill from the building where I taught as a graduate assistant; some evenings after class I'd climb to it and walk along the rutted pathways as warm wind rose from the desert and the edge of the moon dazzled over the mountain rim. I imagined the tribespeople living along the shoreline, who knew the mountains as islands and witnessed the deluge, the opposite of the flood that set Noah adrift—the shoreline lengthening as the water rushed away, the rocky slopes smothered in algae, the bleached floor, mammoth tusks rising out of the sediment, and cutthroat trout flapping head and tail as they suffocated in the desert air. It amazed me to think that everywhere I went below the trail, from class to the supermarket to the bookstore, had once been under that water. Riding my bike down the steep hills between campus and my apartment, I'd gather enough speed to feel momentarily weightless, as though I could dive over my handlebars and swim into the open sky. I watched the runners pumping their arms and knees along the roads, the Mormons streaming into Temple Square, and the traffic streaming away from the city center, the buses and dogs and baby strollers, and imagined them all as fish, schools of colored trout, silvery eels along the bottom, millions of bodies in motion.

I lived in the attic of a ramshackle Victorian house, three unlit flights of stairs to the top, an open, airy space with angled ceilings and a fire escape outside the window from which I could climb onto the roof and look out over the valley. It was more space than I needed. I'd rented it with a fellow graduate student I'd met via email, but six weeks into our first semester, he dropped out and moved home to Ohio.

One Saturday morning I was reading on my couch when I heard a knock on my door. I opened it to find a large, perspiring teenage boy. He had a mop haircut and glistening peach fuzz on his top lip. He wore a Boy Scout shirt, a sash filled with coin-shaped patches, a blue kerchief knotted into a perfect triangle. The shirt was tight around his arms and chest, as though he'd gone to sleep in a child's body and awakened in a man's. He gave off a musky, elemental odor. He was surprised I answered the door; I was surprised he'd made it to the top of the stairs. He said he was collecting nonperishable food items for his Eagle Scout Service Project. I gave him two cans of tomato sauce and a can of corn, and in exchange, he thrust into my hand a stapled packet of paper. A ward directory, he said. Each page contained a hand-drawn map of the neighborhood, my street and the surrounding streets served by the local Mormon church. The houses were drawn as triangles atop squares, and inside each box were the names and telephone numbers of the people who lived there. I couldn't believe so many people were so trusting with their information, but most of them probably liked knowing how to get in touch with their neighbors, who to call when you needed help with a leaky faucet or a ride to the hospital. I flipped the pages until I found my street, my house. The downstairs tenants had their names on their mailboxes, so their names were listed. My name wasn't on the mailbox, and the upper triangle representing my apartment read, simply, Apt. 3.

More than I wanted to find a church, I didn't want to *not* find one. Apathy about God, I'd learned early and often, was its own choice. Before I left California, a friend from the campus fellowship had given me the name and phone number of a friend of hers in Salt Lake City. She'd been part of the campus fellowship at the U, but now she was in her first year of medical school. Her name was Lindsey. One Saturday afternoon, I went by myself to the football game and tried to talk to the people I sat beside in the stands. But no one would reciprocate, and full of indulgent self-pity, I came home and called Lindsey up. She invited me to church the next morning.

The church turned out to be Baptist, and hardly different from the Baptist churches I'd known as a kid in Texas: chunky gold-rimmed Bibles spread across every lap, the men in jackets and ties, a moon-faced preacher who spoke with a drawl and wiped his forehead with a hanky. The service lasted an hour and forty-five minutes, the sermon alone was an hour, and afterward we filed down the hallway for the singles' Bible study. That hour was dominated by a pair of twins, Evan and Justin, both six-five and stock boys at Target. When we went around the room to say our names and where we were from, Evan stood up, his thin hair rising in a static charge toward the low ceiling, and said, "I'm just passing through this life on my way to the next, hoping to take as many people as possible along with me."

To be an evangelical, or a Baptist, in Utah is like being a Catholic in Belfast or a Jew in Medina: a member of the true faith surrounded by an enemy. Mormons and evangelicals have more similarities than differences, but similarity can be the catalyst of discord. Because Mormons *seemed* so Christian, carrying leather-bound books of scripture on their way to meetings, bowing their heads when they prayed, mingling with the Baptists as they crossed through the church parking lot, it was often impossible to tell who was Baptist and who was Mormon. Because a spiritually inquisitive heathen might mistake one for the other, evangelicals labeled Mormonism a cult and spoke its name with the same venomous condemnation as the word *feminist* or *liberal* or *communist*—just as the Mormons saw any faith besides their own. My students had one day asked me if I was Mormon (the class was mostly freshman and most of the men had just come off their own missions and didn't see the question as improper), and when I said I wasn't, they looked at me with a judgment I knew only too well: They knew something I did not and felt bad for my not knowing but were also pleased with themselves for figuring me out. Some of the students saw me as untrustworthy, others as a potential

convert. I saw very clearly, painfully clearly, how their own sexual abstentions made them fidgety, their eyes hungry. They watched each other all
the time, trying to match physical attraction with enough nonnegotiables
as fast as possible so they could get married. I had students my first year
who met on the first day of class and had tied the knot by Thanksgiving.
I worried I gave off the same look, the same pheromonal hunger, and that
everyone around me knew exactly what my look meant.

One member of the singles Bible study at the Baptist church said
Mormon girls with their honey blond hair and eagerness to marry were
a snare set loose by Satan to tempt true Christians away from their faiths.
He'd been on his way to buy his Mormon girlfriend an engagement ring
when God laid a burden on his heart. Evan and Justin nodded their
heads, as though they knew exactly what he meant. I thought of Julianne,
but stayed still.

I thought I'd never see another tract again, but here they appeared, the
same size and shape as the KGP, only recast as refutations of Mormonism.
One began with a quote from the First Book of Nephi, from the Book of
Mormon: "Behold there are save two churches only; the one is the church
of the Lamb of God, and the other is the church of the devil." The verse
was written in old English calligraphy, like the cover of Ozzy Osbourne's
Prince of Darkness album; beneath the scripture were photographs of
inverted pentagrams on the Salt Lake Temple, as if the upside down stars
were proof the Mormon church was the *other* church, the church of the
devil. A second tract claimed Joseph Smith was unqualified to lead a
church because of his many wives—many of whom were teenagers or
taken from their husbands—and that he died young because he boasted
in his own strength, and God had struck him dead. Sitting with these
booklets on my lap while Evan raised his fist toward the water-stained
ceiling and declared that God had brought each one of us to Utah to be
warriors for Christ and that we needed put on the full armor of God,
just like Paul says in Ephesians, I couldn't stop myself from laughing. It
came like a hiccup, an involuntary gasp. I tried to push it down, but the
more I did, the harder it came. I pretended to cough and excused myself.
Evan was still on his feet when I returned. The guy beside him wore a
fedora and a wooden cross around his neck. A woman in the circle wore
white pantyhose beneath her flowered skirt, her blouse buttoned to her
throat—Christ's soldiers in the war for Utah.

Lindsey, however, was good company. She had a boyfriend in Illinois, and she made it clear that I shouldn't get any ideas about the two of us becoming more than friends, but after church let out, we'd change into shorts and spend the afternoon hiking in Big Cottonwood Canyon. Rather than tough it out in the Bible Study, I volunteered to teach the first grade Sunday school. Not long after I started, I told one of the children, the daughter of the associate pastor, that her crayoned fish swimming beneath Noah's ark looked like Princess Ariel from *The Little Mermaid.* The girl looked up at me with a scowl. "What?" I said. Had I let my tongue slip even here? The other teacher, a lanky brown-haired woman, pulled me aside and explained that the Baptist church had boycotted Disney for being "anti-Christian and anti-family."

"Anti-family?" I said. "Disney?"

"They have 'Gay Days' at their theme parks," she said, full of contempt. Her eyelids were coated in purple. "The gays wear red."

"Like The Bloods," I said.

"Who?"

"The street gang," I said. I turned back to the table, the fleet of wooden ships on the crayon sea, the children's downy necks like a basket of peaches. I wasn't fit to tend even this flock.

My best friend my first year of graduate school was a poet and fellow student named Claudia. She'd come to Utah from Arizona, where she'd left behind a man she loved very much, one of her former students. Unlike more liberal cities, Salt Lake offered her a kind of purgatory, a reprieve from old temptations. Claudia surmised she'd have no chance of falling in love with a student here. Some of her students complained she was too provocative, her language too profane, her above-the-knee skirts an insult to decency. "As if I wake up in the morning scheming to give those Mormon boys a hard-on," she said, her lip curled in an Elvis snarl. "God, how hard up for sex can they be?" I felt her question in my stomach, as though she'd asked me because I might have an answer. She knew I went to church but not where; I said as little as possible about my faith for fear that if she knew I'd proselytized overseas and had pledged to abstain from sex, she'd see me as a joke. But I was beginning to understand how unsatisfied desire could eventually turn on itself. The force that through the green fuse drives the flower one day pools into a sour puddle, turning brackish, deteriorating the ability to connect. This was the deadline my students raced to beat. How long did I have before it was too late?

Claudia spent the last month of the semester making a stained-glass window for a seminar she was taking in narrative and poetic theory. When I held the window to the lamp on her desk, the face of her ex-boyfriend, scissored from old photographs, emerged between the triangles of glass. The day after classes ended, Claudia put the window in her car, and we drove out to the shore of the Great Salt Lake. Mid-December, windy and cold, the sky and the shore and the rippled water were the same ashen gray. Bergs of wind-whipped foam, like gigantic dollops of meringue, floated on the lake, and the small islands across the water still bore the streaked layers of their drowned millennia. The fine gravel rising up through the melted snow felt like the sediment that collects around a bathtub drain. It felt like exactly what it is: the floor of an ancient sea, the low point in the Great Basin. The geography for the first time felt personal. I'd been descending for months, like a diver in an antique suit, my head inside a copper bell.

Claudia held the window flat between her hands. I expected her to send the glass wheeling into the cloud light. I expected rage, catharsis, but at the edge of the water, she unceremoniously opened her hands and let the window fall. It splintered on the ground and she kicked the large shards into the lake. Before returning to graduate school, she'd worked as a counselor for battered women, and she still worked part-time in a home for drug-addled teens. She had a talent for befriending the worst off, though she, too, sometimes slipped into darkness. She'd hold her temples between her fingertips, as she was here now, staring down at the pieces of her broken window nested in the powdery sand below the water. A pained looked washed across her face—more menacing than sad, a kind of horror. It scared me. "This is a weird place," I said. "It's creeping me out."

"Kids from the teen home say they used to come here to do mushrooms," she said, staring at the water, pushing on her temples. "I can see why."

I wanted to put my arm around her and tell her everything would be okay, but I didn't know if I should. I ground my heel into a blue polygon of glass. It crunched beneath my foot. "Want to go get drunk?" I asked.

"I have a better idea," she said. "Let's have a party."

〜〜

Dusklight illuminated the dust in the air as I walked to Claudia's apartment on Saturday. The golden Angel Moroni atop the Temple flashed as the sun dropped out of the clouds and into the Great Salt Lake. Farther to the west, over the empty desert, a bank of dark clouds was piling up. The wind smelled briny, almost like mold, as it often did before it snowed. Paper trash spun up into a cyclone before scattering across a yellowed lawn. I arrived dry-throated, thirsty. The kitchen counter was crowded with bottles, six packs, and harder stuff, as well as cranberry and orange juice and Coke. Claudia lived on the bottom floor of an old house, a small kitchen sandwiched between a small living room and a small bedroom, the bathroom at the back. More than a hundred people crowded inside. The windows and the crossbeams of the ceiling were festooned with colored lights shaped like chili peppers. With the dog-shaped piñata on the bookshelf, the photographs of Tucson, Arizona, scattered about the apartment, and the lime wedges rising from the Corona bottles like green crescent moons, the party felt more like Cinco de Mayo than Christmas.

I stood in the doorway between the kitchen and the bedroom talking to a woman with curly brown hair and a sing-along Arkansas accent. She wore a black top with a plunging neckline, and a tiny silver cross lay inside the space between her collarbones, a statue inside a shrine. I'd noticed her two parties ago. Moist snowflakes drifted against the windows and clung to the screens. The orange tips of cigarettes floated in the parking lot behind the house. Three classmates sat cross-legged on Claudia's bed, arguing about Julia Kristeva. "Possession can take the form of a single love absorbing the entire universe," hissed a woman with ink black hair. In the living room, a man stood with his hand against the wall and whispered into a woman's ear, and another couple kissed on the sofa. Claudia leaned close to a fellow graduate student, her painted eyelids heavy, half closed. In theory or in practice, the whole world was in love.

The woman told me she was moving to Nashville on Monday. She'd earned a master's in psychology from the U, but was going to be a French teacher in Tennessee. Utah was okay, but not what she'd hoped for. The relationship that had brought her here had ended, and she was ready to get back to the South. I said I was happy to stay away from the South for good. She dug inside her front pocket and extracted a small canister of lip-gloss, Floozy Fruit. "A friend gave me this as a joke," she said. She swirled her finger in the center and smeared the gloss across her lips. Her mouth glistened beneath the chili bulbs. She held the canister out to me, and I pressed into her fingerprint. I smoothed the wax on my lips. I could taste the wild berry and could almost feel the transference: her finger, her lips, my finger, my lips.

"I have another one at home," she said. "Virgin Violet. I wear it to church."

"Oh," I said. "So you're making a statement."

"You calling me a floozy?" She slapped my arm.

"I'm not the one with gloss," I said. "What you see is what you get." The margarita pitcher was upside down in the sink. She pressed her shoulder against the doorframe, leaned in. "What's your number?" she asked.

"My number?"

"How many women have you slept with?"

Since the party in Newport, I'd learned to avoid this kind of drinking game. When it started up, I excused myself from the room to refill my glass or took refuge in the bathroom. I'd become an escape artist. There was a line outside the door to the john and my cup was more than half full. My back was against the doorframe. "A gentleman never tells," I said.

"Ladies never tell," she said. "Gentlemen read *Playboy*."

"Not me," I said.

She leaned a little closer. "Come on, tell me."

I shrugged, sipped from my cup.

Her number was three. "I waited till I was nineteen for Bible Belt reasons."

"I know what that's about," I said. I added, "I grew up in Texas."

"You're Baptist?"

"Not exactly," I said. "But I've been known to congregate."

Her look said, *I thought so.* I gulped my beer. "I thought I'd go to hell if I did it before my wedding night," she said. "God would strike me dead with a bolt of lightning."

"What happened?" I asked.

"As it turns out, getting hit by lightning's a huge rush," she said. Her smile widened, and the ice rattled at the bottom of her cup. "You think less of me now?"

"Of course not," I said. She was the only person I'd met in the last year who might not laugh if she learned my secret.

"Then let's hear it," she said.

I guzzled the rest of my drink and told her she could guess.

"One," she said.

"No."

"Zero." I didn't respond. She smiled.

Her face promised to keep the knowledge between us. She rubbed her hand against my arm and leaned her head against my shoulder. I felt nervy and daring. When the line to the bathroom cleared, she made her way toward the back of the house. I followed her and waited outside. I had to go, too. I heard the toilet flush and then she opened the door and pulled me inside and closed the door behind us and fell toward me with her eyes closed. The water was still swirling in the toilet. I wondered how much she'd had to drink, but I didn't wonder long enough to stop her. I leaned into her, braced her back with one hand and worked my other hand up inside her dark curls. I could taste the cranberry juice on her lips.

A fist pounded on the door. "Hurry up in there! I have to go!"

"I don't want to stop," I said.

"Let's go somewhere else," she said.

I told her my apartment was close enough to walk. She pressed her keys into my hand. "Drive my car," she said. "I don't want to walk back here in the morning."

I felt farther from myself than ever before. Australia was a make-believe land I'd visited in a dream, and for much of the last year, I'd been searching for a way to arrive at this place—looking through windows, leaning into women at parties, all the while mourning my own lost experiences, the wild nights, the uncalculated risks, the hasty testing of my so-called fragile heart. My goodness had become a sickness, and I wanted to heal myself of it. And here I was, locked inside a bathroom a week before Christmas, kissing a woman who was moving to Nashville in two days, on the verge of becoming, at last, an actual human being. I could let this happen, she wanted it to happen, and when it was finished, it would be as though it never had happened in the first place. No one would have to know.

She followed me up the dark stairwell, past the doorways of the lower apartments, rooms from which I'd heard the echoes of argument and lovemaking, sounds that made my stomach tighten whenever they rose through the floor. Climbing the stairs, I felt as though I'd slipped out of my skin and into the body of a man capable of bringing a woman back to his apartment. I watched him separate the keys on the ring. I watched him open the door. I watched him lead her inside.

The windows were open and the city lights bobbed like boats on water, the snow still falling. We were light-years from anywhere, my bed a raft in the ocean in the middle of the night, drifting and alone. I removed her shoes as she climbed across the duvet. She lay back and her hair mushroomed over the pillow. She slid her hand into my waistband and pulled up my shirt. Her blouse floated over her head and off the ends of her arms. Her fingernails raked my chest. Our mouths crashed together until I felt as though I could slip between her teeth and slide down her throat.

The clasp of her belt dragged against my stomach. I set my hand on it. All I had to do was unfasten it. Momentum would carry me the rest of the way.

What happened next is hard to explain. Mentioning Jeremy now will sound as though I'm pulling a narrative trick or else trying to stop myself from going forward by thinking of the worst possible thing—though anyone who's lost someone they love can attest to the fact that the dead return to us when we least expect them to, in the very moments where they ought not to appear. The truth is, I did think of him; or more precisely, I thought of his mother standing beside the table in the neighbor's house at the reception following the memorial service, eating from her plate of cantaloupe and crackers. How I promised to mow her lawn and how I failed to live up to it and how from that failure came a larger promise: The promise I was now about to break. At a certain point, the vow to preserve my virginity had become freighted with evangelical rhetoric; sex was a chip I'd traded for a bigger prize—for membership in the faith, and in my father's life—and now that I was ready to give that chip back, I saw there was something more to it, something older, something that preceded even faith itself. My need to wait for sex originated not in the jargon of evangelicalism, but in the need to counteract the devastation and senselessness and blood lust wrought by the murders. Did I think of Jeremy lying on the floor of his living room, his shoulder visible through the open front door? No. But I did think of the commitment that scene made necessary, and I understood that it was the one aspect of my faith that came from no one else but me. Among the epic and artificial pretensions of my life, this vow touched a part of me that was real. I'd held onto my virginity for all these years because I'd needed to believe I was more than the demands of my flesh. Because I'd needed to make choices and believe that it would one day mean something to have made them. What, exactly, they would mean, I couldn't say, but I knew to discard it now, with a woman I hardly knew and would never see again, would render the declaration, and my reasons for it, meaningless.

All of this moved at the speed of the brain, in nanoseconds. I saw Mrs. Woodley lifting a cantaloupe ball to her mouth. I saw myself promise to mow her yard. I was here, in my bedroom, my hand on her belt, my mouth on her neck. I registered it as instinct, not epiphany. Epiphany rolled in more slowly, after I'd rolled onto my back and was staring at the ceiling. "I'm sorry," I said. "I can't."

She leaned up on an elbow. Her sternum glistened where I'd kissed her. "Really?"

How could I explain it? How could I ever explain any of this without making it sound like an excuse? I was tempted, for a moment, to try, but I didn't. "I'm sorry," I said again. It sounded hollow the second time, like I was hiding something. I expected her to get angry.

"It's okay," she said. "You shouldn't rush it." She scooted close and worked her head into the soft spot between my clavicle and shoulder. She draped an arm across my chest and fell asleep. I was grateful she didn't leap up and run away. I lay awake until dawn, smelling her hair, my groin in flames, half hoping she'd wake up and ask me to reconsider.

In the morning, I sat on the floor while she wriggled into her shirt and brushed her hair in the mirror. Watching her dress, I felt both hungry and empty. The city and mountains slept beneath a white blanket of snow, the sun kindling the amaranthine clouds above the peaks. I'd like to say I felt some sort of pride, some newfound resolve, but I didn't. I still felt unmoored and uncertain, and vows, like scenery, tend to amplify loneliness, not abate it. My imagined new life was all the more imaginary. "If only you weren't leaving so soon," I said. I asked her to stay for coffee, but she said the movers were coming on Monday and she had so much to pack.

She kissed me one last time, said, "If you're ever in Nashville." I heard the staircase creak as she disappeared around the corner. "Au revoir," she called up as she descended. "Au revoir, Utah. Au revoir."

The Hoary Deep

William Faulkner writes: "A man always falls back upon what he knows best in a crisis—the murderer upon murder, the thief thieving, the liar lying." I first heard this line in a song and then went hunting through *Absalom, Absalom!* until I found it, and I've carried it in my pocket ever since. Faulkner implies that we're each endowed with certain wily resources that come in handy when the chips are down, but also that our weaknesses have a way of defining us. No matter how hard we try to overcome them, sooner or later we find ourselves right back where we started.

I wasn't in crisis in Utah, not yet, but after months of loneliness, I knew something needed to change. My religious options seemed reduced to two: I could go on living miserably as an evangelical, pretending I had something in common with guys like Evan and Justin and that Disney movies contained subliminal messages advancing the pro-gay agenda, or I could find a different evangelical church I liked better. It didn't occur to me that I could attend a church that wasn't evangelical, or no church at all. My definition of Christianity had been too strongly conjoined with evangelicalism for me to conceive of a faith by any other name, and I took seriously the notion that having given my life to Jesus, I was unable to take it back. I was married to my faith whether I liked it or not.

Thankfully, Lindsey was tired of the Baptist church, too. She suggested we head farther south, to a nondenominational church at the far end of the Salt Lake Valley, not far from the Utah State Prison but also close to the highway that snaked up Little Cottonwood Canyon toward some of the best skiing in the country. Were it not for the big steel cross bolted to the church's façade, the building might have been mistaken for an elementary school. There were other evangelical churches closer to the city, but not many, and this church had a fellowship group for singles in their twenties. Danny and Trudy, the fellowship leaders, both physical therapists who'd moved to Utah from the Midwest in order to ski, had a garage filled with gear for every kind of outdoor excursion, from spelunking caves to ice climbing. Some members of the congregation came to church dressed in snow pants and parkas, their skies already on top of the car. I made friends. The fall of my second year of graduate school, I moved out of my attic apartment and into a house with one of them.

But something was missing. I hadn't swum on a regular basis in the last two years. My senior year of college had been the end of the road: I'd milked the sport for my college tuition, and I'd long ago relinquished my dreams of going to the Olympics, unless it was as a spectator. Swimming, like faith, seemed pointless without a goal to work toward, without something tangible to accomplish. I didn't miss it when I still lived in California because I swam in the ocean almost everyday, and for most of my life, swimming in the ocean was something I'd done on my days off from workout and in a way that felt distinctly not like training. The ocean lacked protocols for how long I needed to stay in the water or in which direction I was obliged to move. No one ever told me while I was surfing to elongate my stroke recovery or that by letting a big wave pass me by—choosing to float over it just so I could feel it lift me out of the water—I was hurting not only myself but also my team.

In Utah, however, water was scarce and opportunities for swimming were harder to come by. Whatever fantasies I'd harbored about the Great Salt Lake as a kind of inland ocean were dispelled the moment I took a close look at the water and got a good whiff of its rank smell. I found myself thinking about water, dreaming about it, looking for it wherever I went. Walking to class in the mornings, I noticed the grounds crews hosing down the sidewalks, and I stopped to watch the water pool over the cement squares. As the winter snow melted, the culverts that followed the streets near my house filled up, and as I walked around my neighborhood I could hear the run off barreling through the city, a loud and constant gurgling like a gigantic bathtub drain. Whenever the fellowship group went hiking, I suggested trails that led toward high mountain lakes, the amoeba-like depressions in the map beckoning me to come toward them, even though the water there was too cold for swimming. Even on the hottest days, the water temperature barely cracked forty degrees, and thin films of ice floated in the shady spots. I missed the rhythmic slosh of water flooding my ears, the way it synchronized my breaths with my heartbeat. My skin missed it, too: After all the years of chlorine and salt water drying out my pores and bleaching my hair, I now felt greasy, oily. My T-shirts turned yellow. My bed sheets, once blue, turned green.

One day I went to the county pool a few blocks south of the university and bought a pass. The pool was housed in a vast tiled room with windows on three sides that overlooked the mountains to the east, the city to the west. The desk attendant informed me that the pool also had a masters team. Masters was the adult branch of USA Swimming—competitive swimming for what I thought were latecomers to the sport, pot-bellied and gray-haired men who splashed around in the pool each morning before my college workouts started, even though we started at 6:00 AM. Waking with the sun rather than in the inky depths of the night was the one benefit of no longer being a swimmer, and the masters swimmers I'd seen in California appeared more interested in shooting the bull on the wall than in actually swimming. I needed to swim so badly that I didn't care what time I dove in or who I was in the water with—so long as I was in the water.

I showed up the first morning at six o'clock, thirty minutes early, and stood on the deck feeling awkward and lurpy in my Speedo, suddenly conscious of the ten pounds I'd gained since college and the fact that my skin, no longer exposed to sunlight for four hours a day, had returned to its natural shade of alabaster. It was still dark out, the first thin bands of dawn orange lighting over the mountains, and my reflection glowed in the natatorium's big windows. Then the other swimmers started showing up, men and women in their thirties and forties and fifties. I was the youngest by at least a decade. A few of the men were big-gutted, and the women who'd had babies had purple veins along the backs of their knees and pearly stretch marks in their thighs, but other swimmers were sinewy and tan and, I could tell, no slouches in the water. No one seemed to notice my body one way or another. That is, until the coach showed up.

He galumphed in right at 6:29, in washed-out jeans and a leather jacket so weathered that white dendrites showed through the cracks in the cowhide. Broad shouldered and boxy, he bounced on the balls of his feet and walked with a slight shake to his shoulders, a little shimmy and jive. He caught sight of me from the other side of the pool and kept his eyes on me all the way around. I could see him appraise my wooly chest and stomach, sniffing out my self-consciousness before I ever had a chance to pretend I wasn't. It was a familiar feeling, his gaze the same look I'd received the first time I walked onto the deck in college. I could sense the zinger taking shape in his mouth. He had my number before he even knew my name. *Oh, shit*, I thought. "Good morning, everyone," he said to the crowd amassed behind the blocks. He turned to me. "Yo, Bear," he said. He reached out his hand. "Grrr-eat to meet you."

His name was Matt Walters. He was from New Mexico, but it turned out that he'd gone to Texas Christian University where he'd swum with a guy and a girl from my high school team, both of whom were seniors my freshman year. Swimming, despite its relative ubiquity across the country, remains a small world, and meeting someone from that old world—the fact that he'd once shared a lane with someone I'd once shared with myself, and who'd shared a lane with Jeremy—felt like reclaiming some essential part of myself. Matt built and maintained the website for the Salt Lake Organizing Committee for the 2002 Olympics, still a year and a half away, and was married to a pretty blond physical therapist named Darlene. Our friendship, unlike my friendships with Jeremy and my high school and college teammates, was mostly confined to the quips and monkeyshine between sets and in the locker room. He had a wife and closer friends, and was devoted to his widowed mother, who still lived in Los Alamos. I had my roommate, the church group, my fellow graduate students. But Matt always made me laugh, and laughter undergirds fraternity. He was also one of the fastest swimmers in the country; the previous spring he'd won the two hundred butterfly at the U.S. Masters National Championships, a title which gave his humor an aggressive edge. That first morning, I lifted my head to breathe during a hard breaststroke set and saw Matt at the end of my lane, windmilling his arms and sliding his shoes across the tiles like a speed skater, his jaw slack, his hands knifing the air. I laughed so hard I had to stop on the wall to blow the water out of my sinuses. The days we swam together, he'd lean in close and whisper in my ear, the second before I pushed off the wall, "I'm coming for you, you sack of shit."

After swimming ended, if I could get dried off and dressed fast enough, he'd give me a lift to campus in his shitcan Isuzu pickup. The floorboards were littered with empty cans of Copenhagen and an odd assortment of toothbrushes and mini tubes of toothpaste, and on the passenger seat was a pile of yellow Carl's Jr. receipts the size and shape of a sleeping housecat. He wanted to know how much tail I was getting in graduate school. "All those Mormon cuties over there," he said. "I bet you're just rolling in it." He didn't seem to catch on when I laughed the question away. Matt steadied the wheel with his knees so he could use both hands to tell me about the women he dated in graduate school—long before he'd met his wife—the student from whatever class he was TAing. She'd braced her back with the pickup's steering wheel when she straddled him. "Right here," he said, tracing the shape of her body in the air. "Right where I'm sitting now." He honked the horn and rolled his eyes toward the back of head and howled. It reminded me of driving around with Trey Smith and Mike Collins and Chris Mangold, trying to make sense of their pornographic stories, their laughter so dissolute it sounded almost manic—which, back then, it was. The angst of that former life was nine years and two states away, and the short ride in Matt's truck felt like ten minutes of guiltless indulgence in some of the things I'd missed.

Swimming in general felt like a nostalgic return. After two years' absence from the pool, I felt as though I'd been rebooted. Rather than the four or five hours each day I used to spend at the pool, the workouts now lasted a single whomping hour—from six thirty to seven thirty two mornings a week, or from twelve until one Monday through Friday. I could be intense in the water, but I was no longer controlled by the teeth-gnashing need to win at all costs. One of the lifeguards swam with the team during her lunch break, and after climbing down from the stand, she clocked out by sliding her key card through the machine on the wall. Its small beep echoed off the tiles. The whole hour felt that way: off the clock, unaccounted for and unaccountable. My skin dried back out. I liked the perfume of chlorine that filled my bedroom when I unzipped my bag at the end of the day. I liked dawdling on the deck with the other swimmers before workout started. I wasn't the only one who used the water like a drug, who came to the pool sick or hungover or sleep deprived because doing so felt better than staying away; I wasn't the only one who got there early in order to sit beside the water and stare off into space while the old women bobbed back and forth in the shallow lanes or the pregnant women floated on their backs with their eyes closed. During the winter, the doors and windows fogged with condensation; the pool would get so hot some of us would go out the door to the outdoor patio to pace in the icy wind. Moving through clouds of one another's breath, steam curling from our bare shoulders and backs, we'd relive the workout, the side cramps and anaerobic huffing, the pain we endured together.

When one of the coaches moved to Colorado, I asked if I could take her place. I coached the lunchtime workout on Mondays and Fridays.

The first Monday in March, I showed up to coach on the first day of spring break. After several weeks of icy, tubercular fog trapping every mote of ash and dust in the valley, the sky was bright, the mountains were as white as cake frosting, and the parking lot shone with melting snow. Matt walked out of the locker room with goggles looped around his thumb and his towel in his teeth. He gave me a high five. He and Darlene had been trying to get pregnant and had spent the weekend in a mountain cottage. "Did you make a baby?" I asked.

"I tried my best," he said. He bumped my shoulder. He smelled like a cheeseburger.

"I'll keep my fingers crossed," I said, holding up both hands, digits intertwined.

"What do you have planned for today?" He said it like a warning. I composed the workouts and watched over the team while they were in the water, but my small authority ended with the hour. Whatever I dished out today I'd pay for tomorrow.

"Get warmed up and you'll see," I said. "You're going to regret that burger."

"I was hungry," he said. "I skipped breakfast."

I stepped toward him with my palms open, but he dove in before I could reach him. I stood for a moment with my knee against the starting block. Vernal sunlight flooded the windows along the ceiling and bent to green against the floor of the pool, liquefying the black tiled stripes in the center of the lanes. Matt's scapula and spinal ridge pulled tight as he extended his arms above his head. He streamlined into deeper water, crossing out of sunlight and into shadow, his wake flowing into the lane ropes. He shrugged his shoulders; his feet separated and fluttered and propelled him up, up, up toward the water's ceiling, then through it, his elbow bent, and his mouth turned to breathe. Four more strokes and his feet slapped against the wall. I clapped my hands and the remaining stragglers entered the pool, one after the other until the deck was empty and

every lane was full. I stood still a moment longer, listening to the centrif-
ugal rhythm of the water churning, the steady splash over the coping—a
contentment I didn't trust anywhere else but at the pool. I turned to the
whiteboard to write out the day's sets.

The natatorium was full of sunlight, and while the marker floated over
the board, I let my mind wander. I don't really know where my thoughts
went; I only really remember the sound of the water purling through the
gutters somewhere in the background. Whatever I was thinking about
isn't important; what's important is that for a few minutes, I got so lost
in my reverie that I didn't see Matt drape his arms over the lane ropes or
his face fall forward into the water. Another swimmer lifted Matt's head
and yelled for someone to call 911. I turned around only after I heard him
shout. I saw Stephanie running for the phone. Carl was kneeling on the
deck where I should have been kneeling, his hands reaching for Matt.

A coincidence too rich to fabricate: The man who pulled Matt's face
from the water and yelled for help was an emergency room doctor. Bruce
cradled Matt's chin between his thumb and forefinger while I knelt
beside Carl. We gripped Matt's armpits and slid him from the water.
Matt's eyes were closed but his mouth gaped. His hands flapped. He was
seizing. Bruce yelled, "Hey, Matt! Come back!" and dropped his ear to
Matt's lips. Matt opened his eyes and tried to gasp, but his tongue pro-
truded between his teeth. It didn't look right. Hadn't he been swimming
a minute ago? I kept thinking, *This isn't real. This isn't happening.* How
could this be real? It wasn't simply the fact of Matt turning blue and purple, but of my standing there, my watching it. One of the two couldn't be
happening. I told myself to wake up. Or for Matt to wake up. *Open your
eyes*, I thought. I prayed it. *Please God, open his eyes.* I said it aloud: "God."

"Think good thoughts," Stephanie said. "He needs your energy."

Bruce pressed his ear against Matt's chest, said, "He must have inhaled
water. Roll him over." We did, and a thin string of foamy saliva streamed
down his cheek. Matt's face turned green, then blue, then a blue so dark
it was purple. The veins in his head and neck bulged. "I can't find a pulse,"
Bruce said. The lifeguard straddled Matt's waist and began compressions.
Bruce pinched Matt's nose and breathed into his mouth. Bruce's ribs rose
through his skin with every breath. Matt's chest didn't move at all.

I stood with my hands on my knees, my back humped, sweating.
Stomach acid filled my mouth, and the grouting between the square

white tiles began to widen. I was tilting forward, nauseous. I backed up to the window, sat down on the sill. "Calm down," I told myself. How many times had I seen swimmers black out from holding their breaths for too long, or knocked out cold after running headfirst into the wall? How many gallons of vomit had I seen in the water? When my head cleared, I stood back up, resumed my place in the circle. I watched Bruce administer CPR with every ounce of my concentration, as if by watching I could compensate for the minutes I'd stood with my back to the water, when Matt's heart stopped and his head slipped under.

Ten minutes had passed since Stephanie had run for the phone, five minutes since Carl called again, and still the paramedics had not come. Time slowed to the pace of the compressions: fifteen, followed by two breaths. After four cycles, a pulse check. At the first check, Matt's pulse was there, faint but palpable. I exhaled. Then it was gone again, and the lifeguard dropped her head. Her dark hair fell forward over her eyes as she pressed her weight into Matt's sternum. She rose on her knees as she counted, gritting her teeth. "Where's the goddamn ambulance?" I said.

Thirteen minutes after they'd been called, the paramedics arrived. Five medics loped through the door, slow as mules, five fat slobs paid by the hour, five bellies overhanging five belts. "Run, guys!" Bruce said. He reached out and yanked the stethoscope from the neck of the first medic to reach him.

My terror turned into rage. Hatred took hold. I hated the paramedics for their lazy shuffle across the deck, for their blank, dispassionate faces and slow moving hands, for taking nearly a quarter of an hour to respond. I also hated the dispatcher for not conveying the gravity of the situation, though she was told and told again. I hated the faceless patient who'd occupied the medics' attention before Matt, for taking his place in the ambulance. I hated all the television shows that had portrayed paramedics as hyperalert men and women who slept with one eye open and spent their free time lifting weights beneath the fire bell. I hated the Red Cross for devising and teaching a skill that didn't do what it promised to do. I hated myself coming back to swim, for letting my guard down, for believing the lie that life was trustworthy again and that I wouldn't lose anyone else to anything other than old age or sleep, the gentlest departures.

"Step back, sir," one of the paramedics said to me. His wide frame obstructed my view, and I could see only Matt's bare feet hanging over the edge of the coping. "Okay, there's his pulse," a voice said. "Okay, let's go." My rage abated; Matt had a pulse. His feet rose in the air as he was hefted onto the gurney. A medic squeezed a ball-shaped rebreather, and the other four pushed the gurney through the door. Bruce jogged behind, still in his Speedo, and climbed inside the ambulance. I tossed him his pager and told him I'd get his clothes from his locker, drive his car up to the emergency room.

I parked in front of the hospital and carried Bruce's bag over my shoulder. In the waiting room, Carl's tie hung below his open collar, and Stephen was in his undershirt and jeans, bare feet shoved into his loafers. Stephanie's wet hair darkened the shoulders of her jacket. I expected to wait for hours until a doctor came to tell us everything was all right, that Matt had fainted and inhaled water, and though it got a little scary for a minute, there was nothing to worry about. They had defibrillators and ventilators and epinephrine. The emergency room could give a tree a pulse if it wanted to. Matt was thirty years old, a national champion. His heart was beating when he left the pool. He'd be fine.

I knocked on the sliding glass window and told the admitting nurse I was a friend of the doctor who came in with the ambulance, the one in the Speedo. I asked her to let Bruce know I had his clothes. She began to write on a pink message pad. Then the doors swung open and Bruce was there, in a blue scrub top and black nylon shorts, both suctioned against his skin. His face was red, his eyes swollen. He shook his head. Shaking your head in a hospital is a symbol, no explanation required. It possesses its own horror, that tiny twist of the neck.

Bruce pressed his hands to his forehead, smoothed his salt-and-pepper hair against his skull. "They tried," he said, shaking his head some more. "They tried to pace his heart. There was no current, and nothing in the echo."

I heard Bruce speak, I gathered in the words, but I couldn't translate them into anything meaningful. Surely he didn't mean Matt. I must have heard wrong or asked the wrong question. I scratched the back of my neck. My shoes were a long way down.

"They tried everything?" Stephanie asked next. "*You* tried everything?"

"He was gone before he got here," Bruce said. "I could tell in the ambulance, but I prayed for a miracle."

I saw Priscilla, a fellow coach and matriarch of the team, pass behind the nurses' station. She was followed by Matt's wife, Darlene, her blond hair fanned over the collar of her chocolate-brown jacket. I stood there as the women turned the corner, and a few seconds later, maybe ten, I heard Darlene scream. Her scream was a combination of the word "no" and a sound straight from the stomach. Stephen and Stephanie fell into each other's arms. "Oh my God," Carl said. He cupped his hand over his mouth.

I stood there, still not talking, thinking. I thought about the morning after Jeremy died, how I'd sat on the bleachers beside the pool and listened to the school psychologist tell my swimming team that sudden traumas can bring to the surface other losses, older griefs. I dismissed the idea at the time, but only because I could not imagine anything as terrible and violent as the murders and so could not believe that any other loss would warrant comparison with them. Jeremy's murder was also my first death, so the proposition was academic anyway. For the last year or so, I'd begun to think I had the murders managed; I saw my two years away from the pool almost as a kind of buffer zone that separated the swimmer I was now with the swimmer I'd been back then. But now, standing in the ER waiting room, the devouring memory of that hot September night came rushing back, as sourceless as the desert wind: sirens flashing in the windows, Jeremy's white shoulder beyond the sheriff's boot, his face beside his father's and brother's in the morning newspaper. My high school teammates in their letter jackets, girls wearing T-shirts decorated with puff-paint and ribbons around their ponytails, the stained carpet in the classroom where I sat with my friends and tried to cry.

Stephanie lifted her head from the huddle, a springy coil of dark hair hanging between her eyes. She reached out her arm, my invitation to join the grieving circle. Her face looked hot, as if she and the others stood over a steam vent. The shock was airborne. I couldn't go toward her, couldn't allow myself to breathe their same air. I felt, for a beat, like I might throw up, but then that passed and I realized, more alarmingly, that I felt nothing at all. I felt as though a tide was sweeping me out to sea; any minute it would pitch up and crash. I needed to get out of there. I shook my head and stepped backward, toward the chairs, the table with its magazines arranged like a peacock's tail, the lighted EXIT sign.

I moved in a jog, not frantic enough to cause alarm, but fast enough for people to move out of my way. I followed the hallway down a flight of stairs and around a corner until I arrived at the glass skybridge connecting the university hospital to the children's hospital. The coffee cart sat like a checkpoint at the university end of the bridge. There were paintings on the interior wall of the bridge of striped umbrellas on beaches, boys and girls in sandboxes. A little girl came walking down the corridor, stiff-legged and encumbered, her hand gripped around the rolling IV stand. A translucent tube connected the hanging bag of clear fluid to her neckline, and her head was turbaned in gauze. The nurse's scrub top was covered in Mickey Mouse ears, and she smiled as though this wobbly, faltering walk was a medical breakthrough. Hospitals are terrible places, I decided. They loom over their cities like cathedrals, waiting for us to fall on our knees at their doors and beg for mercy, as if the secret to eluding death might lay somewhere inside when in truth, inside waits only more dying, more death.

I took the elevator to the bottom floor and hurried through the hallway, past the pharmacy and the Outpatient Clinic and the vending machines and through the sliding glass doors and into the open air. A minivan waited in the parking circle with its side door open. To the left, a woman sat on a wooden bench reading a novel, her fleece zipped all the way to her chin. I moved downhill, across the parking lot to the sidewalk alongside 1900 East, the main artery connecting the University of Utah campus to the medical center, and sat down on the retaining wall beside the bus stop. Cars whooshed by. Across the road, the evergreens dotted the brown golf course, and beyond the trees the valley fell away toward the city, the Oquirrh Mountains on the other side, the Great Salt Lake as flat and metallic as a sheet of foil. I leaned my hands on my knees and worked to suck in air.

A cold wind kicked up. I'd left my jacket at the pool. I cupped my elbows in my hands and began to shake. I tried to make it stop; I didn't think I had any right to shake, to feel the terror that kept waving through me. I wasn't as close to Matt as I was to Jeremy. I was, however, closer to the dying. I'd actually watched death swoop down and pluck Matt's life right out of the water, the way a pelican dives for a fish. The worst part was that death seemed indifferent to who it claimed. There was no evil to it, no agency at all. *It happened so fast*, I thought. I couldn't believe how fast it happened.

It wasn't something I could make sense of except to recast it in the terms I'd used for years. I thought of the stories Matt told in his truck, his bacchanalian exploits as a younger man, and for a moment I entertained the idea that he was being punished for a sin. I pushed my index fingers into my temples, and I tried to think of the verse. "When lust has been conceived, it gives birth to sin, and sin brings forth death," or something like that. In recalling the verse, I realized what the real problem was: I was afraid. I needed to reassure myself I was safe. It's a psychological trick I'm still given to: When murders show up on television or children go missing, I find myself hoping for the killer to turn out to be the husband, the ne'er-do-well ex-boyfriend, the babysitter, the drug connection no one knew about—praying for a way to separate the crime from the conditions of my life. I could accept a world which metered out punishment to bad people doing bad things; what I could not accept was randomness. Which was exactly how Matt's death seemed. Death had made an arbitrary choice, and it very easily could have taken me. I looked at the steady stream of cars going by. Not a single driver seemed to notice me, some guy hyperventilating beside the bus stop, and so none of them had any idea that I'd just watched someone die. Then I thought—a thought I'm still ashamed of—I'm glad it wasn't me. I struck my chest with my fist, as if to declare some idiotic defiance to death, but really just to feel my hand thud against my breastbone. I stilled my hand and counted my pulse. "I'm alive," I said.

A woman came down the sidewalk pushing a little girl in a pink stroller. The girl's blond hair was tangled up like a bird's nest, and her pink nylon jacket was scuffed and dirty. The girl squinted at me in the sunlight with a cool, almost antagonistic regard, as if to chide me for my ugly and selfish thought. As if to say: *You're not as safe as you think.*

I turned and looked up at the hospitals—the white walls and mirrored windows of the children's hospital, the brown-and-white checkerboard of the university hospital above it. All those rooms where people were begging God to save their lives, and somewhere among them, the room where my friends were holding vigil for the battle lost.

The chairs in the waiting room were empty. I asked the admitting nurse where everyone had gone. "Who?" she asked. Behind her desk, two nurses in green scrubs pushed a gurney down the hallway.

"The friends of the man who died swimming," I said.

"He's been moved to the Meditation Room on the second floor," she said. She pointed toward the door. "Follow the signs."

The Meditation Room had the same blue-gray carpet that covered the corridors; the furniture was the same wood-trimmed, blue upholstery love seat and chairs found in every other room. In the counter along the wall was a sink. Matt lay on a gurney covered in a mauve blanket, his feet pointed toward the door. He'd been wheeled in and would be wheeled out. Darlene sat with a ball of Kleenex in her fist. A round Episcopalian priest sat on Matt's other side, his red prayer book on his knee. Priscilla sat in a chair near the door.

The swimmers had assembled in the chapel next door. The stained-glass panes were lit by electric bulbs, a constant glow rising from a recessed panel. Nothing in the room pointed to a god with a name, no crosses adorned the walls, no scriptures filled the pews. The images in the stained glass were of birds and snowy mountaintops. A chaplain stood in the doorway, dressed in olive slacks and a yellow oxford—the same business-casual, we're-all-friends-here style the pastor of my church sported on Sundays. I heard him say, "This is a time for family and friends." It was his job to offer words in crisis, and I knew it, but it nevertheless irritated me that his need to remain neutral forced him into bland clichés. The trouble was, as I sat down in one of the pews and knit my hands together and closed my eyes, I couldn't think of anything better to say. I could, however, think of many things worse. I didn't know everything about Matt, but he'd told me once his mother was a devout Episcopalian. He went to church with her when he visited her, but not so often the rest of the time. In the evangelical universe, a nominal faith was worse than no faith at all, for it allowed someone like Matt to call himself a Christian even if he'd never invited Jesus into his heart. This verse was easier to recall, for I quoted it often while I roamed around Brisbane, passing out tracts: "Not everyone who says to me, 'Lord, Lord,' will enter the kingdom of heaven, but only the one who does the will of my Father who is in heaven." At the end of passage, Jesus himself says, "Away from me, you evildoers." Which meant, if I adhered to my evangelical beliefs, if Matt's soul lingered in an afterlife, it didn't linger in heaven, but in hell.

Fear of hell—far more than the promise of heaven—had launched the Crusades and sparked the Inquisition; hell had the power to drive protestors into the streets. In Australia, my friend Josh feared hell in a real way and harnessed his fear as a tool for winning souls. Hell, for me, was real but nothing I feared on a day-to-day basis. I thought of hell as something akin to Chaos in *Paradise Lost*: "a dark illimitable ocean, without bound, without dimension"—a vast, disorganized realm that was simply, logically, the universe deprived of God's presence. Eternal solitude. A proposition informed by the same classical ratiocination as abstinence, so simple it seemed almost mathematical: Entrance to heaven came down to a single choice to know Jesus; it had nothing to do with being good or bad. Avoiding hell was, in the end, a small problem with an equally easy solution, and I clung to the notion that everyone, including the most stone-hearted, would call to God, even if in their final, dying moments. A thousand times I'd imagined Jeremy closing his eyes in his living room that night, his brother beside him already gone, praying for God to ferry him safely away while God's angels descended to receive him. But Matt's death I had watched, watched him wheeze and flap his hands and spend his final dying moments fighting to live, not calling out to Jesus. He was a good man; he loved his wife, loved his mother and sister, and he was my friend. The thought that Matt's wife and priest prayed over a soul adrift in hell was unacceptable. My tower of logic was leaning, wobbling. It was one more crack in my faith, as if a pebble had ricocheted off a car windshield, leaving behind a quietly expanding web.

I left my chair and went to stand with Stephanie, Carl, Stephen, and Bruce. Stephanie reached her arm around my shoulder and pulled me in, completing the embrace I'd rejected an hour before. "Where'd you go?" she asked.

"I needed some air," I said.

"I'm glad you came back," she said. "I was worried."

I rested my shoulder against the wall and crossed my ankles. My friends told each other what they knew. Matt's father had died of a heart attack when he was fifty-three. Matt had gone to a cardiologist in January and was told he was in fine shape. They wondered what the cardiologist missed, and they talked about Matt's long hours at work, the nights he came home to kiss Darlene goodnight before going back, and they remembered the mornings when he showed up at the pool unshowered and unshaved, his hair in nine directions. I remembered him on those mornings, too. I remembered he talked about giving up coaching. I remembered the month he didn't swim. I remembered he'd had pneumonia last fall. "If only we'd seen," Stephen said, rising on his toes, then settling back down. I felt the same way. Matt had died right in front of me. Saving him should have been easy, if I'd only turned around.

I must have said so out loud. "You can't think that way," Bruce said, working the buttons through the cuffs of his dress shirt. He explained the causes of sudden heart failure: hypertrophic cardiomyopathy, pulmonary edema, aortic stenosis, all complex and variable and dependent upon a number of factors. "Too much salt and exercise can cause the heart to arrest," Bruce said. "The marathon runners you hear about, who collapse on a jog around the block? Sometimes the heart just stops." For Matt, the cause might have been the fast food receipts piled on the seat of his truck, or been encrypted in the workout scrawled on the board at the pool, in my handwriting. Or his genetic code may have been wired with a bomb, programmed to explode from the first division of his cells. "The pathology report will tell us more," Bruce said. "It will take a few days."

"Can they donate his organs?" Stephanie asked.

"No," Bruce said. "Organs have to be taken while the heart's still beating. Bone and tissue are possible, maybe his cornea. If Darlene wants that."

Stephanie said, "Maybe he'll help a burn victim." She was uncomfortable talking this way, but what mattered was that we were talking. It's what the chaplain knew. I needed the people standing around me. I needed someone to notice if I disappeared. I needed someone to breathe for me if I stopped.

Priscilla came into the chapel to tell us she was taking Darlene home. We filed into the hallway and formed two rows, one against each wall. Darlene's nose and upper lip were bright red when she opened the door, as if she'd come in from a long run. Her hair was a mess, but her ivory blouse was still tucked into her khakis. The nurse standing by the door touched Darlene's back, and Darlene slowly pressed the door closed. She smiled and said, "Hi," dabbing at her eyes. She was taken in and embraced and released, and soon she was standing before me. She was holding a clipboard, and up close I could see on it the autopsy authorization form, Darlene's loopy signature across a line at the top. I spread my arms and pressed my face to her neck. I didn't know what to say. She stepped away. My tears dissolved into her blouse.

I walked to the window of the Meditation Room. The nurse stepped out of the way so I could see inside. Pink skin folded over the priest's collar as he read from his prayer book. Matt lay unmoving beside him. The curtains were drawn across the windows, and the sunlight through the twill stood in the room like sediment in a jar. "You can go see him, if you like," the nurse said.

The priest rose from the chair when I stepped inside. He shuffled toward the door with his hands clasped at his belt. I stood next to Matt. The blanket had been tucked beneath his shoulders. The elbow of the breathing tube still rose from his mouth, held in place with surgical tape. Dried flakes of blood and the wiped-away residue of a smear clung to his nostrils and the corners of his mouth. I leaned closer and saw blood inside his inner ears. I saw what Bruce meant when he said the doctors tried everything. They'd compressed and shocked Matt's heart until blood oozed from every orifice. His eyelids weren't completely closed, and his eyes were soupy, the vitreous gel congealing, so thick it reflected the overhead light. In his cheeks I could see the fingerprints of the doctors and nurses and medics who'd held his head and squeezed his nose.

I placed my hands on his chest. His body felt filled with liquid, as if I pressed harder he'd pop. I tried again to think of a prayer, but instead I thought about the autopsy form. When Bruce said pathology report, he meant autopsy—a dissection. Matt would lie beneath a bright lamp while a pathologist opened his skin down the axis of his sternum and sawed apart his breastbone. His heart would be extracted and weighed, his lungs and kidneys, each organ cradled in the hanging scale and then moved to a different table. He'd be reduced to ever-smaller pieces, rinsed and peeled, studied beneath a microscope. His deficient cells, his muscles and blood, would become the conclusions, the end of the story. We, his friends, would remember Matt squirting beer through his teeth, dancing at the Halloween party in a tutu, but he was slipping away even as I touched him. I'd spent my life exchanging the flesh for words, for the Word, the temporal for the eternal. But with my hands on Matt's chest, his hair still wet, words amounted to nothing. I felt something inside me shutting down.

That night I lay in bed with my hand over my heart. I watched the blue numbers on my clock and counted my pulse and envisioned my heart stopping, as suddenly and as soundlessly as Matt's. If death came for me while I slept, I might not even stir. How long would it take before I was missed, before my roommate opened my door to check on me? I pulled the blankets to my chin and prayed, aloud, "Please God, save my life."

I rode my bike to the pool the next day. It was spring break; I had nowhere else to be. I got there early, and was the first one in my suit, first onto the deck. The workout we never swam yesterday—my workout, in my handwriting—was still on the board. I sat on the bench and watched an elderly woman in an old-fashioned bathing cap tread in a shallow lane, her arms sweeping the water as she stepped forward. She moved so slowly the exercise couldn't do her much good. The lifeguard twirled her whistle around her fingers, pleasantly bored. My arms and shoulders felt heavy. I wondered if I'd come back to the pool too quickly, if I should have ever come back at all. Then they began to emerge from the locker room—the swimmers, my people. They wore their suits and caps, carried their goggles like rosaries. I stood to meet them, and we wrapped our arms around each other. I felt their warm skin against my own. I heard myself breathing. We whispered Matt's name.

Priscilla arrived at five minutes to noon. It was her day to coach. She stopped at the edge of the pool when she came through the locker room door. I followed her eyes to the water, and stared into it as I had the day before: the early spring sunlight, the liquefying tiles, though today the bottom looked deeper, the water buzzing with an electric charge. I glanced over to make sure the old woman was still moving. I stared into the water until I saw Matt circling up from the bottom of the pool, bubbles streaming from his nose. He rose slowly toward the surface, but just before he broke through, he turned and plunged back down and disappeared through the grates of the drain on the floor—slipping through the open door that joins this world with whatever comes next. I'd swum with a ghost for almost ten years, and now I had another. I lowered my goggles and dove in.

Wandering in Zion

The day Matt died, two women I'd never seen before showed up to swim. I could tell their suits had never touched chlorine and their caps, still dusted with talcum, had just recently been unwrapped from the cellophane. They swam together in the first lane, reserved for the slowest swimmers, and were hardly wet when we pulled Matt from the water. To my surprise, they followed the ambulance to the hospital along with the rest of the team. They were standing in the hallway when I fled the emergency room and were there in the chapel when I returned, their heads inclined toward each other, silent and crying. I didn't know what to say to them, or even who they were, so in the end I said nothing. It turned out they were Matt's coworkers. He'd been hounding them to come swim for months, and the day he finally talked them into it was the day he died. It seemed like one more cruel irony in a series of cruel ironies: The moment they lowered their defenses enough to take a leap of faith, try something new, was the moment the floor disappeared. I watched for them when I coached—hoping they'd risk the water one more time but also wondering if they would ever again go near a pool without thinking of Matt seizing on the deck. Neither one of them returned. Their first swim had been their last.

Not swimming was never an option for me. In fact, in the months that followed Matt's death, I felt pulled toward the water more strongly than ever. I swam in the mornings, coached at noon, and returned in the evenings after my classes let out. At night, after the windows went black and the underwater lights turned on, the pool gave off a lambent blue glow, like the cooling tank of a nuclear reactor—a supernatural quality less eerie than a cemetery, but nevertheless pulsing with a strange vibration, the certain knowledge the dead were near. I told anyone who asked that I needed to burn off stress, though I'd already handed in my master's thesis and wouldn't start work on my PhD until August. The extra swimming brought back some of my speed. In May, I won the five hundred–yard freestyle at the U.S. Masters National Championships—a greater victory than I'd ever had in college. When the summer came, I took a job teaching swimming lessons to children, at minimum wage. I had to teach eight hours a day—one after another in half-hour blocks—in order to pay my rent, but it felt good to spend the day in the water, the sun on my scalp and back, the children's heartbeats drumming as fast as hummingbirds as they floated against my palm. I lost most of my post-college weight. My skin regained a little color.

The county aquatic facility doubled in size during the summer. The Olympic-sized outdoor pool, drained and empty throughout the winter, was bleached and refilled and watched over by a constantly rotating herd of lifeguards and swimming instructors who roamed the deck in mirrored sunglasses and red bathing suits. There were so many of them that I didn't learn most of their names. One name, however, I made a point to learn. Katherine was the lifeguard supervisor and occasionally lifeguarded herself, perched above me in her canted chair. She had dark eyebrows, a wide smile, and a clover patch of freckles across her nose and cheeks that darkened the longer she sat in the sun. The other guards read *Cosmo* on their breaks, or else weathered paperbacks with wizards on the covers, but Katherine read *Jane Eyre* and *Housekeeping*, novels I taught in my own classes. The books gave me an excuse to talk to her.

I learned she was majoring in English and was taking summer classes to finish her degree early—in three years instead of the usual four. In addition to the pool, she also worked nights as a unit clerk in the children's hospital and did volunteer work with Planned Parenthood. After graduation, she planned on becoming a social worker. I couldn't help thinking of my college Bible study: All the negotiables were lining up. The tougher question was the nonnegotiables: where religion factored in, and how. It was a question I didn't want to ask. I feared her answer almost as much as I feared my own reaction to whatever answer she gave.

One morning between swimming lessons, I was sitting in the hot tub with the other instructors when Katherine approached to ask if anyone wanted to pick up an extra lifeguarding shift. I squirted her with the rubber duck I used to coax the children into the pool. The water hit her elbow. She looked down at me, her dark eyebrows arched, her pursed lips a mixture of seriousness and sarcasm. She wasn't easily fooled or easily persuaded, but she was willing to see how things played out. I knew next to nothing about her, but looking up at her standing with her back to the pool, her hair pulled into a knot, I imagined her giving me that same look years from now, decades from now, lines around her eyes, gray streaks in her hair, as though it was the sextant by which I'd chart the worth and peril of every act from here on. It didn't feel like a fantasy, but calmer than that—like pulling up the driveway, for the first time, of the house where I was destined to live.

She turned and walked away. I climbed out of the water.

Katherine wasn't Mormon, she was Presbyterian. Her family, though, had been in Utah since the beginning. Her grandfather's grandfather had had a fling with one of Brigham Young's wives, which got him banished to the desert side of the Oquirrh Mountains. The town he founded was still there, but Katherine's family hadn't been Mormon for eighty years. Her own church was small, and most of her friends had gone out of state for college, which she would have done, too, except that she was paying for college herself. The Sundays she went to church, she went alone. I asked if she wanted to come to church with me. She said okay.

After a year in the most proto-California evangelical church in Utah—where more people wore fleece jackets than blazers—my faith was on life support, though I could not easily say why. All my friends, including my roommate, went there. Three of us in the fellowship were working on doctorates, two more on master's degrees. But the service itself felt sort of like a time-share presentation. The pastor preached in an open collar and used PowerPoint in his sermons—sermons replete with the evangelical stock phrases I'd learned as a teenager, used as a college student, and propagated as a missionary. As though he typed into his computer a few loaded keywords like "moral relativism" or "family values" or "how God tests our faith," and a few seconds later a website generated forty-five minutes of Bible verses connected by bad jokes and sappy anecdotes. Communion was celebrated once a month with little square crackers and Welch's grape juice brought forth from the kitchen by two women in their late fifties who resembled primary school teachers (a resemblance undoubtedly fueled by the all-weather carpeting on the floor, the econo-sized jugs of juice, and the tiny paper cups into which they poured it). And yet no one else seemed bothered by any of it. Whenever the band took up their instruments at the front of the room, every man and woman around me closed their eyes, opened their palms to the air.

Within our first few dates, I'd figured out that Katherine made sense for me. I felt all the novelty that accompanies an early closeness, but I also felt plainly, and delightfully, normal. Each layer we peeled away was both revelatory and ordinary—like learning the water used to boil eggs also worked as a plant food or that Picasso once painted on brown paper bags. I hadn't dated as much as some, but I'd dated enough to know the difference between my previous efforts to arrange myself in the best possible light, and being simply in the light, revealed. When I finally told her about Jeremy and tried, awkwardly and incompletely, to explain how the murders had affected me and the vows I'd made in their shadow, she'd listened in a way other people had not: not with shock or artificial sympathy but with recognition. She'd lost a friend, too, during a rafting trip—the boat had flipped in the rapids; her friend went under and never came up—and her ambition to become a social worker came, in part, from the impotence of watching it happen. She understood that some commitments actually meant something, and believed that once made they should be kept. Listening to her talk was invigorating and lovely and right, and by inviting Katherine to church with me, I hoped the feelings I had with her would transfer to church simply because I was with her there.

For a while, it seemed to work. The fellowship took Katherine in, made her their friend. She joined a women's Bible study; the men's group met at my house. We went camping at San Rafael Swell and hiked to the top of the Pfeifferhorn, high above the Salt Lake Valley. I have an entire photo album filled with shots of the group: a dozen men and women in their twenties, dark-haired with dark sunglasses, in fleece vests and hiking boots and bandanas around their foreheads, their arms around one another's shoulders, their backs to the slickrock, the ski lifts, the Wasatch valley from the top of Hidden Peak just as the sun's coming up on Easter morning, squatting beside an orange campfire, straddling mountain bikes with streaks of mud up to our chins, my roommate Aaron climbing Storm Mountain in Big Cottonwood Canyon with a belt of colored carabineers dangling from his waist, the lot of us lifting our cups to toast through the steam while we soaked after a day of waist-high powder in Danny and Trudy's hot tub, Katherine with a flaming marshmallow inside her open mouth, laughing so hard the woman standing beside her in the photo is pointing and saying something about flames coming through her nose, a look on Katherine's face that says: *This is the most fun I've ever had. This is what it's like to have friends. This is what it's like to be young and in love.*

I quit worrying that the sermons were fatuous or that the praise band couldn't sing. I ignored the pastor when he encouraged the congregation to "vote our values," and I ignored the Operation Rescue and Love in Action flyers pinned to the bulletin board near the front entrance and the Focus on the Family magazines stacked on the counter beside the coffee urn. When we could no longer ignore them, Katherine and I started skipping the services and showed up just for the fellowship meetings—the real meat and potatoes, where the discussions weren't so empty and the company was easier to keep.

But even in the fellowship, the rhetoric turned fiery. We read and discussed a book challenging Christians to swear off dating in favor of "courting": A man and a woman interested in a relationship ought to join a couples' Bible study and spend time with each other's families. Giving up sex before marriage wasn't enough; the entire enterprise of affection needed to go. A member of the fellowship who worked with the junior high youth group decided to give up beer, not because beer was sinful, but because he needed to be a witness to the kids. "What would one of the youths think if they saw me drinking a beer?" he said. "As Paul writes, 'all things are permitted, but not all things are profitable.'" So many abstentions were rationalized this way. Because a child cannot understand complex moral issues—that alcohol consumption in moderation is different than in excess—Christians should refrain from "gray area" pleasures that might cause a child someday to stumble. Every week, someone proclaimed yet another thing to avoid.

In June, Danny read Psalm 104 during the fellowship meeting and declared that before the Fall in the Garden of Eden, no rain had fallen on the Earth. A vapor cloud had hovered above the trees, providing a constant source of moisture and nourishment. Katherine looked at me with one cocked eyebrow. Then Danny pointed to 1 Timothy 2:12 and talked about Paul's dictum that women not teach men. Women could teach other women and children, but not men. Unlike the vapor cloud, I'd heard this song before. It came up at least once a year, an annual booster shot of sexual politics. This lesson was a one-two punch: The Earth didn't begin the way contemporary science describes, therefore people, starting with women, shouldn't behave the way contemporary culture dictates. I'd always loved the Apostle Paul: first among sinners, blinded by God on the road to Damascus, who gave his life to roaming the world and encouraging the dispirited, who wrote in First Corinthians that love was more important than healing or prophesying or any other spiritual talent. Now Paul sounded like a Luddite, a sexist, a eunuch who begrudgingly allowed marriage as a concession even as he held that the truly faithful would stay celibate forever, become missionaries, preach the word day and night. I listened with my hand resting on Katherine's knee. I meant it as a gesture of affection, but the longer Danny talked, the more my hand felt like a manacle. Katherine crossed her legs and brushed my hand away.

"Is *rain* sinful?" Katherine asked me on the way home. We had taken the hardtop off her jeep the day before, and she had to shout to be heard over the wind. "Seriously!" she yelled. "When Adam and Eve sinned, rain was punishment?"

"I've been reading the Bible a long time," I said. "I've never heard of the vapor cloud before. The Psalms are poetry. It's a metaphor."

Katherine changed lanes, shifted into fifth. The wind, as we came around Mount Olympus, died down a little. She said, "Danny didn't make it sound like a metaphor."

I felt weirdly compelled to defend Danny—not Danny himself, but his point of view. What I couldn't do was admit Danny, or whatever Bible study guide told him about the vapor cloud, was full of it. "It takes courage to read the Bible literally," I said.

Katherine turned her eyes from the road, crunched her brows together. Her nights in the hospital had sharpened her ability to sniff out a lie. "Do you believe in it?" she said. I believed in evolution, I said, and I had no problem with women teaching men. "They're tangential things," I said. "Neither one is essential to my faith."

Our exit was next. Katherine downshifted and merged toward the off-ramp. We wondered aloud if we should grab something for lunch. I rooted through the glove compartment for a Subway coupon. With the wind gone, we could hear the radio, so I turned it up. But the question stayed with me. For the last year, I'd volunteered two nights a week as a coach for a gay swimming team—the team had spun-off from the masters team, and did charity work with the Utah AIDS Foundation and Operation Shine America; as my friendships with the men and women on the team deepened and I saw how much most of them had had to give up in order to admit who they were—cut off from children, excommunicated from churches—the less I believed homosexuality was a sin, or a choice, and I felt embarrassed about being a part of a church that didn't welcome them. Katherine had started at Planned Parenthood because the director had gone to her old church—"a *Presbyterian* church," she intoned—and the organization prevented far more abortions than it promoted, yet she'd never told the fellowship group that she worked there. All these things joined the vapor cloud and women teaching men under the banner of THINGS NOT ESSENTIAL TO MY FAITH. The question that remained, which I was right then unable to answer: What things *were* essential?

One thing I knew: I was still a virgin. Now that I'd met Katherine, I was glad I'd made it to her without a truckload of bad sex trailing behind me, or even one extravagant mistake. Falling in love was, for me, evangelicalism's reward, the whole reason I'd sacrificed the fleeting pleasures of youth in the first place. After a decade of resisting temptation—even after eleven months of kissing Katherine into the purple hours of the morning—my virginity had fused itself to my remnant faith the way a barnacle fuses with the hull of a boat. It had become the symbol of faith itself.

In the non-evangelical world, virginity is preserved only by time, by youth and awkwardness, rather than by deliberate commitment. The loss of virginity is a story everyone's heard a thousand times: the transgression that is not at all a transgression but a rite of passage, the moment the adolescent molts from his or her baby skin and becomes a full-fledged citizen, capable of both love and disobedience. The event happens and is over; life becomes about other things. Virginity is reduced to a postcard from the past. But for evangelicals, the virgin body is the living metaphor of submission to Christ, a nod to the burning wheel in the sky. It divides the faithful from the fallen, those who seek God's will from those who seek their own. Long after virginity has been given up, even for the married, it remains not a postcard but a point of origin. It stands always behind us, like Einstein's clock tower, glowing bright no matter how far or fast we move away from it.

This narrative was especially true for me: Virginity had defined my faith from the beginning. It had steered me around the destruction that had taken down my friends; it was Article One in the code by which I sought a good life and informed my every assumption about how I might obtain such a life; it was my shield against divorce and calamity; it kept my heart from suddenly giving out; it protected me from murder. I knew it was a superstition, one I couldn't defend, and it led me to wonder, sometimes, how my life might have played out if Jeremy hadn't been killed. If I ever would have swallowed the hook of my father and stepmother's faith. Yet even as I felt my foothold in the evangelical world slipping, even as I ground my teeth on the word *virgin*—even then, I madly clung to the belief that depriving my body for the nourishment of my soul was, somehow, the key to keeping God's favor. Letting go of it would result in exile. I'd be cast into the wilderness.

The weekend before fall-term classes started up again, and I switched from teaching seven-year-olds how to swim to teaching twenty-year-olds how to write, Danny and Trudy organized one last hiking trip to Zion National Park. Twelve of us spent the night in St. George and set out for Zion beneath the stars, a full two hours before dawn. We left two cars at the trail's end and squeezed into two others to snake our way up the mountain to the trailhead. We were a mile in before the sun made it over the peaks; in its angular shadow, the slickrock appeared to flow into the canyon, as though the water had receded from an ancient sea floor, and the exposed sand had petrified instantly. We moved east and south as we descended into the canyon. Once we hit the bottom, we followed the river. For six hours we slogged through opaque green pools briny with juniper silt and bloated squirrel carcasses, pools sometimes waist-deep that we crossed with our packs above our heads, pools without bottoms we could cross only by swimming. In the less-traveled slots forking off the main trail, the canyon walls narrowed to less than eighteen inches wide, lit by shafts of light so slim and removed it felt as though we were hiking in the bottom of a well. At the end, we rappelled into the hundred-yard stretch of canyon that gave the hike its name—the Subway—undercut by floodwaters into a near-perfect cylinder, large enough for a railcar to pass through, its tubelike interior glowing orange as the afternoon sun worked down through the sandstone.

When we came out of the tunnel, Danny gathered the guys to run ahead to the parking lot, pile into the cars we left there that morning, and drive to the upper trailhead to retrieve the other two. If they made good time, they'd complete the loop in two hours. Six men ran ahead, though only four were needed, as if staying behind was an admission of weakness. The women could take their time hiking out. I remained behind so I could hike with Katherine, and I was the only man. My roommate, Aaron, had promised to stay with Jenny, his girlfriend, but he changed his mind at the last minute and left without saying good-bye. Ten minutes later, ditched and pissed off, Jenny slung her pack over her shoulder and set out by herself.

I looked forward to killing time with Katherine, lingering in the first open sunlight we'd seen all day, laying my socks and T-shirt over a rock to dry. But if I'd learned one thing from living on the fringes of a desert, it was that no one, especially not a jilted heart, should walk through it alone. "Maybe we should go with her," I told Katherine. I meant it, at first, only as a suggestion. Then, a quarter-mile downstream, I saw Jenny step from the shoulder of the river, onto dry trail. We'd lose her if we didn't leave now. "Get your shoes and socks on," I said. I clapped my hands, a little more like Danny than I intended. "Let's go." Katherine frowned. I knew I was out of line, but I was also impatient and stubborn and trying to be responsible, so I didn't apologize. Katherine went silent and stuffed her feet down inside her wet socks and wet shoes. We set out in pursuit.

Jenny moved with purpose, as if trying to keep pace with the men. I could see the dust clouds popping up behind her shoes, but it still took us a good half hour to reel her in. Not long after we overtook her, we came upon another hiker, Joe, a gray-bearded, barrel-gutted man who had gotten separated from his hiking group. He wore long khaki shorts and tall hiking boots that reached almost to the center of his meaty calves. On his left knee he wore a black neoprene athletic brace, a little window cut to allow his kneecap a chance to breathe. We were all headed for the parking lot, and I told him it was fine if he wanted to hike with us. He fell in line, and for close to an hour we followed the western bank of the river, in the long part of the canyon shadow, marching in a slackened single file, and in silence. I listened to the stream eddy against the scrub and watched the sego lilies begin to close up for the night. We watched for the trail marker, but we weren't quite sure of what to watch for. All day we'd charted our direction by watching for conical piles of stones placed by the park rangers to mark the trail without looking man-made. A single cairn in solitude looked like a natural oddity, a study in miniature of the whorled rock formations and arching bridges indigenous to the landscape. Only the frequency of their occurrence gave them away.

At last we spotted a trail climbing away from the river. My eyes followed it to the base of the canyon wall where it disappeared beneath a rockslide. Joe pointed to what he said was a cairn about fifty yards uphill. We figured we'd hiked far enough. The trail looked trampled. We decided to take it.

The trail switched through a small riparian stand of cottonwoods and rose out of the shade into a terrain that knew no water. The piñons were hardened against the heat and thrust forward in the afternoon sun like stage props under a spotlight. The rockslide to the ridge was a long tongue of loose debris. Each step was like climbing a staircase in an abandoned house, the floor shifting and slightly fluid beneath our feet. Most of the hike had been like this—impossible passageways and dangerous scrambles across unsteady ground. After nine hours, I was only slightly accustomed to it.

We ascended until we came to a gap in the ridge wide enough for a foot to anchor. I pulled myself up and then turned to pull Katherine, then Jenny, and finally, Joe. He curled his big hand around my wrist, and I leaned back to hoist him. When he was up, I turned and looked around. An empty grassland mesa spread before us, west onto nothing, no parking lot, no cars, no road. "Uh-oh," Katherine said.

"Should we turn around?" Jenny asked.

"Now that we're out of the canyon that doesn't make much sense," Joe said.

"Maybe the parking lot is in a ways," I said. "We need to hike in to find the trail."

None of us realized how far off course we'd strayed. A winding access road skirted the perimeter of the wilderness between the lower and upper trailheads. The road curved sharply east as it climbed from the canyon and then immediately tracked several miles to the west. Hiking west, as instinct told us to do, would lead us parallel to the road rather than perpendicular to it. We didn't realize the right trail out of the canyon was two miles farther downriver than where we'd ascended. Now that we were above the canyon rim, I could see the thunderbank building in the southwest corner of the sky. There was no telling if it would hit us, but if it did, it was sure to be a heavy, late-summer monsoon. Even a small rain could cause a flash flood in the canyon, those tumbling brown-and-white avalanches of water that scythe off trees and deposit boulders at Martian angles. Hiking in a canyon or down-climbing on loose gravel was no place to be in a storm.

"I'm really nervous about this," Jenny said.

"It's fine," I said. "Our best option."

"I need to pray before we go on," Jenny said. She turned her back to us and lowered her head, knit her fingers, and held them at her waist. Her green shorts rode high on her hips. Her lips moved, but she didn't utter a sound.

I stood beside Katherine, but I was careful not to stand too close. I gathered her in with quick, furtive glances, the glittery dust on her calves, the dark outline of her purple bikini top through her T-shirt, and then turned to study the rocks and sky. I was afraid of what Jenny would know if she caught me staring. Neither of us said anything, nor closed our eyes to join Jenny's prayer.

Joe adjusted his sleek blade sunglasses, a mirrored band across his eyes. I could tell he was watching Jenny pray and was trying to listen. "You guys Mormon?" he asked.

"No," I said.

"What are you then?" Joe slid his boots backward in the dirt.

"We're evangelicals," Jenny said, coming back to us. "We were hiking with a group from our church. Up in Salt Lake City."

"I see," Joe said.

We hiked west on the mesa for another two hours before we stopped and passed around the water bottle—a gray, transparent Nalgene that'd been riding all day in the meshed webbing of my pack. The water line was halfway up the hash marks, about eighteen ounces. I shook the bottle and held it to the sky, as if the sunlight passing through the water would cause it to multiply. Floating specks of dust and saliva bent into the redshift, tinting the water violet. It was still as hot as noon, but once the sun lost the horizon the temperature would plummet. My socks were damp from the hours we'd hiked through the river, and I could feel blisters forming on my toes and heels. I unscrewed the cap and sipped and passed the bottle. We each took only enough to kill the thirst. No one had to be told to take less. I replaced the cap and slid the bottle back against my hip. We stood and argued.

Jenny wanted to go back. She thought we could manage the slide and the down climb. "It's not that far from the rim to the trail," she said. "And it's a way we know." I was tempted to declare myself licked and backtrack, though it was after five now, and if we turned around, even under the best circumstances, we wouldn't hit the canyon floor until eight. By then it would be pitch black. Lightning struck in silence over the western mountains, followed twenty seconds later by a low rumble, like an unlatched car trunk bouncing down an unpaved road. I felt it in my chest.

Joe lifted his sunglasses from his eyes and placed them atop his head. In his tall hiking boots, his gut like a boulder, he exuded the authority of a police officer—his former profession. He pressed his finger into the soft, empurpled flesh bunched over his kneecap. The skin whitened around his touch. "My struts won't make it down," he said. "And I'm too big to piggyback."

"That settles it," I said. "We hike on."

"Maybe I'll go back," Jenny said. "If I can get back to the trail, I can find my way out. You three can keep going."

"No," I said. I looked her in the face so she'd know I was no longer talking to everyone. "No one's going off alone."

We ascended a knoll covered in whiskers of pale tamarisk and scooted down the other side. The southern wash shallowed out, and at the bottom we spotted a stand of cottonwoods. Between the trunks, I could see a brown rectangular sign on a green metal stake. "Look at that," I said. "That's got to be a trail marker." I skidded down the gully. The juniper scratched at my thighs, and my socks filled with thorns, but I didn't slow up. Jenny moved fast behind me, tiny avalanches from her feet flowing around my shoes as I stepped and slid. Katherine and Joe descended more slowly. I circled the sign and saw it had the logo of the National Park Service—the cypress tree and mountain peak on an inverted arrowhead. It wasn't a trail marker. The stake marked the boundary of the park. On the other side was land governed by the Bureau of Land Management, earmarked for natural gas drilling and winter grazing leases, unpatrolled and untouched all the way to Nevada. I was standing outside Zion.

"This isn't the way," Joe called out, side-stepping down the slope. "The gully won't lead us out."

"It could lead back into the canyon," Jenny said. "An easier way back to the trail."

"It's hard to say what's between here and there," Joe said. "If we get stuck, we'll be awfully hard to find down there."

"I'm tired of this," Jenny said. "It's been three hours, my underwear's all up my butt, and I'm tired."

"Back up," I said. "Damn it."

We climbed back up, pulling on the trunks of the cottonwoods to keep from backsliding. I felt the panic wave in, each sweep climbing a little farther up the beach of my reason. I'd heard of bodies found naked in the desert, clothes folded into neat little piles beside them. I'd heard of people who died with their own flesh clenched in their teeth. Would that be me? Would we wander until I lost my senses and began to howl? I tried to focus on what I knew now: this hill, this ascent. I followed the backs of Jenny's knees. Veins spidered across the creases between her calf and thigh. Her socks were caked in mud, and I could hear her crying, softly. "This is all my fault," she said. Exertion prevented her from sobbing louder. "How did I get us into this mess?"

I was winded, too, so I didn't argue. But I knew it wasn't Jenny's fault we were lost. It was mine.

A hot night at the end of July, Katherine and I had gone to a party for a friend moving out of state. The sky above the mountains throbbed orange and black. South of Provo, a forest was burning. The branches of the oak in the backyard were adorned with hanging paper lanterns intricately lettered with Japanese characters and lit from the inside by small incandescent bulbs. An orange extension cord wrapped the trunk of the tree, snaking toward the kitchen door through a disordered assembly of chairs. By the back steps of the house stood a folding table crowded with bottles, its downhill legs not quite snapped tight. One of the bottles was Belvedere Vodka, which I liked because it was expensive and didn't often drink for the same reason. I scooped ice into a red plastic cup big enough for a beer and filled it halfway with vodka and a splash of 7UP. I drained it and poured a second, which I sipped more slowly, sitting in a lawn chair while I watched the oak list and creak in the wind.

The music was loud, coming from a boom box propped in the kitchen window. Contrails of smoke drifted across the sky. The wind smelled like an extinguished match. The stars fell through the oak leaves and landed on my shirt. I was awash in starlight, in golden haloes from the lanterns and smoke, and when I lifted my hand to touch this dazzling, star-spangled firmament, my hand dragged along in time. I closed my eyes, and when I reopened them, the firmament was still there, and I understood I wasn't hallucinating. I was drunk.

Katherine drifted across the yard, her sandals sloughing through the weeds. She stopped and turned her eyes to me. I stood and lunged toward her. "I'm hammered," I said. "You've got to get me out of here before I make an ass of myself."

"I've had a few myself," she said.

"Can you drive?"

"Probably," she said. "For a while at least."

Her jeep was parked on the street. I stepped up onto the rear tire, took hold of the roll bar, and swung into the backseat. Katherine climbed in, started the engine, and took a head-clearing breath before releasing the brake. A Salt Lake City native, she knew the roads where the police were least likely to park, the winding shortcuts along streets without lamps. I leaned my head against the spare tire bolted against the rear and watched the stars wheel in the sky. The moon rose and sank, the night passing before me. The jeep climbed a hill and swung around a corner. I could see only Katherine's hair whipping around the headrest.

We parked in front of my house, and Katherine held my arm as I jumped to the lawn. I fumbled my keys out of my pocket and tossed them to her. She dropped them on the grass and bent to collect them, and when she leaned up we were laughing. We made our way toward the door, and through it, and through the house to my bedroom. We fell down laughing on the bed. We kissed. My roommate was out and we kissed with impunity, the lights on and the blinds open. At first our kissing was playful, but all at once it turned serious, two gears higher, as though we'd come to the end of our little country road of affection and merged onto a new interstate. I felt her belly in my hands, her breasts, and before either of us thought to stop, our clothes were on the floor.

It happens a billion times a day, people coming together like this. How many other couples left the party and ended up this way? I was twenty-five, and I was the last of my kind. My friends from college were married. My few previous girlfriends were married. My non-evangelical friends had shucked off their innocence long ago. I was the only one left, and

I was in love. Every event in my life, every victory and disappointment, every yes and every no, felt like a prologue to this instant. Our clothes were entwined on the floor like dance step footprints showing us what to do. My heart hammered so hard it made me queasy. The swamp cooler clanked in the window down the hallway. I pressed my eyebrows against Katherine's. Her lashes made a faint wind against my cornea. I leaned back and saw her silver necklace pooled into the hollow of her throat, like a coiled rope. She bit her lip, and I saw she was afraid. I was afraid, too. We could turn back. We could say we drank too much. And though it may be true that the vodka loosened my inhibitions, I was not, at the moment I made the decision, drunk. I was responsible for everything. I could have stopped as I'd stopped so many times before. I looked at the hair sweeping across Katherine's forehead, the tiny crinkles where her nose met her cheeks, the hardly visible delta of blood vessels beneath the skin of her chin, and I saw the illuminated path of my future. I reached out and touched the life I'd been waiting years to begin.

Only afterward did I think of my old promises and inhabit the fears of what would happen now. I watched Katherine disentangle her clothes from mine in terror, certain that this one instance of coming together would become the spark of our estrangement. After all those years of hearing how God repays sin with misfortune, punishing men and nations alike, how could I think I was different?

I didn't say any of this to Katherine as I walked her out to the jeep. I didn't want her to leave, but I was afraid to have her spend the night. Anyone driving past my house would see her car parked on the street and know what had happened, my sin exposed. We held each other and kissed hesitantly. She climbed in and rolled down the window. The mountains were veiled behind a curtain of fog, and moisture beaded on my arms. I was shivering. I said I'd call her in the morning; maybe we could go for a drive. She touched my wrist with her warm fingers, and the only thing I wanted in the world was to not lose her. I leaned in to kiss her once more, but before my lips touched hers, I said maybe we should go on the hiking trip with the group from church. A weekend with other "strong Christians" would be good for us. Help us avoid future sins.

~~~

We'd been hiking for twelve hours, if we counted the miles before we got lost. A full turn of my watch. Katherine suggested we break for dinner. We kicked the stones out of the tamarisk and stomped the ground flat and sat down in a circle. We unzipped our packs and took inventory: ten ounces of water, as well as half a pouch of Jack Links Beef Jerky, a plastic jar filled with raisins and peanuts and M&M's, a Ziploc baggie of gummy bears. Not enough to drink, but more food than I expected, and miraculously dry despite being dipped in the river throughout the day. We passed the jerky around and each pulled out a chew. Jenny dumped the gummy bears into her hand, laid the baggie flat on the ground, and spread the bears on the plastic. She leaned over her crossed legs as she counted. "Thirty-eight bears," she said. "Nine apiece, with two left over for the men."

"We get extra?" Joe asked.

"You're bigger, you need more. We need to ration anyway. Three now, three in the morning, three for later tomorrow."

"Jenny, they're gummy bears," Katherine said. "They have, like, ten calories each."

"We still need to think about what we'll eat tomorrow."

I fished three M&M's from the jar and cradled them in my palm. I stared down at the three colored candies nesting against my lifelines, and wondered if the end of my story was already foretold. I knew nothing of astrology, gleaned no meaning from my sign or the signs of others, and lacked any ability to decipher the secrets inscribed in my skin. But I knew people died out here. It happened every year. Last autumn, two women went for a day hike in the mountains east of Salt Lake City, an early snowstorm struck, and they weren't found until spring. Just some tattered clothing and a few bear-licked bones.

Before I could gobble the M&M's, Jenny asked if we should pray. Joe shrugged, "Be my guest." Jenny and Katherine looked to me, perhaps because I was male but more likely because I was known to pray aloud during Bible study. I set the M&M's on my pack and closed my eyes. "Lord," I said, "thank you for this food. Help us have the strength to keep hiking. Help us find the road." It was a small prayer for a meager meal, but rather than say "amen," I kept talking. I asked for forgiveness, for our arrogance in thinking we could find our way without God's guidance, for not praying the moment we got lost. I prayed for all our unrepented sins, for all our lusts and hungers. Jesus lived for forty days without food; surely we could endure a night on three gummy bears and a strip of jerky. My prayer became a chant, words flowing over words like water over stone. I felt myself rising, looking down at the tops of our heads, the part in Katherine's hair, our packs in a circle. I no longer felt the ground, and I no longer felt hungry. I promised God if we made it out of here, I'd give up every fleshly desire, every bodily need. I'd cut ties with the world and all its trappings. I'd never touch Katherine again.

It was a promise that, even as I made it, I knew I could not keep. For a long time, I'd believed that the Christian life meant a life of choices not my own, that happiness meant a will bent toward God's plan, all individuality erased, all humankind funneled into a single, unified chorus chanting praise and glory. It was never a plan I found attractive, but I accepted it as part of the bargain. I'd tried for years to believe I needed no family other than a spiritual one, that I could be so filled with *agape* I didn't need *eros*, that I could go without touch, or late-night phone conversations, or romantic meals in out-of-the-way diners. For the last several weeks I'd tried to convince myself that what happened with Katherine was the result of a lapse in faith: I'd sought my will before God's and had fallen into sin. But I hadn't lapsed. I was fracturing. My convictions were changing shape, like an origami crane being unfolded and smoothed flat and refolded into a different animal. The world was too big to spend my life with my back to it.

As if sensing where my thoughts had gone, or maybe to prod me to shut up so we could eat, Katherine reached over and set her hand on my knee. Her palm was gritty, and her heat radiated up my thigh. I cupped my hand over hers. I squeezed until I felt her pulse in her fingers, and I recalled the moment that brought me here—the falling stars, the lighted oak tree, the hollow of Katherine's throat. I thought: God could leave me out here. He could lay me down to sleep beneath the juniper tree night after a hungry night, and still I would not let go.

God did not leave us wandering in the desert all night long. About a mile past where we'd stopped to eat, we found an unpaved service road that led to the highway where a man in a green minivan was kind enough to give us a lift back to Danny and Trudy and the other members of the fellowship. The twelve of us talked for a minute in the parking lot, but it was now past 8:00 PM, and we had a long drive back to Salt Lake City, so we divided among the cars and set out for home. Danny listened to heavy metal on his headphones so he'd stay awake while we drove. Katherine leaned her head on my shoulder and fell asleep. I stared at the highway through the car window, the mountains one with the starless night, and pondered the fact that God's wrath had not come. We'd made it out of the desert and were on our way back to civilization. Katherine's love was the sturdy rock I leaned against. The world was not radically changed by my actions. I, however, was.

Back in Salt Lake City, Katherine and I would sit on my couch and cry and finally admit that we could no longer go back to the church or the fellowship group. I was no longer an evangelical, and I'd known it for a while, though somehow this day of wandering in the desert would come to reside as the moment I at last understood it. After a dozen years, it was not easy to part with an old life. It wasn't simply a matter of enlightenment, of wising-up, but rather a deep, sorrowful resignation—reminiscent of the night my father and mother agreed to divorce. My father drove out to the house, but rather than come all the way inside, he stood and talked with my mother in the front entryway. My sister and I were in our bedrooms down the hall. My mother's and father's voices were measured and matter-of-fact, and when they were finished, my mother said, "Okay, I'll tell them." As though we wouldn't know unless she did. My father left without saying hello or good-bye to Devin and me. I remember looking through my window as he sat down inside his car. He paused for a long moment with his head bent toward the steering wheel, the dome light a yellow moon above the rearview mirror. He'd failed to keep the marriage together and now looked more disappointed than sad. I'd sit with the same posture, weighted with the same sense of failure, for weeks. Years later, I still feel the echo of that failure.

A few weeks later, Katherine and I followed a procession up a narrow, wooden staircase to a tiny chapel in the upper floor of an Episcopalian grammar school in downtown Salt Lake City. The plaque on the door said the chapel was built in 1910, and a daguerreotype photograph showed how a vaulted roof had been added to bridge the empty space between two freestanding buildings. The brick walls still bore the water stains from their years of outdoor exposure. Tiered choir pews lined both walls, a narrow aisle between. The sun backlit the stained glass clerestory windows. At the front of the line, the acolyte carried the cross with her nose pressed against it; a few paces behind her shuffled the priest who'd come to the hospital on the day Matt died. It was September 16, 2001, and after nearly a week of sitting on my couch in the dark, glued to the news, watching the firemen in their black coats and helmets ferry away from the smoldering wreckage the recovered bodies wrapped in American flags—I woke up on Sunday hungry for church, for music, for someone to say something, anything, and the priest who'd prayed over Matt's dead body was the only clergy member I could think of who wasn't evangelical.

Katherine and I found a seat near the back. The man who settled in beside me smelled faintly of cigarette smoke, a peppermint rolling around in his mouth. Children yawned and fussed on their parents' laps. Candles burned the air. I rose to sing, knelt to pray. At first these motions were perfunctory and mindless, but when I followed the line toward the altar for the Eucharist, I felt the shell around my heart begin to crack. The people kneeling at the rail were sobbing, sobbing, gusting breaths and heaving shoulders. Two-thousand miles from Ground Zero, this grief had been held in for days, and now, here, at last it had found a space in which to come. The small flames inside the votive cups were trembling, and the sunlight through the stained glass turned in a kaleidoscope on the floor and wall.

The priest placed the wafer in my hands and said, "The Body of Christ, the bread of heaven." I set it on my tongue, cracked it against the roof of my mouth. An old wind moved through me. It was a primitive sensation, a breath blown across the back of my neck—the voice I'd heard on a beach when I was fifteen, silent for so long I thought I might never hear it again. Kneeling at the altar, I touched the ninety years of prayer that had occurred in this room, Christian belief arcing backward for millennia more. For the first time, I felt I was stitched into the broad cloth of humanity, not unraveled from it. After so many years of hearing how the world was antithetical to God, how the world and all it contained should be rejected and abstained from, the idea that being a Christian located me within the tide of history—though obvious to many—came as a revelation. And a relief. My faith and the fevered vows I'd made in its name were gone forever. But not, I realized, my will to believe. That I heard God's voice, and not merely an echo of my own, was the one thing I knew. From that tiny truth—a hope smaller than a mustard seed—I might grow a new faith.

Rogue Waves

The priest kissed the Gospels before opening to The Beatitudes, the last words to be spoken before the marriage vows. "Blessed are the poor in spirit," she said, "for theirs is the kingdom of heaven." Katherine and I stood facing each other at the top of the stairs leading to the altar. The front of her dress was embroidered with a complicated opalescent pattern that, in the bent light through the stained glass, shimmered like fish scales. From our elevated position, a half turn of my head was all it took to see the expanse of the old Episcopalian church. Afternoon sunlight flooded the narthex through the open rear door and washed across the stone floor, the empty pews in the back. The right side of the church was filled with faces from my past: my uncles grayer and fatter than the last time I saw them, my grandmother in a wheelchair, my college teammates in gray suits and colored ties, light-years removed from their overgrown beards and waxy, chlorine-bleached hair. A few friends had not made it and I noticed their absence, and I imagined, briefly, Jeremy standing among the crew. Or possibly beside me, in a tuxedo, my rings in his front pocket.

"Blessed are the peacemakers, for they will be called sons of God," the priest said.

My stepfather and mother, father and stepmother stood together in the front pew. My mother and father stood side by side for the first time in fifteen years. They'd seen each other at my college graduation, and at my sister Devin's graduation a year ago, but they hadn't been shoulder to shoulder since my seventh grade band concert. An entirely different life. Yet the thought flickered by, like the picture of Jeremy a moment earlier, of what it might have been like had they stayed together. My stepmother wore a champagne colored suit, a big string of pearls around her neck. Her wrist looped through my father's elbow. She held her mouth closed in a pose of absolute neutrality, neither frown nor smile, an expression I'd learned over the years to recognize as evaluative, if not exactly critical. She was watching, gathering. I wondered what she thought about this church, where Katherine and I had attended for the last two years—a denomination my stepmother had once said did not follow Jesus—or about the priest, a stout woman with a trilling English accent, among the first class of women ordained to the Anglican priesthood. I wondered if my stepmother heard The Beatitudes the way I did, for I had picked them for our Gospel reading with her in mind. She'd communicated with Bible verses for as long as I'd known her, verses serving as epigraphs in birthday cards, scrawled across the backs of photographs, the last word in any argument. I hoped these verses would speak what I'd struggled and failed to say to her face. That she would hear in The Beatitudes both my rebuke and my plea.

"The Gospel of the Lord," the priest said.

I turned back to Katherine and the rest of the sanctuary, the people present and missing, left my mind. Katherine set her hands in mine. To Jesus' list of blessings I added a few of my own: Blessed are the dressmakers for fashioning such a thing of beauty; blessed are the florists and organists and candle lighters for filling this room with color and sound and light. Blessed am I, married.

Later, at the reception, my uncle Don pulled me by the elbow and backed me up against the door to the men's room. His cheeks and high forehead were bright pink, and I could smell the beer mingled among his Skin Bracer, a smell as old as time. "All this religious hoopla is fine," he said, "but if you really want to know the secret to a happy marriage, I'm here to tell it to you."

"Fire away," I said.

"Dependable income. A steady paycheck. Got that?"

"Got it," I said.

He turned and looked into the reception hall, toward my mother. My stepfather had lost his job, and the tension between him and my mother was palpable. "Get a job," he said.

"I have a job," I said. In fact, I had several. I taught my classes at the university, two each semester. I taught swimming and coached the masters team. In a few weeks, I'd start as a counselor at a summer camp for young children, herding them to archery and figure skating lessons and to field trips at the Kennecott Copper Mine—a job that would pay $8 an hour, $2 more than minimum wage. That was the problem: None of my jobs paid very much. "I just don't make a lot of money," I said.

"Income isn't dependable if it doesn't cover your monthly nut," he said. "Read Edgar Allan Poe on your own time." The bathroom door fell away behind me, and I stepped inside. When I came out, my uncle was spinning on the dance floor in my grandmother's wheelchair, a fresh beer in his hand.

His advice wasn't completely lost on me, for I'd been thinking about money a lot lately. Katherine had a full-time job at the children's hospital, as the clinic and outreach coordinator for the Spina Bifida Clinic, but she'd need a master's degree to get licensed as a social worker. She'd keep the job through the summer, but would have to quit when school started in the fall. For a while we hoped she could keep the job and go to school, but both were full-time commitments. She'd sit twenty hours a week in class, work twenty more in an unpaid field internship, study around that. Her boss told her if she wanted to stay, she needed to stay full-time. Katherine waffled, but I didn't. We were young, about to get married. I had three years to go on my PhD and then who knew where we'd end up. I promised we could make it, if we lived cheaply.

Three months later, Katherine came home early on her last day of work. It was a Friday afternoon, the end of August, and she was beat. She dropped to the couch, but it was too hot to lie there, so she was up again digging in the refrigerator for something to drink. She wasn't ready to talk yet. I watched her move through the kitchen, heat clumping her hair together at its ends, the back of her neck flushed red and hot. Even with the windows open and the swamp cooler on, the house smelled like her lavender and her hair spray, her blouses taken hot from the dryer and shaken in the air. I was still a little surprised she came home to me every day.

She sat down on the kitchen floor in the path of the window cooler and craned her neck to catch the breeze. The swamp cooler's bottom was rusted, the rust had worked up into the pump, and the air it blew across the linoleum smelled like rust. It also smelled like her shampoo. She pointed to the flimsy paper box on the counter. Inside was a half-devoured circle of chocolate cake covered in white icing, GO and KAT written in blue jelly. "Want some cake?" she asked. One of her officemates had baked it, and since she was still, technically, a newlywed, her coworkers hadn't yet grown tired of suggesting bedroom games involving the leftover cake.

Spina bifida was caused by a lack of folic acid prior to and following conception. "Sex and green vegetables make a better pair than cake," she said. "Forget frosting, healthy babies are made from broccoli and cabbage." We laughed. She was feeling better. She lay back on the linoleum and stretched her arms above her head, and I glimpsed in her a sign of that tingling sensation that the thing she was supposed to be doing, the career she'd sidled up to and backed off from for years, was about to begin.

Katherine stood up from the floor. "Let's go eat," she said.

The wind blowing through the jeep windows was as hot as a hairdryer, dry enough to make my nose bleed. The Great Salt Lake had been shrinking all summer. The wind smelled of the brine shrimp frying on the exposed flats and alkaline salt marshes. We ended up at a burger joint with neon tubes ringing the ceiling and a clock moving backward across an airbrushed picture of Elvis. We sat against the windows, next to the air-conditioning vent. I set my bare foot over the grates and felt the moisture between my toes evaporate. We ordered two burgers, fries, two large Cokes.

We turned over a paper placemat and used a crayon to scribble out a budget. My teaching stipend and swimming lessons would cover about half of our rent and half of our groceries. Coaching swimming bought pizza one night a week. On Monday, Katherine would begin nannying for one of the hospital's physicians, watching over his two-year-old and six-month-old twins, all girls. She'd been promised $12 an hour, twenty hours per week. If we each made a thousand a month, we'd be okay. Half of that would go to our rent and utilities, the rest toward food and gas and car insurance. There was also the phone, Katherine's textbooks, notebooks, an occasional odd-and-end. I recalled my uncle's advice from the wedding: "dependable income, a steady paycheck." I didn't want to cut it too close. Katherine made an appointment to see the gynecologist and the dentist one last time before her insurance ran out. She'd already canceled her cell phone. I made a list of other things that would have to go: movies, concerts, eating out. "Enjoy the burger," I said. "It may be our last for a while."

She shook her finger at me and arched her dark eyebrows. "Don't think you're the only one with fiscal discipline," she said. She kissed me, breathing ketchup and red onion into my mouth and ears. "Relax," she said. "There's no need to turn into Gandhi quite yet."

~~~

But soon, there was. The nanny gig wasn't the money we hoped for. Instead of a thousand a month, it came in under six hundred. Some months it was under four. The doctor's wife sometimes calculated the hours wrong or multiplied by eleven instead of twelve, and Katherine felt awkward handing the check back and asking her to rewrite it. The family flew for free (the doctor's wife had been a flight attendant before she quit to have babies), and their frequent travel left whole weeks without pay. I picked up extra swim lessons and coaching sessions and helped medical students with their personal statements for their residency applications. Katherine babysat for anyone who asked.

We could have made it easier on ourselves by borrowing more. Had we been medical students or law students or even business students, we could have borrowed without limit and felt assured of our ability to pay it off. But debt scared me. My mother and stepfather and a number of friends kept their credit cards afloat by paying only the monthly minimums; if we wandered down that road, we might never find our way back. Katherine's parents hadn't helped her with college, and though she'd worked full-time and finished in three years, she'd had to take out student loans. We'd taken out more loans to cover her master's tuition. I was determined not to borrow a dollar more than we had to.

Instead, we trimmed. We gave up going to bars. We gave up dessert. When my jeans ripped, Katherine sewed a patch over the hole. When my boxer shorts wore thin, Katherine wore them to sleep in. Over the winter break, I taught extra swimming lessons and Katherine nannied in the morning. In the afternoon, she tied a green apron around her waist and drove out to a kitchen store where she'd been hired on for the holidays. She was on her feet until after nine, answering questions for the customers maxing out their credit cards to buy expensive Christmas presents — bread machines and commercial blenders, glazed terra-cotta tea kettles unfit for boiling water, Japanese Ginsu knives sharp enough for surgery. Our Christmas presents for our family came from there, cheap trinkets made cheaper by her employee discount. For my mother, stepmother, mother-in-law, sister, and stepsister, we bought $9 aprons; for our fathers we bought stainless steel grilling spatulas, for my brother-in-law, a book of cocktail recipes. The job was going well. The owner liked her and she liked working there. He sent her home with a box of lemon-iced biscotti, by far the most extravagant treat we'd had in months. She planned to ask to stay on after the holidays, working on weekends and in the evenings when she wasn't in class or at practicum or nannying. She could fit in the hours on the weekends, and the extra cash would be helpful. We ate the biscotti with milk while we added up our day's wages. I slept soundly that night, the first time since the summer.

The week before Christmas, a stack of cookbooks, an apron, two tins of Christmas sprinkles, a box of Altoids, and a meat thermometer were found in the back of the store, stuffed behind the shopping sacks. Nothing was missing as far as the owner could tell, but there were a million tiny things in the store, and it wasn't possible to keep up with everything. But he knew Katherine had been working in the storeroom earlier in the day. He searched Katherine's bag before he called her into his office and found it empty, but he took the empty bag as a sign she intended to fill it with merchandise. "I had my lunch in there," Katherine explained. "I came here from my other job."

"Well, where's your lunch now?" he asked.

"I ate it."

"That's not good enough for me," he said.

"Do you have a security camera?" Katherine asked. "It would show you I didn't touch those things."

"I don't like to reveal my security measures," the owner said. He sat across the desk in his office, tapping his meaty fingers on his mouse pad. The floor manager had seen Katherine working in the back, but couldn't say she *didn't* see Katherine put the items there. "She could have," she said, standing with her arms crossed behind the owner's chair. "I don't know. I'm sorry." The owner asked Katherine what she did for her other job. She said she was a nanny and was working on her masters in social work. "Before that," he asked, "what did you do?"

"I was the clinic and outreach coordinator for the Spina Bifida Clinic."

"The what?" He snapped, the term "spina bifida" foreign to him. Katherine wanted to snap back, tell him her last job was a real job, a better job than this one, a job that paid enough for her to shop in this store without guilt for the money she spent. But she knew we needed the money, and she didn't want to get fired, so she explained spina bifida and the job she'd once performed at the hospital. "Well, I've never had a problem with my other employees," the owner said. "All signs point to you. Let's go ahead and call it a night. We'll mail you your check." On the way out he put his hand on her back, like a father, and patted her shoulder.

"Kleptomania is caused by a lack of impulse control," he said. "Counseling would help you make better decisions."

Katherine walked into the frozen night, away from the owner's condescending hand, got into the jeep, and drove away. At home, she collapsed on the couch and sobbed.

I used to think going broke resulted from catastrophe: a job shipped overseas, an addiction taking hold, a lump beneath the skin discovered one morning in the shower. An event that empties jewelry boxes and pawns away family heirlooms. I'd never thought it could happen more gradually—money not rushing out the door in a flood, but slowly leaking away. The week after Katherine lost the job at the kitchen store, I returned to the jeep after class and found a parking ticket on our windshield. The next week, the dentist's office called: Katherine's insurance had ended earlier than her health insurance, and her appointment last August wasn't covered. The office had let it sit for months, but they now demanded $200 by the end of the year or they'd put her account into collection. The spring before we were married, a car in front of us slammed on its brakes in traffic, going up a hill, and the jeep dented the other car's bumper. Not a big dent, but dented nonetheless. The owner of the car left Utah for a few months and seemed to forget about the whole thing, but now she was back and wanted her bumper fixed by New Year's. We couldn't afford the insurance premiums to go up, so we paid out of our savings. I looked at what we had left to make it until January and tried not to panic.

But it was Christmas and we'd made it this far. Katherine was at the top of her class, perfect her first term. The doctor and his wife gave us a gift certificate to an Italian restaurant in the back of a bookstore, a cozy little place with only ten tables and windows looking onto a courtyard filled with twinkling blue lights. I wore a jacket and tie and Katherine wore her cashmere sweater. We ordered shrimp ravioli and pumpkin risotto, skirt steak over linguini, two glasses of red wine. For two hours we touched noses across the tiny table and talked about next Christmas and the Christmas after that and about my idea to run a marathon in the summer and how Katherine missed seeing the kids at the hospital and we were happy. There was a snowstorm blowing in, and we agreed we had it good. We'd eaten, we were someplace warm on a cold night. Many people, Katherine said, didn't have that much. Many people had it worse.

A single mother and her son rented the basement of our house. Emmeline was two hundred pounds overweight, addicted to painkillers and sleeping pills. She collected disability and watched *Little House on the Prairie* most of the day. A former Mormon, she'd been born again as a fundamentalist during rehab, and her dark basement apartment was filled with porcelain figurines of Jesus and posters of Calvin from the *Calvin and Hobbes* cartoon kneeling before a cross. Her son, Truman, was the fruit of her former addiction to cocaine and heroin, a skinny, buck-toothed kid way too small for his age. He was fourteen but looked no older than nine or ten. His attention deficit/hyperactivity disorder was so severe his legs and hands twitched when he talked. His daily medications could have sedated every kid in his class. He hated the drugs and refused to take them, which made him violent and short-tempered. I watched him destroy a juniper bush with a pocketknife. He broke into the neighbor's house and stole a piggy bank. He came into our kitchen while I was mowing the back lawn and stole a box of cereal and a can of cake frosting. In the early hours of the morning, we'd hear him banging on the walls with a two-by-four he'd whittled into a sword. Through the heating vents, we heard Emmeline call him a little fucker, a dickhead, a shit. We shouted through the floor for both of them to pipe down but it was no use. Truman kept banging away, and Emmeline kept shouting.

Before she bought her van, Emmeline used to come to our door every day to ask for a ride somewhere—to the hospital, Wal-Mart, McDonald's. Her cheeks were fleshy, but her skin was clear and her eyes were marble blue. "Are you a Christian?" she asked me once.

Hesitantly, I said I was.

"Born again?" she asked. She reached for my hand. "Do you know Jesus?"

"We go back a ways," I said, sliding my hand inside my pocket.

"Then you're my brother in Christ," she said. "God tells us to help one another. My son needs a father figure. He's too much for me to handle on my own."

At the end of the Gospel of John, Jesus tells Peter, the first pope, to "feed my sheep." Tending to the needy wasn't something a church ought to do, one good among others; it was the point of existing in the first place. Our own Episcopal church in downtown Salt Lake City had a food pantry, an emergency daycare, an interfaith hospitality network for resettling homeless families. The downstairs neighbors had bounced from one state-subsidized apartment to another, and the boy changed schools every year. They were the outcasts, the modern-day lepers forced to live outside the city gates. I wondered what was wrong with me that I'd feed Christ's sheep by bureaucratic means but not in person, one neighbor to another.

So one day I'd asked the members of my swimming team each to donate $5 to buy Truman a summer pool pass. I raised the money in a single day. Truman and I rode our bikes to the pool together, and I stood with him while he waited for his ID badge to slide through the laminating machine. I walked him outside to the pool. Dozens of kids his age splashed in the turquoise water. "Maybe you'll make some friends here," I said. We stopped at the Rite-Aid on the way home to buy a lock so he could park his bike in the racks at the pool. My gift to him, I said. But in the drugstore, Truman begged for candy and Pokémon cards, and when I said no, he tried to shove them down his pockets. He never returned to the pool, and for weeks afterward, Emmeline knocked on our door to ask for money. "You bought my boy that pool pass," she said. "There are things I need, too."

It was the parable turned bitter: Rather than thank the man who saved him, the beaten traveler demands the Good Samaritan's donkey, a new set of clothes, another two denarii. The priest and the Levite, passing by the man as he lay dying, seemed to have made the smarter choice. I watched Emmeline ferry home sacks from McDonald's and Taco Bell and unmarked brown paper sacks with grease stains along the bottom, and then ring our doorbell to complain that her disability checks didn't provide enough money for food. A strange smell, like a bowl of fruit gone bad, seeped through our floor. I lifted the outdoor trash can lid and found a discarded frying pan swarming with maggots feeding on a white substance I couldn't identify. Truman's hands were always sticky, Emmeline's shirts always stained, and as our savings dried up, they went from pitiful to revolting to menacing. I wanted to be merciful, but I couldn't. Mercy required a security we didn't have, money we couldn't spare. I said to Emmeline, "You could try the food pantry."

"It's all canned goods there," she said. "I don't have a can opener. And I hate tuna."

"Better than going hungry," I said. I gave her a Diet Coke, hoping she'd take it and leave me alone. She handed it back. "I don't like Diet," she said. "Tastes like plastic."

All charitable impulses gone, I called the landlady and complained. When the pounding didn't stop, I called the police. The cops wrote Emmeline a ticket for a noise violation. The next morning, she pumped my doorbell until I answered. Truman was at her hip. She asked if they could come inside to talk. I refused. "I'll forgive you," she said. "But one day you'll stand before God."

"Okay by me," I said.

Katherine and I came home from our Christmas dinner and found Emmeline's van in the center of the front lawn. The engine was running and she was in the front seat. The dome light was on because the dash light was out. The steering wheel creased the center of Emmeline's stomach. The headlights illuminated the path she'd cut across the snow while trying to back out, our kitchen windows splattered with ice and mud. She tried to rev up and slam her way out, but spinning the tires only bogged her down farther. She asked for my help. The snow was falling in silver-dollar flakes and the air smelled briny, like the Great Salt Lake, a sign of a big storm. If Emmeline didn't get out now, the van would have to be towed, and who knew when that would happen. I took off my jacket and tie and pushed her van out of the yard, yelling that the next time it snowed, she damn well better park on the street.

Katherine went inside and threw up. I found her lying on the bathroom floor with her skirt hiked above her knees. Frozen air slithered in from the bathroom window, opened one slim inch.

Snow fell for the rest of the week, through Christmas Eve and Christmas morning and for three days after. The sidewalk disappeared, then the street, then the flowerbeds. Katherine weathered the storm on the couch, intermittently nauseous, her elbow tented over her eyes. She felt better on Saturday and we made plans to snowshoe, but on Sunday afternoon, Katherine crawled to the sofa and lay shivering beneath a blanket. "You go," she said. "Enjoy the snow. I need to rest awhile." She waved me out the door with a limp wrist.

I drove up the canyon and parked at the entrance of a golf course, its cart paths and fairways doubling during the winter as a cross-country skiing circuit. I crossed the plain of the sixteenth hole until I reached the lower foothill of the mountain, then shoed up through the leafless aspens and still-dark firs, a forty-minute climb to the top. The Salt Lake Valley spread out below: its orderly, gridlike streets dotted by amber lamps, the stoplights changing from green to yellow to red. In the other direction, the white-capped sea of peaks, the Wasatch and Unitas, stretched all the way to Wyoming. Everything was white, the sky, the ground, the road, the jeep parked beside the highway far below. Christmas lights were turning on, colored skeletons of rooftops and trees and candy canes. I thought of the collage of Christmas cards taped to our kitchen cupboard and fastened with magnets to the refrigerator, photographs of old friends, some of them now with spouses and children. Their glad tidings seemed another profit of marriage, an echo of the handshakes and "welcome to the families" extended my way as Katherine and I floated from table to table. I wondered then what Jeremy's card might have looked like. I pictured him someplace warm, palm trees in the background, in shorts and a Hawaiian shirt and his bare feet in the sand. The image rode in on the stinging wind, so sharply I was sure I'd seen it before: the braided ivy circling the border, *Happy Holidays* in a loopy cursive beneath the glossy photograph, the rectangle of transparent tape holding the card against the cupboard door.

I was alone, the snow was near my waist, and the city lights spread out like a gigantic circuit board. I let the idea of him take shape, and for the first time, the thought of him didn't plunge into the hive of buzzing memories about the murders. Instead the picture was of his life had he lived: a brick house with a wide lawn, lost among the Houston sprawl, a job with an engineering firm that let him wear polo shirts to work, a cement patio out back with an inflatable pool for his children, a dog slobbering at the sliding glass door. Maybe all of these projections were overblown, and we wouldn't have stayed friends after high school. Maybe I would have succeeded in moving to California my sophomore year and that would have been that. On the other hand, maybe we would have roomed together at the University of Texas, like we'd once talked about, and a different college might have led to a different graduate school, or to no graduate school at all. I likely wouldn't have been here, on this hilltop, had he not died; I never would have met Katherine. I thought of Katherine watching television wrapped in a blanket, her socked feet pinning the blanket's hem to the arm of the couch, heat from the furnace blowing across the floor and melting the snowflakes that fall through the chimney into the fireplace, and I felt I owed Jeremy—owed his death—my life. I felt guilty at first for thinking this way, but I stopped myself: The greater betrayal was to not think about him, to pretend that none of it mattered anymore, that his death hadn't made much of a difference. The better response was gratitude.

Katherine was gone when I got home. Snow was falling again, and I worried where she was, sick, with no car. I made a cup of tea to warm up. Maybe she'd trudged to the store for medicine, I thought, but after an hour she still wasn't home. I showered, brewed another cup, and sat by the window. I regretted canceling her cell phone. I called her parents' house, but no one answered. Finally her mother's car pulled up. Katherine kicked through the snow on her way up the walk. "I felt better," she said, hanging her coat on the hook. "So my mom came, and we went for coffee."

She carried her purse into the bathroom. I heard the door shut, the toilet flush. For a long time I heard nothing. Katherine had been bulimic as a teenager—a secret she'd never confessed to her parents and still rarely spoke of—but she could still make herself vomit in total silence. For the four years we'd been together, including the week of our honeymoon, I'd watched the movements of her fork and mouth with a careful worry, reading her body for signs of an old woe. I stood at the door. I knocked. "You okay in there?"

"Give me a minute," she said.

I leaned against the wall. When the door opened, her face was as white as the windowsill, and her eyes were round and dark. I tried to see past her to the toilet, but she blocked me by extending her arm. Between her body and mine was a pregnancy test, stained with two pink lines.

We looked at one another, confused. She was on the pill. I asked if she'd missed one. She said she didn't think so. I lifted the test box from the sink. It wasn't a name brand. "In this case," I said, "we need to spend the money." We pulled on our boots and gaiters, bundled up in our ski parkas, and hiked back to the pharmacy. I knocked on the metal grating rolled down over the pharmacy counter. I asked the pharmacist to come out. I told him we'd had a positive pregnancy test but doubted the results and wanted to find a more accurate brand. He told Katherine to stop taking the pill immediately. The hormones weren't good for the fetus. "That's not what I meant," I said. "I think we had a false positive."

The pharmacist's silver hair was combed back over his head in straight, glistening rows. He looked out of place in a Rite-Aid. He belonged in an old-fashioned Woolworth's, calling his customers by name, giving candy to their children, jerking the phosphate levers and scooping ice cream between prescriptions. It was nine o'clock at night, the thirtieth of December, and I was on the verge of something I couldn't quite measure. Nostalgia is the balm of fear. We were the only three in the store, Christmas music played soft and low over the speakers in the ceiling, and all the red-and-green candy was marked down in big bins at the front. The pharmacist slapped a big hand over my shoulder and chuckled. "False positive? Not a chance."

Without insurance, we couldn't afford prenatal care, let alone a stay in the hospital. I suggested that we do a home birth and that Katherine's mother, a pediatric nurse, could deliver the baby—a proposal Katherine shot down within seconds. Thankfully, both she and the baby qualified for Medicaid. When I looked up the maximum allowable income for a family of three, I saw a number three times greater than what we earned. The caseworker sent us across town to apply for a nutrition program for women, infants, and children. We went to the clinic and waited for our name to be called in a large room filled with chairs. A mentally disabled woman in a painter's cap blinked and argued with the television screen. Three women stood outside smoking, their backs to the window, their babies crawling across the dirty floor in black-kneed pajamas, their filthy hands in and out of their mouths, their faculties of speech and mobility delayed by poverty and hunger. Truman, the boy in our own basement, had once been an infant in this clinic and had probably crawled over this same floor. The children here today were likely to inherit his problems, his attention deficits and night terrors; they'd grow up stunted, banging on walls and breaking into houses. Katherine wanted to become a social worker so that she could protect children like these, though, for the moment, we weren't protecting anybody. We were the sheep asking a state agency for charity.

We were led into a room where a woman measured Katherine's weight and height, pricked her finger, touched the sides of her belly. A second woman led us into a second room where she gave us pamphlets on healthy eating during pregnancy and a recipe book for cooking beans. She circled the pictures of the vegetables, told Katherine to eat all she could. Vegetables would prevent diseases like spina bifida. "Ever heard of that?" she asked.

Katherine nodded. She worked to hold her eyes straight, away from mine. The woman pressed a button on her keyboard and out of her printer spit a sheet of food vouchers. "These will buy milk and cheese, beans and juice," the woman said.

"No vegetables?" Katherine asked.

"Only beans," the woman said. "Green vegetables are too costly for the program to cover. So is peanut butter."

A part of me felt ashamed leaving the clinic with the vouchers, but more of me felt guilty. I felt like I'd duped the state government into thinking we were hungry. Hadn't I always taken my food for granted? But as we walked around the grocery store, it began to dawn on me how hungry we really were. We had to decide which foods we needed the most, which we could afford, which we could do without. Katherine put Wheat Thins back on the shelf in order to buy bread and lunchmeat. Since Thanksgiving, we'd denied ourselves afternoon snacks for the sake of the main meals. We were hungry in other ways, too. We were hungry for stability. As soon as one month was settled, we worried about the next. We were hungry for movies and a pizza, a six-pack of beer, clothes to cover Katherine's rapidly expanding stomach.

Katherine handed me a coupon for a free package of pasta and a tube of ground beef. "See if you can find these," she said. I looked down at the pictures of the food the store was giving away and felt like I'd won the lottery. I wandered the aisles, collected the pasta, the beef, and turned down the baby aisle. For the last few months I'd walked this aisle with a strange sense of belonging, two whole shelves of enigmatic things about to fill my house. Now I felt staggered by the costs. I'd always expected cribs and car seats and strollers and glider chairs to be expensive. Those price tags didn't surprise me. It was the diapers that got me, how quickly infants went through them, how few came in a pack. I figured diapers would run $12 a week, $20 if we bought the fancy brands. Then there were wipes and rash creams, powders, special body washes, and no-tears shampoos, lotions, bottles, nipples, reduced-dosage cold medicines. I stepped back from the diapers, no-name pasta in one-hand, no-name ground beef in the other, and I felt the full weight and grief of the hunger I'd been trying not to admit. In the diapers I saw not the miracle of childbearing, but an extravagance I could not afford.

Emmeline and Truman finally moved out in March, a trail of wreckage in their wake. Deep ruts gouged the lawn from the van's tires, and granules of broken glass glittered across the driveway and back porch from the nights Truman pounded on the storm doors with a broom handle, then with his fists, then with his forehead. Scraps of paper and slivers of wood from their punished furniture flew out of the back of the pickup truck that hauled away the last of the loads. The truck turned out of sight, and Katherine and I went down to the basement. Food was smeared against the walls and stamped into the carpet. Soda had hardened in the circle where it had spilled. In the corner by the heater, milk had turned solid; a shovel could scoop it up. Fast-food wrappers and salsa and ketchup packets oozed in a pile behind the washer and the dryer. On the shelf above the washer was a stack of little fundamentalist comic books—the same size and shape as the tracts I had used to share my faith in Australia— about how pretty much *everyone* is destined for the pit of burning flames. "This must be where they got their decorating ideas from," Katherine said. The walls and shelves of the refrigerator, next to the washer, were an organic, lake-bottom green. The ceilings and the walls were pocked with holes from a year's worth of rages. Truman's bedroom, in the rear corner of the house, smelled so overwhelmingly like urine that Katherine ran out of the basement with her hands clasped over her mouth.

The landlady announced she was going to unload the house. She wanted us to sign an agreement to move out if the house sold to someone who didn't want to rent it. Then she decided to fix up the basement and try leasing it one more time. The carpet came up and so did the linoleum. The fridge, the ceiling, the drywall, the faucets, the baseboards were all carted away. Professional cleaners in white masks scrubbed the basement with undiluted pine cleanser, a smell so pungent we opened all the windows in the house to let the odor out. We piled blankets on the bed and slept with our bodies touching.

For the next month, saws and drills rattled the dishes in the cabinet and the glass top of the coffee table. Sawdust piled around the base of the heater vents. When the basement was finished, everything was new—new linoleum, recessed canister lighting, plush carpet from wall to wall. The place was the nicest I'd ever seen it. "It looks good," I told the landlady the night Katherine and I went downstairs to have a look. "The workmen did a nice job."

The landlady was in her seventies, a big white head of hair atop a big chest and skinny legs, like a teakettle releasing a cloud of steam. She asked us about the baby, patted Katherine's tummy, told us she loved us. She apologized for renting the place to bad tenants and promised not to do it again. "Oh yeah," she said, sliding it in, "the utilities went up again, so we're going to need to raise your rates." We paid our utilities with our rent, all in one check. It was a good deal when I first moved into the house with a roommate. When Katherine and I re-signed the lease before we were married, the utilities went up $50. When I pointed this out, the landlady said, "I know, son, but they went up again. You can call the utility companies if you don't believe me." The rates had gone up in January and now it was March, and she wanted us to pay $25 more per month, retroactively from the first of the year.

I'd seen this coming, and the week before, I'd asked the neighbors on our street how much they paid for their utilities. The family next door occupied the whole house; they had two kids and ran a business out of the basement. They said their total bill was slightly over a hundred a month. They kept the house warm enough that even in winter they walked around in shorts. I cranked down our thermostat each morning when we left and each night when we went to sleep. I told the landlady the basement was occupied all day and I often saw the doors left open during the winter. The landlady pressed her palm against her stomach and told us she thought we were getting "a darn good deal" on our house. "This is the *most exclusive* neighborhood in the city," she said, as though this fact alone would conclude the discussion. The Salt Lake Country Club was a few blocks south and there were some expensive homes over there, but our street was postwar cookie-cutter, small houses all built together in 1949. The couple on the other side of our house had taught high school for fifty years. The man across the street was an unemployed alcoholic.

Desperation bends logic, and it bent mine. I begrudged the landlady her money, how she made it and how she spent it. Because we were locked into our rent, I figured she wanted to use the utilities to recuperate what she spent on fixing up the basement. With the extra money from us, and a steeper rent for the basement apartment, she could make back the costs in eighteen months. She said she was on a fixed income, but she'd owned the house outright for more than thirty years, so her fixed income included our rent, the downstairs rent, her husband's pension, and their Social Security. They'd recently bought property in St. George, Utah, and Star Valley, Wyoming, as well as a new motor home to shuttle between the two. Twenty-five dollars a month was the last of our margin. I felt she owed us something for sticking it out while Emmeline and Truman tore the place to shreds. "We've been good tenants," I said.

"For the most part. You should have asked me before you painted the living room."

"It would have cost several hundred dollars to have a professional paint it," I said.

"Which we'll have to do when you move out," she said. "The colors you picked aren't neutral enough."

Maybe I was affected by the basement, Emmeline's former lair, the underworld beneath my own living room, but Emmeline's shameless ploys for sympathy now seemed like my only option. I set my hand on Katherine's belly. "We're on Medicaid," I said. Katherine stared at me, and her eyes told me not to say another word, but it was too late. "We buy our groceries with food stamps."

"Call the ward," the landlady said. "The Relief Society will bring you dinner any night you want."

That night, as I lay in bed, I recalled the time that my father and I saw a family trying to shower at a gas station. A boy my age and a girl my sister's age stood in their bathing suits under the water hose used for refilling car radiators. Their mother was bent over beside them, massaging shampoo through her hair. Their Oldsmobile station wagon was full of clothes and cardboard boxes. Grimy pillows pressed against the windows in the backseat. I was eleven, and the Houston economy was in a tailspin. My father was out of work then, and I could see the fear in his face as he watched that family, stripped of the dignity of bathing in private. I'd seen plenty of homeless people around downtown, half-lucid old men with unkempt beards and missing teeth waddling between doorways, but this was the first homeless family I'd ever seen. I knew no one who worked harder than my father, yet the company he worked for had gone bankrupt. By the time he'd found another job, he'd moved three states away.

Watching my parents' financial discord avalanche into acrimony then into betrayal and finally into divorce, I learned the destructive power of money, the way the numbers in a checkbook register could incite panic and fury. I'd been married for less than a year, and already I could feel our monetary worries widening the fissures between Katherine and me. We argued over whether we ought to buy generic or name brand laundry detergent, over the necessity of a book for school, over the number of eggs in an omelet. Our lives had become governed by a thousand small economies. I pilfered the coupon inserts from our neighbors' recycling bins rather than pay for the Sunday paper. I pocketed great handfuls of sugar packets from the coffee carts at the university and put them in a jar in the kitchen. Anything that could go back to the store, went. I returned six packs of soda. I returned my instructor copies to the large bookstore, and on Friday nights, Katherine and I wandered around the shelves, read magazines and *What to Expect When You're Expecting*, and used our store credit for dessert at the café.

I slept fitfully—a half-sleep in which my worries about bills morphed into shallow dreams about the cashier at the supermarket cutting up my debit card due to insufficient funds. I woke up startled and worried. I used the toilet, paced the house, and eventually settled into a chair at the kitchen table. The street was silent. Downy fog settled over the crusted brown grass.

I turned on the light and began reading the Psalms. Reading the Psalms, back when I was an evangelical, used to calm me down, but now it only heightened my anxiety. As I worked my way through the verses, I started to feel a certain kinship with David, the Psalmist, and not just because we shared a name. Stung by false accusations, burdened by fatherhood, he was exiled to the desert. The principalities where he sought refuge had names the Mormon settlers would later borrow for their own settlements. The longer I read, the more I began to wonder if everything that had happened in the last few months was my fault. I'd brought our misfortunes upon us by going to a church that didn't read the Bible literally and allowed women to teach men, by registering to vote as a Democrat. It was the logic I'd learned long ago, the world as I knew it: Obedience to God yields blessings overflowing; rebellion leads to torment and punishment.

For a long time I sat at the table, feeling every tremor of regret that had conspired to bring us to this place—flat broke, a baby we hadn't planned on, a landlady threatening to evict us. The night was stubbornly long. Eventually faint gray light began to separate the silhouette of the mountains from the frosted sky. The cold air seeping through the swamp cooler rustled the photographs on the refrigerator, the Christmas cards we'd never taken down. I stared up at their cheerful faces, all the friends who'd witnessed our wedding ceremony. I wanted to call someone, but it wasn't yet five AM, an hour earlier in California. Durden and Rich, my groomsmen, were both sound asleep and likely wouldn't answer the phone anyway; I hadn't talked to Jake or Tommy Baker in years. My father woke up at five each morning, and often earlier, so there was a good chance he was awake. I thought of him lying on the couch in his underwear, watching CNBC in the dark with the quilt draped across his chest. I went to the phone and lifted it from the cradle and stared at the glowing numbers in my hand. It was his voice I most wanted to hear. But he was the one person I couldn't call.

The Christmas before we got engaged, Katherine and I had flown to California to spend the holiday with my father and stepmother. They knew I intended to propose, and they knew we'd been attending an Episcopalian church, a place so synonymous with liberalism my stepmother couldn't fathom why we'd go there. "How can you meet Christ in a church like that?" she kept asking me. My stepsister Stacie drove up from San Diego with her four-year-old daughter and year-old son. September 11 was still raw, Stacie's husband was on an aircraft carrier in the Persian Gulf, and the talk around the table was heightened by the prelude to the apocalypse we'd witnessed three months earlier. "Jerry Falwell shouldn't have apologized for what he said about 9/11," my stepmother said. "The secularists led God to lift the veil of protection. Madalyn Murray O'Hair got prayer taken out of school. Look what happened to her."

"I didn't think God murdered," I said, though I recalled past debates about the Tribulation, when three quarters of the Earth's population was projected to die directly from God's hand. Four and a half billion people, if it happened today.

"God doesn't," she said. "But when wickedness and sin go unchecked, sometimes vengeance is necessary."

Family arguments are like rogue waves: They begin with tiny shifts in the continental plates, imperceptible on the surface, and then rise out of nowhere, unpredictable, impossible to surf. Innocent comments build upon assertions that build upon sarcastic asides, building and building, into a towering wall of recrimination and grudges. The argument on New Year's Day began this way. There was orange juice on the table, and bacon, and halved grapefruits sprinkled with sugar. It was sunny outside. By the time I caught on, the wave was above my head and I couldn't stop it. My stepmother had watched me over the past week decline an invitation to church, to *her* church, and had seen the novels and *The New Yorker* magazines on the table beside my bed. She'd grumbled whenever I whispered into Katherine's ear and feared we were whispering about her. She feared the faith she'd worked to instill in me had changed, maybe even had been abandoned, and she was convinced Katherine was to blame. She decided to test her. "Does your faith inform your job?" my stepmother asked.

"Of course," Katherine said.

"Do you ever share Christ at the hospital?" she asked.

"Well, I can't do that," Katherine said. "The hospital could get sued."

My stepmother frowned. "I have a friend who's a physician. He shares his faith with his patients all the time. People have prayed with him minutes before passing away."

"It's not really appropriate," Katherine said.

"What about domestic partnerships?" Stacie chimed in. She was standing in the doorway to the dining room, my nephew on her hip. With her free hand, she made air quotes with her index and middle fingers. "Does your hospital treat people in those relationships?"

"Of course," Katherine said. "We treat everyone. It's the law."

"That really burns me up," Stacie said. "Why should I have to pay *my* tax dollars for something I find repugnant?"

"Your husband's in the Navy," I snapped. I was growing impatient. "Your whole life is paid for with tax dollars. You bought a car with tax dollars. What if people find *that* repugnant?"

"I can't believe you'd say that," Stacie said. "Homosexuality is a sin."

I'd had enough of the inquisition. These debates had always seemed to me a kind of shibboleth, a way of separating the real Christians from the fakers. Real followers of Christ knew God hated homosexuality and Planned Parenthood and stem cell research and the separation of church and state, and anyone who thought otherwise was deceived by Satan. I thought of the gay families who attended our church, the men and women who couldn't hold hands in public, who, even in a church that welcomed them, were careful not to sit too close. I'd put off telling my father and stepmother I was no longer an evangelical for fear of the argument that would surely ensue, the argument I was now embroiled in. But I couldn't believe in something and allow my silence to imply agreement with its opposite. "Enough," I said to Stacie. "I don't believe the same things as you. Not anymore." I turned to face my stepmother. "I don't think homosexuality's a sin," I said. "I haven't thought so for a long time."

My stepmother's eyes grew wide. She set her napkin on the table. Nothing I said, from that moment forward, mattered. We were lost to each other.

My niece ran around the table. She pressed three fingers against my nose. "Three Gods in one," she said. "That's the answer."

"It's a good answer," I said.

After three hours, our juice glasses and coffee mugs emptied, refilled, and emptied again, Katherine headed to the bathroom behind the kitchen. "That was rough," she said.

"Let's talk about it later," I told her.

I came around the corner from the kitchen. Stacie and my stepmother were whispering with their arms crossed. Lines had been drawn. My father was outside watering the plants. He came back in and told us to get our shoes, we were walking to the beach. He hoped changing locations would end the standoff. I didn't want to go, but this time I didn't object. Or speak.

The conflict went underground until May when Katherine and I met my father and stepmother in New York so we could drive together to Philadelphia for Devin's college graduation. I'd proposed to Katherine the day before, in Central Park, and when we met them at Penn Station, I sprang the news. Katherine held out her hand to display her ring, the tiny diamond in the center. My stepmother hugged us both, but something wasn't quite right. At breakfast the next morning, my stepmother admitted she was nervous about seeing my mother. All morning she was short-tempered, unsettled by the rain in New York and, as we moved south, the gray pall over the Philadelphia skyline and its narrow, unnavigable streets. She said almost nothing in the car. From the backseat, I looked over Katherine's shoulder while she turned the pages of a wedding magazine.

Toward the end of the baccalaureate ceremony, a student read a blessing from the Qur'an. My stepmother sat forward in her chair, incredulous, then stood up and marched out of the auditorium. I found her in the quad afterward, watching the students and their families descend the auditorium's stairs. She stood with her arms crossed. I wanted her to tell me she'd left because she had an upset stomach, not because an innocuous, minute-long reading from the Qur'an had offended her. I wanted her to tell me she was sorry for her bad mood, for not greeting the news of my engagement with more enthusiasm. I wanted her to tell me that after some fresh air she was feeling better. I'd been engaged for less than twenty-four hours, and I wanted everyone to be happy. "Everything okay?" I asked my stepmother. "Did you enjoy the service?"

"Definitely not," she said. She kept her arms folded.

"I thought it was nice," Katherine said. My stepmother glowered at Katherine, then turned her back. She didn't speak to either one of us again until we said good-bye at Penn Station, two days later.

In the airport and on the plane back to Utah, Katherine and I replayed the exchange. I couldn't figure out what, besides not sharing my stepmother's disdain for the Qur'an, we might have said to make her so angry. I said we should apologize anyway. If we said we were sorry, I told Katherine, I was sure my stepmother would tell us what went wrong and apologize for her share in it. We'd share the blame and the forgiveness and could get back to normal. Katherine and I sat on my bed and called my stepmother. Katherine talked on the bedroom phone, and I was on the cordless. If something we said upset her, we said, we were sorry. "I value your opinions," Katherine said. "Even if we don't always agree."

"We always wanted David to find the right woman to marry," my stepmother replied. Her voice was soft, almost conciliatory. "You just weren't who we had in mind."

Katherine set the receiver on the bed. She lay her head on the pillow, but then slid to the floor and went into the bathroom. Something jarred loose inside me. "I think you need to explain that," I demanded.

"She's led you away from your faith. All the things you've believed since you were a little boy," my stepmother said, misremembering when my faith had begun, and why. As if the horrors that had made faith necessary—Jeremy lying in his doorway, the bloody pile of carpets behind his garage—had been forgotten. As though at twenty-seven, I remained so manipulable and lacking in independent thought that I couldn't tell the difference between truth and want. Yet it was the way she said *"we"* that most inflamed my rage, the insinuation that she spoke not only for herself but also for my father, and that his silence at the breakfast table on New Year's morning and his silence in the car between Philadelphia and New York and now his silence in the background was his tacit assent. That he felt the same way as she. I couldn't bear it. I struck the mattress with my fist, stood up from the bed.

My stepmother handed the phone to my father. I swallowed my urge to scream and said to him, "If you can't accept Katherine, I'll never come there again. Ever. You won't see me anymore." Telling him that broke something inside me.

"I respect that," my father said.

Katherine and I drove back to California at the end of the summer, twelve hours across the desert in the jeep, without air-conditioning, in the hope of making amends. I'd spoken to my father only sporadically during the past months. My stepmother I'd talked to only twice, and both conversations had ended in a rehashing of the argument begun on New Year's. Both times I'd hung up the phone angrier than before. Katherine and I brought my stepmother sea lavender in a small terra-cotta pot, a peace offering. We sat in the living room. Positions were clarified. I told them I hoped they'd come to the wedding. "We wouldn't miss it," my father said.

My father's mustache was nearly white, my stepmother's hair an electric blond. I remembered her crying the morning I left California for Utah, my bed and desk and boxes of books packed into a U-Haul with a lot of room to spare. My father and I had moved away from each other before; he shook my hand and told me to call him when I got there. My stepmother, though, wept and hugged me hard. She stopped short of asking me not to go. It was a more tearful parting than when I said good-bye to my mother the day I moved away from Texas. My mother could rely on our nominal endurance; she'd remain my mother wherever I went. My bond with my stepmother, however, was not as ironclad. Our most intimate years had been my most zealous; the more my faith resembled hers, the more attitudes and assumptions we shared, the more we had in common. So long as I'd needed her spiritual direction, she'd been more than my father's wife; she was my own proxy mother. For years I'd called her "Mommy," and she'd often told me that I couldn't have felt any more like her own son. But what would happen if I no longer needed her guidance? If my faith no longer resembled hers? The morning she stood crying in the driveway as I was about to drive away, she seemed to know I was beginning the process by which she'd return to being my father's wife, a step removed from motherhood, a step from necessary. Now I was getting married and had declared my break with evangelicalism. She was losing me for good.

I see it this way now, but I didn't then. That day in their living room, my defensiveness, coupled with my stepmother's unwillingness to apologize, obscured my capacity for sympathy. I thought I was being rejected, not the one doing the rejecting. I felt my old dream of family—of returning to my father's house with a family of my own, the brood of us camped at the beach, my father teaching my children to surf, our rendezvous in Las Vegas or Palm Springs—evaporating like the sea fog. The rug and coffee table between the couch where they sat, shoulder to shoulder, and the chair where I was felt as wide and impassable as the ocean. I tugged at the hair on my wrist. I loved them, and told them so, but everything was different—a difference I still felt a year and a half later, sitting at my kitchen table while the room lighted around me. I wanted my father's help, but I couldn't ask for it. More to the point, I swore I wouldn't ask, no matter how bad things got.

The end of the next week, our bank account dropped below $100. Katherine was crying when she picked me up from school. I asked if she'd seen our account. She hadn't. She had, however, gone to the baby store and had seen the crib bedding she wanted. It was the choice of celebrities, plush and soft in all the ways she'd imagined a baby's bed. "I shouldn't have even gone in there," she said. "That was my first mistake. My second mistake was imagining what it would be like."

She was crying so hard she could barely drive. She came within inches of a car turning left in front of us.

Broke and pregnant, we'd become the inheritors of the patchwork visions of the mothers and fathers who preceded us. Our friends had been generous with their hand-me-downs, and we loved them for it, but they weren't the things we imagined for our child. When pregnancy was brand new and strange to us, we consoled ourselves by walking around the baby stores and watching the procession of fat, expectant women and the milk-drunk infants slung against their mothers' breasts. Katherine would hold the tiny clothes against her chest and feel filled with mystery. But slowly that vision was eroded by the reality of what others had given us. To be down to $100 and not accept whatever was offered would be more than rude; it would be irresponsible. So Katherine surrendered her vision for her child in sadness but without complaint when clothes, a stroller, a car seat, and a rocking chair were handed down from family and friends. Even when the baby girl she had hoped for turned during the ultrasound and showed us his penis.

By the time we got home, I was frazzled by Katherine's crying and the close call on the road. "Don't hold so tightly to the idea," I said. "They're just sheets."

My words sent her to the bedroom, the pillow. "They're not just sheets. The baby should have some things his mother picks out. He shouldn't have to be carted around in everyone else's old stuff. That's no way to start out in life."

"There are worse ways," I said.

She rolled to her back and cupped her hands around her belly. Her eyes were narrowed, chiding. "Look," she said, "the bedding is soft and light and *so* baby. It's like my wedding dress. It makes the whole experience. You don't want it to, but it does anyway."

"Sheets are like your wedding dress? *Sheets?*"

Her cries were inconsolable. "They're not just sheets," she said again. "They're everything. It's everything."

"I'm sorry," I said. I tried to go to her, to wrap my arms around her.

Katherine pushed me away and buried her head again. "I need some time alone."

It was after five, the sun behind the Oquirrhs. I changed out of my jeans and into my shorts and sneakers and synthetic long-john top, the only shirt I had that wasn't cotton or flannel. I laced up my Nikes and went for a run, the only thing I could think to do that didn't involve re-tabulating the check register or sniping at Katherine. The irony struck me as I closed the front door behind me: I'd gone back to swimming after moving to Utah, in a sense, to temper desire, punishing my body instead of yielding to its urges. Now I was running to combat the wor-ries of marriage and pregnancy, the result of desire fulfilled. It wasn't fair. I'd bought into the rhetoric, the ceaseless obsession of the campus fellow-ship, that abstaining from sex until marriage would yield a better, stron-ger marriage. Reliable, happy. One of the chief "sociological" arguments for abstinence was that it would reduce unintended pregnancies, thereby rendering abortion unnecessary. I'd held out for the right woman and had been handed a baby I wasn't ready for while my friends who'd enjoyed the pleasures of youth went on enjoying their freedom as adults.

I ran along the poplar-canopied streets bordering the Salt Lake Coun-try Club, followed the chain-link fence along the west side of the golf course, dipped beneath the freeway and headed south in the bike lane along 2100 South. The last two days had seen rain, snow in the mountains. The peaks of Mount Olympus were streaked white against an iron-colored sky. The wind bit my bare thighs and neck and hands.

I headed south four more miles, turned west, and dropped down to Highland Drive, and then wound back up into the neighborhoods where the runoff from the mountains flowed beside the street in wide cement channels, swift and dark, only a few degrees above freezing. The absence of traffic left me free to look at the brickwork and the blooming tulips. But looking was dangerous, too, because it made me start to want, and my wanting was painful. I passed by my favorite house, a blue-and-white cottage that appeared small from the front, but from the side stretched back into a grove of cypress trees, the lot descending into a ravine where a stepped rock wall was filled with flowers, a wrought-iron bench sat between two shady pines, and a wet patch of lawn stretched out at the bottom, out of reach of any van. I looked upon the house with a longing not unlike the longing I felt the night I watched Katherine unfasten the tiny hooks on the back of her wedding gown. Bodies, sexual touch, had once seemed impossible, something other people took for granted but that I was never meant to have. Now it was houses.

I was past the house and starting my climb. The light was almost exhausted, and the temperature was dropping. I folded my hands inside my sleeves, zipped the collar on the top of my long johns. My ankles were stiff, and I could think of little else besides dinner and getting warm. I'd been out for well over an hour, and I felt hunger deep inside my chest and belly and in the back of my throat. I was at the bottom of my last and steepest hill, a ball-breaker. I was burning for rest, but I had two miles to go.

My ankles throbbed as I climbed past a wide white Colonial, two cars parked in its circular driveway. The smell of the dinner cooking inside the kitchen hit me in the face. I picked up my knees and chugged, working hard, emptying my last reserves. The wind rushed through me, cold and wet from the canyon, strong enough to pitch me into the middle of the road. I tucked my head to cut through it. I held out my hands and felt myself lift. I was all surface, no inside, transparent as a leaf. I got ahead of the wind, and the wind pushed me up. At the top I could go no farther. I doubled over and spit and gasped. I had nothing in my stomach to lose. Acid trickled from the corners of my mouth in thin, yellow streams. I walked in slow circles clutching my stomach. I held my hand to the streetlamp and saw a muted flash as the light passed through my skin.

Katherine was in the bath when I got home. She was round and naked, and the water was unable to surmount her belly or her breasts. Our son was less than a season away. He kicked against her skin, little bounces that rippled the water, his first exertions against the world. Katherine touched the rise of his foot and smiled. I peeled off my shoes and socks, my top and my shorts. I was red from scalp to toes. Katherine bent her knees. There was room for me here, for the three of us, our tiny family about to be. I reached for Katherine's belly as I sank my foot into the tub. Water spilled over the side.

Hydrophobia

I watched our new downstairs neighbors as though they foretold our future. Britney and Dylan's son was due three months before ours. By the time they finished angling their furniture down the basement stairs and unloading the boxes from Dylan's 1970 Chevy truck, classic white with turquoise paneling, they had less than a month to go. I eyed Britney's heavy belly through the kitchen window and wondered how Katherine's small frame would carry something so large. Britney's mother brought over packs of diapers, and her father tuned the furnace and water heater. They had a baby shower in the backyard while lilac bloomed along the fence, tulips in the planter boxes. Fleece sleepers and short-legged sailor suits floated out of their tissue wrappings, held aloft by a chorus of sighs.

Their son Cole was born a week before Memorial Day, but the doctors had trouble controlling Britney's bleeding following the delivery. She became anemic, which weakened her immune system, which led to bronchitis and pneumonia and three extra weeks in the hospital. By the time Dylan's truck thundered up the driveway with Britney in the passenger seat, she hadn't seen her son in nearly a month. Dylan had cared for Cole by himself; I don't know how he worked. Dylan guided Britney down the basement stairs, Cole's bucket car seat hanging from his opposite elbow, but a few minutes later I heard his truck roar back to life and zoom down the driveway. For the rest of the afternoon, we listened to Cole's rhythmic wailing through the floor while in the background his mother's cries were quieter, sadder. The next day, Britney's mother came and took her home to Ogden, leaving Dylan again alone with the baby. Britney began sleeping at her mother's house without Cole three nights a week, then four, then all seven. The nights she slept downstairs, Dylan went out with friends, often returning after one in the morning with a truckload of beer and men in baseball caps. His friends sat in the backyard, smoking and talking too loud.

Britney called Dylan a deadbeat asshole. He fired back that she was a dumb bitch who didn't know how to use birth control. Emmeline and Truman had called each other kinder things.

"I hate that basement," Katherine said, lying in the dark beside me. "No one ever gets along down there."

"There's no natural daylight," I said. "None of the windows open. I'd go crazy, too."

"I hate you!" Dylan hollered beneath us.

"God," Katherine said. "Should we call the police?"

"Not yet," I said. "I haven't heard anything shatter."

"Is that going to happen to us?" She rubbed her orb of her stomach, rolled over and draped her arm across my chest. I felt the baby kick between us.

"We'll be okay," I said.

"This is the last place we live with people in the basement," Katherine said. "I'd rather camp in the woods for the rest of my life than listen to this." She leaned up on her elbow, looked me in the eye. "Swear."

"I swear," I said. "No more people in the basement."

The closer we got to our own son's birth, the more I worried about what might go wrong. Britney and Dylan were proof of how quickly luck could turn. After the baby was born, Katherine would begin her second year of practicum at the children's hospital, where she used to work, a position with a stipend—a laughably small stipend, but combined with my teaching and coaching, and the food vouchers for formula, it was enough to get by. Barely. The baby would have Medicaid for a year, but Katherine's coverage would end with his birth. I hadn't been insured in years. Riding my bike to campus, I made sure to brake at every stop sign for fear I'd spill and break my arm and have to take out a loan to have it reset. After we paid our bills at the end of the month, we had less than $10 left over.

Despite the doctor's assurances, the night Katherine went into labor, I worried that the nurses would treat us differently because we were on Medicaid. Katherine sat upright in her hospital bed to watch the baby's heartbeat on the fetal monitor. I tried to sleep in the chair in the corner, but after a few hours, I got up and wandered the halls. I told the nurses my wife worked in the big hospital up the hill and that my mother-in-law was a nurse there, too. I hoped nurses, like wolves, would look after one of their own. I shook hands at the ice machine with two other men, one who was still in his twenties but already balding, his blond hair as fine as the babies' in the nursery window, and another, brown-skinned, his dark hair slightly gray at the ears. His denim jacket smelled of raspberries. Down the hall, a woman was screaming her lungs out. "*Dios mio,*" the man in the denim jacket said. "Ouch."

"That's my wife," the blond said. "She's doing this 'natural.'"

"You better get in there," I said.

"She's in transition," he said. "This is our third. It's better if I'm not there for this part." He crossed his ankles and leaned against the wall, impervious or simply accustomed. He'd witnessed enough new lives spill forth into the world that he no longer found the event remarkable. I leaned with my ankles crossed too and tried to believe I belonged to this communion of fathers, that standing between these men I could participate in their optimism. The obstetrician would make it to the hospital on time, the insurance would cover the bill, the baby's final push, along with the cutting of the cord and the circumcision—rites from the beginning of time—would go forth without incident. Brahms's "Lullaby" played every time a baby was born. I heard it every five minutes. It was dizzying, so many babies with my son's birthday. Would God remember me in this mass whelping, the ex-evangelical in the heart of Mormon country, the consumer of state-purchased bread and cheese? I was restless, antsy. Scared.

I brought Katherine a 7UP in a Styrofoam cup. She drank it and immediately reached for the plastic basin beside the bed and threw it up. "You want something else?" I asked.

"It's okay," she said. "I'd rather do this on an empty stomach."

The nurse came in. "That's a good sign," she said. She carried the basin to the toilet and poured it out. "It means you're ready to push."

Galen slid out fifty-four minutes later, caked in blood and vernix. The nurse laid him on the scale, pressed his foot into an inkpad and then onto a blue index card. She clutched my wrist, hauled me to her side, and pressed Galen's footprint into my forearm. She slid her fingers beneath my hand and looked up at the clock. She was checking my pulse. She said, "Take a breath, Dad. He's here."

"I was nervous," I said. "I've never done this before."

The second nurse in the room was shorter, rounder, from Alabama. I liked her best. "Oh, honey," she said, patting my shoulder. "This is just the beginning."

~~~

By the time we left the hospital, Galen's skin had turned the color of a ripe peach. The doctor diagnosed the problem as jaundice and wrote a prescription for a home phototherapy unit, which would help break down the bilirubin in Galen's blood. A few hours after we carried Galen through the front door, a van from a medical device company arrived. The driver walked to the door carrying an old hardside suitcase, the kind of thing a door-to-door salesman carried around. He wore a mechanic's shirt with the company logo stitched to the breast pocket. I smelled cigarette smoke when he stepped across the threshold. He set the suitcase on the coffee table and cracked open what looked like a miniature, portable tanning bed—a hard plastic basin on the bottom, four slim cylindrical bulbs in the ceiling, a flimsy transparent shield that, the deliveryman explained, helped to hold in the heat and to prop open the lid. The deliveryman fit the plug into the socket on the wall, and the lights flickered to life with a buzz as loud as a microwave oven. Harsh blue light filled the basin, revealing all the scuffs and scratches and discolorations in the plastic. The bitter odor of rubbing alcohol wafted out. "You need to keep his eyes covered while he's in there," the deliveryman said. From his pocket he produced a cotton eye mask sealed inside a crinkled cellophane sleeve. "Keep him in just his diaper. The more skin the lights touch, the better."

Katherine stepped back, into the doorway leading to the bedrooms. She held Galen against her shoulder, his fuzzy head cupped inside her palm. I watched the panic bloom across her face, and I felt a torque in my spine. The prospect of putting my son inside this box introduced me to a level of anxiety I didn't know existed. The shell of the unit was, undeniably, a suitcase, and the longer I stared at it, the more I foresaw the lid falling shut with Galen inside, a baby snatcher dressed as a medical-device deliveryman blithely whistling as he strolled back to his van, sliding the suitcase back into his rack beside the dozen other phototherapy units—all filled with infants too small to know what was happening. I resisted the urge to kick the suitcase from the table. I asked, "How long does he have to stay in there?" I thought: maybe an hour a day, two tops.

"Other than feedings and diaper changes, he shouldn't come out at all," the deliveryman said, extending his clipboard for me to sign. I watched my hand shakily sign the form, my every instinct shouting for me to tear it in half. "The more time he spends in there, the faster it works. Jaundice usually clears up in three or four days."

"Four days?" Katherine said.

"They sleep most of the time anyway," the deliveryman said. "It'll go fast." I handed him the clipboard. He checked his watch and strode swiftly out the door.

We carried the suitcase into the nursery. If Galen couldn't spend his first night in the bed we'd prepared for him, at least he could be in his room. The eye patches covered his face from his nose to his hairline, and beneath the lights, his skin looked mottled, brittle, like cracking paint. I sat in the rocking chair and watched him. Through the drawn shades, I could see the silhouettes of people moving outside. The old man next door watered his rose hedge. Dylan ferried boxes from the basement to his truck, the floor shaking every time the side door sprang shut. He and Britney were moving out, barely four months after they'd moved in. The basement would soon be empty again, and I worried about who'd come next, whether we'd have another train wreck like Truman and Emmeline or another bad romance like Dylan and Britney. What shouting we — and now Galen — might hear through the floor as we lay in bed at night. The house felt suddenly permeable, the wooden floorboards and brick exterior walls no match for a menace determined to find a way inside.

I thought of the other places I'd lived before this house, the chain of attic spaces and side rooms and tiny cells from which I'd looked down at the street as if from the crow's nest of a sailboat or peered through the dark while the woman in the next window took off her clothes. I saw my old life in those sequestered rooms in clearer terms: I'd been avoiding loss, mitigating chance. I'd ventured out, made friends, and Matt died. Somehow I'd come through that, too (or had I?) — I'd met Katherine, gotten married, had a baby, found my way to a normal, happy life. My dissertation was taking shape, and I was becoming a better teacher. Yet I couldn't let myself feel easy or mindless with happiness. Jeremy's murder had over the years lost its eclipsing stance in front of my mental spotlight and had instead worked down into my bones, into the lower-octane dread stewing in my gut as Galen lay beneath the ultraviolet lights. The tenuousness of every good and joyful thing. My old fears came back with a whoosh, a wave — the tidal force that had thrust me into evangelicalism all those years ago. I was back on the tightrope across Leviathan's yawning chasm, only now there were so many new ways to fall in. I couldn't let my guard down. I had to protect. I vowed to remain vigilant.

~~~

For the next two years, we lived above a string of young families, some with children, some without, all willing to sacrifice daylight and good ventilation for a savings in rent. The neighbors who followed were quieter, though not completely forgettable, and rent prices were climbing, so we stayed put. Katherine finished her degree and got a job working nights as a social worker in the emergency room so she could be home with Galen during the day. I edited a literary journal and taught classes and hacked away at my dissertation at the kitchen table. When Galen was eighteen months old, I was offered a teaching job at a small college in Wisconsin. We didn't have a dime to put toward a down payment, but my new salary would qualify us for a government loan program that would allow us to buy a house with nothing down. My mother bought our plane tickets to Wisconsin so we could look for a place to live. We walked through thirty-two houses in two days before we found one we could afford. The sellers accepted our offer the night before we flew home. Katherine and I jumped on the bed to celebrate. Then we lay down and celebrated some more.

A week before we moved, our living room towering with boxes, Katherine asked me if our new insurance plan required a waiting period for pregnancy. "I don't think so," I said. I was washing dishes in the kitchen sink. I shut off the water. "I'm afraid to ask."

"Surprise," she said.

Since the pill had failed us the first time, Katherine had switched to a different birth control. "The ring was supposed to work better for us," I said.

"It must have fallen out," she said. "I called the doctor's office. The nurse said it happens fairly often."

I put my head on the counter. It had taken two mortgages and private insurance to buy the house. We had student loans, a car already too small for the three of us, let alone a fourth, and were moving fifteen hundred miles away from anyone we knew. I wasn't ready, and I said so.

"At least we have a house to move into," Katherine said.

The first few nights after we moved in, I lay awake listening to the sounds the house made while we were supposed to be asleep. The ice-maker churning out cubes, the plaster creaking, a squirrel running across the roof. None of it was familiar. Once I swore I heard the back door squeaking open and footsteps advancing across the kitchen floor, and I leapt from bed with the phone receiver in my hand. I flipped on the lights and opened the closets. I crept into Galen's room and stood over his crib, his veined eyelids lit by the moon through the window. I thought of Elizabeth Smart, kidnapped from her bed in Salt Lake City, only a few miles away from where we once lived. The thought of a stranger stealing my son made me shake. I called into the empty living room: "Hello?"

"Who's there?" Katherine said, her head covered by the pillow.

"No one," I said. "I thought I heard something."

"Galen keeps me awake all day and you keep me up all night," she said. "I'm about to get crabby."

I double-checked the locks and went back to bed. *Money* magazine had named our town one of the safest small cities in America. Diapers and tampons were made here. So were manhole covers and fire trucks. I thought of the song I'd learned on the beach half a life ago: "The name of the Lord is a strong tower; the righteous run into it and they are saved." It was up to me to make sure my house was a tower for my family, strong and safe.

In the morning, I turned my attention to the maze of water pipes in the basement.

I studied the pipes for hours, their path from the main valve to the heater and away again, up and over the air ducts, into the ceiling, right through the cinder block. The utility space was lit by a single bulb suspended from the ceiling and two opaque windows, each the size of a shoebox. The home inspector had warned me, his tone as strong as a sergeant's, that water was my house's worst enemy. Allowed to stagnate, water would spawn mold, and if it found wood, it would rot the house to dust. Outdoor spigots, left undrained in winter, could explode. Even rainwater was a constant threat. Unlike Utah, where the ground was parched and sloped, Wisconsin was flat and wet. Water stood in the culverts beside the roads, long black strips buzzing with flies, and on windy nights I could smell the algae wafting up from Lake Winnebago. I watched for it. I scanned the rafters. I touched every shut-off valve, hoping my hand would come away dry.

The morning I eyed a puddle beneath an air duct, I hoped for the best-case scenario. The water was condensation from the air conditioner, no big deal. I turned up the dehumidifier. But I turned around at the top of the stairs. I came back and began feeling my way along the top of the duct until my hand detected water, a little pool in a depression in the top of the shaft. A drop fell on the back of my hand. The sewer pipe was beside my head. Above me was the bathroom. Above me was the toilet.

The ceiling creaked. I heard Galen, now two years old, running back and forth. Katherine moved more slowly, nauseous and tired. The toilet flushed, and water rushed down the sewer stack beside me. I cupped my hand around the pipe and felt the water flow inside my palm. I felt something wet land in my hair. I looked up. A steady drip fell from the seam between the toilet and the floor.

The manager of the local True Value Hardware store diagnosed the problem as a worn-out wax seal, the membrane sealing the toilet to the sewer. It surprised me to learn that a $2 wax ring, which I could mold and pull apart with my fingers, was all that separated my family's waste from the house. In photographs of homes ravaged by tornadoes, the toilet is often the one object recognizable among the debris—white and solitary and steadfast. I expected my toilet to be welded to the sewer pipe, and for the toilet and the pipe to be forged from a single seamless length of indestructible titanium running from the bowl to the ground to the treatment plant on the outskirts of town. The manager explained that toilets are held in place with only two screws, which fit bottoms up into notched grooves on the flange capping the sewer pipe; the weight of the toilet—and the weight of those who use it—keep the seal tight. He sent me home with two new rings and a metal scraper, told me to clean off all the old wax before reseating the toilet.

Katherine took Galen to the park, and I got to work. I turned off the water, separated the tank from the bowl, the bowl from the floor, balled up a rag, and shoved it down the open sewer pipe to hold back the gas. I spent an hour scraping away the grayed, hardened wax, digging it out of the tile, from the underside of the toilet, from the top of the flange. I scrubbed the floor with 409. I set the screws and the rings and prepared to heft the toilet back into place. Handling a toilet is like trying to handle a dead animal: Most prefer to lift with their arms extended, letting their backs pay the price for keeping the bowl away from their faces. Katherine and Galen came home just in time to see me hefting the bowl this way, my elbows locked and my ass in the air as I attempted to thread the screws in the flange through the two holes at the base of the bowl. It was no picnic—the smallest tap knocked the screws over. On my first attempt I missed completely, pushing the screws into the wax ring with the base of the toilet. On my second, I got the screws through the holes, but one came out of the groove in the flange, and I had to lift off the toilet and the wax rings, and reset the whole works. The third time, I got it. I spun the nuts into place and slowly cranked them tight, careful not to unbalance the bowl or crack the porcelain. Before declaring myself finished, I knelt before the bowl and wrapped my arms around it until my hands met in the back and my cheek rested on the lid. I rocked back to make sure I had the thing moored. At first the bowl was firm. Then, just as my ass met my heels, I heard a sucking noise, like the peeling away of the waxed-paper backing of a Fruit Roll-Up. I felt the toilet give. It brought with it everything I'd touched: the wax seals, the screws, the flange, the top of the sewer pipe. I'd broken it off. "Oh, shit," I said.

"Oh, shit," Galen said. He squeezed past me to peer down into the sewer pipe.

The plumber fit a plastic flange onto the top of the pipe and bolted it to the subfloor. He reseated the toilet in one try. He gave me a break on the price because the job didn't take the full hour; it was that easy. The speed with which he'd worked only heightened my worry that he was missing the bigger problem, a crack somewhere farther down the line, beneath the basement floor, perhaps, or beneath the yard. A week after moving in, my strong tower was leaking shit and piss. "Think the stack should be replaced, too?" I asked.

"It's holding fine yet," he said. "I wouldn't lose any sleep over it."

After the plumber left, my inspections of the basement became longer and more frequent. After putting Galen down at night, Katherine settled in on the couch, and I grabbed my flashlight and descended the basement stairs like a miner into a coal shaft. I prowled around the cinder block walls and crawled along the cement floor, sniffing the cracks in the mortar for signs of mold. I measured the cracks in the plaster with my fingertips, the distance between my pinky and my thumb, and each day I found new ones: in the bedroom ceiling, in the stairwell, snaking up the wall from the electrical outlets. I ran my hands over the bubbled lappets and worried that water had once penetrated the house and that it continued to do so. Water was leaking in right now. If I stood here long enough, I'd see it come through.

Katherine came to the basement stairs and hollered, "Are you coming up soon?"

"In a minute," I yelled back.

"The basement's dry," she said. "I checked this morning. Come have a drink."

"In a minute."

A few weeks later I was weeding the garden when I noticed the soil sloping toward the house when it should have been sloping away from it. A little digging unearthed a line of heavy paving stones, and beneath the stones I found strips of foam saturated with earth and water and mildew. I dug out the foam and went to Menards to buy dirt to build up the slope. When I told the garden associate what I'd found in the yard, his eyes grew wide. "The last thing you want is water running toward your house," he said. "Except for water sitting *against* your house." He shut off his forklift and climbed down, leaving the pallets of gray flagstones suspended above our heads. He squinted into the sunlight, his three-day-old scruff and narrowed slits giving him a Dirty Harry look. "The foam will draw water to your foundation, where it will freeze and push your basement walls in," he said. "Big mess."

I thought of the ruined farmhouses I'd seen on our drives in the country, the framing rotted and slumped to one side. I envisioned my house doing the same, the foundation walls collapsing, the cinder blocks loosened from the mortar falling to the floor, the tide of water and clay gushing in as the house listed and the Sheetrock splintered and the roof caved in and the kitchen cabinets crashed to the floor. I felt my pulse kick up. "I was thinking I could build up the dirt so it slopes in the right direction," I said.

He shook his head. "That'll be a patch, not a real fix. No telling how long it'll last. What you want to do is dig out the front yard, down at least three feet, fill in the bottom with gravel and the top with dirt. Lay down some plastic before you lay the dirt. You might want to rent a Bobcat, hire some help."

I could hear the bumpy rattle of the wheels and Galen calling my name as Katherine wheeled the shopping cart through the aisles. By the time Katherine tracked me down, Galen was screaming for lunch, and I had a flatbed dolly loaded with topsoil and gravel, a new shovel. My pants were smeared with mud, and the armpits of my shirt were dripping with sweat. I'd get started that afternoon, in case it rained. "This is crazy," she said. "How much is all this going to cost?"

The salesman shook his head again. "Not half as much as water penetrating your foundation," he said. "Your husband told me about the foam he found in the ground. Now *that's* crazy."

"I'm almost finished," I said. "Five minutes."

"Fine," she said, and pushed the cart, Galen waving over her shoulder, through the sliding doors. Her capitulation was a harsher rebuke than her refusal would have been; I'd gone over the edge and wasn't worth arguing with.

The salesman helped me load the last few bags of soil onto the dolly. "You got to do the job right," he said, full of conviction. "She'll thank you for it one day." But Katherine was right. My diligence in anticipating problems before they occurred was becoming an obsession.

As the husband of a social worker, I'd been a proxy witness to myriad forms of madness. Back in Utah, on the nights she was on-call, Katherine had slept with a pager beneath her pillow, ready to be rattled awake at any moment by the crisis hotline, the number people call when their demons have them cornered. The pager chirped and she answered, groping in the dark for her robe and slipping out to the kitchen to the phone and the table and her notebook. She wrote while her callers talked and tried not to interrupt too early or too often. Sometimes she'd advise a caller to go to the hospital, and sometimes the person simply needed an ear to speak into. On occasion, I'd make my way down the hallway to see her facing the windows, nodding and scribbling, fully present at two in the morning, at three and at four. "It's okay," I'd hear her say. "You're not a freak; you're going through a lot. It's only been a few months since he died." I imagined her callers sitting against their bathroom doors with their knees tucked up to their chins, or at kitchen tables not unlike ours. In their fear and trembling, they were my brothers and sisters.

One call came from our neighbor three doors down, a young mother with a sick infant. Her daughter had been in and out of the hospital more than a dozen times in six months with hip dysplasia, a string of unexplainable infections, and sleep apnea that one night caused her to stop breathing. Our neighbor did CPR to revive her daughter and then rushed her to the hospital. The baby lived, but the mother was afraid to sleep for fear her daughter would stop breathing again. Katherine recognized her name and the sound of her voice; she looked out our front window and saw her kitchen light on, saw the woman pacing back and forth in her nightgown, her blond hair in a ponytail. Katherine didn't identify herself beyond her first name. She didn't say, "Hey, it's me, from down the street. Look out your kitchen window!" Nor did she keep looking out our kitchen window. She sat down and listened. The next day was sunny, and our neighbor was outside, pushing her daughter in the stroller. Katherine wanted to invite her in, reveal herself, become the friend she knew she could be and had in many ways already become. But she couldn't. It was against the rules.

When the hospital called, chances were she'd be going in. A patient needed a psychiatric assessment before being admitted or discharged. Katherine dressed in the dark, brushed her hair, and drove through the empty streets to the hospital. I didn't like the thought of her car alone on the road, and I was always a little scared when she went. I also grew so accustomed to the pager that some nights I snoozed right through it. Katherine left without my even turning over, and later I'd wake up to find her already gone.

The night after Thanksgiving, Katherine arrived home late and woke me up. Her eyes and the tip of her nose glowed in the moonlight through the slits of the blinds. I was stuffed with dinner, the turkey and mashed potatoes like a weight in my stomach, but her eyes told me I needed to sit up. She'd gone to the hospital to assess a patient the police had found screaming "H2! H2!" at a stop sign. The patient told her he'd been eating Thanksgiving dinner with his girlfriend's family when an argument escalated into a fight. He'd thrown a glass against a wall and stormed out of the house, tearing off his shirt as he descended the steps. Katherine recognized his girlfriend from high school—a disheveled but pretty blond who'd once played on the soccer team. The patient wore his hair cut short and was clean-shaven; with his shirt off, Katherine could see the topography of veins in his chest and stomach. He was compact and muscular.

Velcro cuffs around his wrists held him to the bed. He admitted to having a history of schizophrenia; he'd stopped taking his medications, he
said, because they didn't do him any good—he still heard voices. Katherine said the psychiatrist could prescribe him a different drug that might
work better and a sleep aid so he could get some rest. He said he didn't
want a different drug. He wanted to leave. His parents were assholes and
his girlfriend's parents were assholes and the police were assholes. Katherine asked him if he'd used other drugs, and his girlfriend admitted they'd
used ecstasy. Katherine could see the muscles in his chest and arms begin
to contract, slowly, like a python tightening its stranglehold. He made a
fist and flexed his wrist, testing the strength of the cuff. "We'll need to run
some tests," Katherine told him. "Draw some blood."

"Am I going to stay here?" he wanted to know.

"We have a psychiatric unit at another facility. They're better equipped.
You'll be a lot more comfortable."

"Can I drive him?" his girlfriend asked.

"Ambulance would be better," Katherine said. If she let them go, there
was a good chance they wouldn't show up at the other hospital.

"I don't want to go in an ambulance," the patient said.

"It's better," Katherine said. "Safer." She sat back on the bed and took
a deep breath before telling me how the tech came in to draw the blood
and couldn't tap the vein with the cuffs around the man's wrists. The tech
undid the restraints, and the moment his wrists were free, the patient
sprang from his back to his knees in one adrenaline-injected motion,
his hands reaching for Katherine's neck. Had he made it, he could have
crushed her windpipe. Fortunately, the tech stuck out his arm, and within
seconds hospital security was in the room, the patient was on his back
with his wrists restrained. "He never laid a finger on me," Katherine said.
"But he got close enough for me to know what it would have felt like if
he had. I felt the air leave his nose. I could smell the cranberry sauce on
his breath."

The euphemisms for madness in the American vernacular—"nervous
breakdown," "cracked up," "lost his marbles"—all connote a process in
which the mind breaks away from the world where the normal live and
takes up residence in a country without logic, where change comes on
suddenly and without warning, where the laws of linearity and orderli-
ness no longer apply. The madman sees things that aren't there. The madman chitters in a language only he can understand. The images of mental

illness that pervade popular culture reinforce the idea: Bipolars vacillate between manic rage and closed-curtain depression; schizophrenics slavishly obey their inner voices; obsessive-compulsives wash their hands until their skin cracks and flakes.

However, the real-life schizophrenic who lunged at my wife showed me madness might be less a fracturing than a concentration: A fixation on one thing that becomes the head of the pin upon which the universe must balance. The one thing becomes the Everlasting Thing: a crushing weight that, when it fails, results not in an explosion but in an *implosion*, leaving behind a black hole that draws to itself all light, all hope, all peace, and all difference. Madness is the overwhelming persistence of sameness; it is the absence of change. For the man in the hospital, Katherine became the concentrated figure of all the voices that had tried to control him—the voice inside his head as well as the police, his doctors, his parents, his girlfriend's parents—and when he lunged for her neck, he lunged not at her but at everyone all at once.

I wasn't violent and I never heard a little voice inside my head, but as the cold weather set in, I became more and more possessed by water. It was the concentrated sign of my vulnerability, of every nefarious threat I could neither predict nor prevent. Playing with Galen on the carpet, I thought about re-caulking the bathtub. Sitting on the couch feeling Katherine's still-flat stomach for echoes of the baby inside it, I thought about installing a piggyback for the sump pump, in case the power went out during a storm, and standing in front of my classes, I thought about the leaves piling up in the gutters along the roof, damming the rain until it spilled over and ran behind the clapboards. I watched the water spiral down the sink and toilet, the invisible tornado it formed in the bathtub, and at night I lay in bed and listened to the creaks in the walls, straining to detect, in the dark, the sound of a trickle in the pipes that separated our bedroom from Galen's. I touched the walls until my palms grew sweaty and created the very water I feared. I was the agent of damage, I feared, and would bring the house down around us. But I still couldn't pull my hand away.

The afternoon we went in for an ultrasound, I sat in a chair against the wall and watched the rain sliding down the window, wondering if the gravel I'd packed around the foundation was holding. Estimates for a Bobcat and crew had come in way too high; we'd have to wait until the baby was born. I wanted the baby to hurry up so I could save up to fix the problem right. It was synecdoche madness, a story Borges might write: my concern for the symbol of my family's well-being eclipsing my concern for the family itself.

The sonographer squirted gel onto Katherine's belly, and the baby's outline appeared up on the screen hanging from the ceiling. There was the head, the back, the beating heart, the penis.

Katherine said she'd had some bleeding in the last few weeks, the toilet paper sometimes pink, other times a brighter red. "A little spotting is normal," the sonographer said. "We see it all the time."

I pointed to the screen, the baby's heart like a clapper in a bell. "See," I said. "There he is. A-okay."

The sonographer leaned into the monitor, then abruptly stood up. "I'll be right back," she said. She closed the door behind her, and I watched the rain while I waited for her return. The door opened a minute later, and the sonographer reclaimed her stool beside the machine. She hit a button, and the machine spit out a line of waxy black-and-whites, as well as three sepia-tinted 3-D pictures of the baby tucked against Katherine's uterine wall. "All set," she said.

"Everything okay?" Katherine asked.

"Fine," she said. "I just needed to ask the doctor a question."

It was raining harder when we left the clinic. Night had fallen. I drove home and parked in the garage. Katherine went inside to pay the babysitter, but I grabbed my flashlight and walked around to the front of the house. My jacket wasn't waterproof, but it was thick enough to keep me dry for a few minutes. My father had told me once if you combined all the holes in the exterior of an average house, the sum would be the size of a basketball. In a sixty-year-old house, the hole had to be larger. The rain was cold, turning slushy, and it slid down the back of my collar, but I didn't hurry. I used my finger to scoop the leaves from the mouths of the rain gutters and shifted the stones beneath the front window until I could actually see the rain slide downhill. Through the window I saw Katherine on the phone as Galen hugged her leg. She walked to the window and cupped her hands around her face. Her eyes, when they met mine, were angry. She yanked open the front door. "Come inside!" she called into the rain. "Come inside right now or I'm calling a doctor."

~~~

Two days later, Katherine called me in my office. "You have a second?" she asked.

"Sure," I said.

"The doctor called," she said. She paused, swallowed.

"You called a doctor on me?"

"Not you," she said. "The baby. The obstetrician called about the ultrasound. I need to talk to you about what he said."

For the next five minutes she stopped being my wife and became a social worker, the calm-in-all-weathers woman who'd cradled the dead in her arms, dead babies and dead children, the woman who'd ferried grieving parents to the morgue and back, who'd pressed tiny lifeless hands and feet into plaster molds in order to give bereft mothers something of their lost children to take home. She took a big clinical breath and told me the ultrasound revealed that the baby was missing a blood vessel in his umbilical cord; he had two when he should have had three. There was also a small spot on his heart, an echogenic intracardiac focus, a mineral deposit, and the radiologist had seen cysts in his choroid plexus, the membrane in the brain that produces spinal fluid. None of the findings, in isolation, were worrisome: Echogenic foci didn't impact heart function and typically cleared up by the third trimester; the choroid plexus isn't a cognitive part of the brain, so the cysts wouldn't affect function or development. Even the two-vessel umbilical cord wasn't a big deal. But the danger was that all three were markers for a genetic disease, Trisomy 18. Edwards syndrome. Like Down syndrome, which is Trisomy 21, Edwards is caused by the presence of an extra chromosome—a third eighteenth chromosome. Like Down syndrome, Edwards affects mental and physical development, with one horrifying difference: While most Down syndrome children live into their fifties, or longer, very few children with Edwards live more than a week. Many are stillborn and many more die within their first hours of life. The more markers that showed up in the ultrasound, the more the odds were against us.

"Could it be Downs?" I asked. "I swam with a boy who had Downs when I was a kid. He was happy most of the time. Downs would be okay."

"Downs has different markers," she said. "If he has Edwards, we'll need to talk about terminating the pregnancy."

"An abortion?"

Katherine let out a long, frightened sigh—a maternal sigh, not a clinical one. I felt my heart tighten like a fist. She'd seen enough to know the difference between imagined worry and real concern. Twenty minutes before my first class met, I felt the implosion begin, the bottom of the universe spinning through a drain, pulling me down with it.

The doctor scheduled an amniocentesis. The waiting room was filled with parenting magazines, every table and empty seat covered with a glossy photograph of a smiling, healthy baby. We found two seats around the corner, away from the receptionist's desk. I gathered up the magazines and moved them away. We sat, staring and silent, until the nurse appeared in the doorway and called our name. We followed her to the same room where a week earlier we'd had the ultrasound. The sonographer this time was a small woman with dark, spiky hair. Her lab coat hung to her ankles. She told us she was from Reedsburg, Wisconsin, "down by the Dells." Appleton felt like the big city to her. Kids? we asked. Three, she said. Two boys and a girl. She smiled and rolled her eyes toward the ceiling, unable to keep from thinking of them. She stopped herself from telling stories and instead slathered Katherine's belly with lubricant. "There's your baby," she said, excited. It was obvious she enjoyed her job. We wondered if she knew why we were here.

The doctor came in, a diminutive Filipino man in his fifties, still combing the last wisps of his hair on his small round head. He kept a hand tucked inside his coat pocket. We'd found him in the phone book the week after we'd arrived in Wisconsin and quickly came to appreciate his unflappable demeanor and the fact that the certifications from the American College of Obstetricians and Gynecologists hanging on the wall were dated 1985. He'd been doing this a long time. He explained the risks of the amnio: infection, acidemia, a loss of amniotic fluid, and, in a small percentage of cases, miscarriage. We said we understood the risks. The sonographer wrapped the transducer in a plastic sleeve, filled the sleeve with lubricant, and tightened it into place with a metal clamp. Attached to the clamp was a small slot through which the needle would slide. She moved the transducer along Katherine's belly until she found a blank spot, a place the baby was not. A dotted line transected the screen, marking the trajectory the needle would follow through the skin and into the uterus. The doctor threaded the needle through the hole. "Are you ready?" he asked. Katherine nodded. "Okay," he said. "I'm going to count to three and then go in. You'll feel a pinch and a tightness while the needle is inside." Katherine nodded again. "Okay, then," he said. He counted slowly, one, followed by a pause, two. He retracted the needle. He got the *th* out for *three* when the baby's head emerged on the screen and crossed through the dotted line, right through the needle's path. "Of course you'd swim over right now," the doctor said. He laughed, lightly. My heart was racing, my mind spinning, but I remained still, holding onto Katherine's arm. The doctor moved the transducer to a new spot and began the countdown again, more quickly this time. He pierced the uterus and pulled back on the syringe. Katherine winced, gritted her teeth. The canister of the syringe filled with a dull yellow fluid. "Good color," the doctor said. "Little frightening there for a moment." We nodded. I exhaled. "For you, not for me," he added.

We'd been debating names for weeks, but now we chose one, Hayden, aware it was a name we might have to bury. That afternoon, I sat on the edge of the bed and thought about the vial of amniotic fluid—Katherine's water—traveling by van to the lab in Milwaukee. I thought of its soft amber color, its protective viscosity, its blizzard of DNA, the helix of the baby's existence a braid of Katherine's alleles and mine. I couldn't help wondering if I was responsible, if it was my DNA that caused the cysts and the echogenic focus and the two-vessel cord, if my lifetime of worry and zealotry had been passed along to my son, mutating, turning pernicious in the process. Katherine stood in the bedroom doorway. Her eyes were wet. Beyond the window the last yellow leaf fluttered on the maple, lit by the sun through the pines beyond the garage. Downstairs Galen was strapped into his high chair. He banged his milk cup against the tray, and the thud echoed up the staircase. We were alone for a moment. She wanted to reach for me, and I for her, but we did not. Instead I lay back on the bed, and she lay down beside me, and we began to talk.

For ten days we talked like this: in the mornings lying in bed and in the evenings sitting on the couch. In the first days we conjured the worst stories we knew. Katherine told stories from the emergency room, nights with the trauma team: of the ten-year-old girl in American Fork, Utah, hit by a pickup truck while she was crossing in a crosswalk. She was kept alive for two days before support was withdrawn, and her heart was allowed to stop and her organs were removed for donation. She told me of mothers backing over their children, babies shaken to death by immature fathers, healthy eight-year-olds inexplicably bleeding out while having their tonsils removed. I told her about my grandmother, who slipped on her kitchen floor, hit her head on a cabinet drawer, and broke her neck, and about a friend in Texas who lost his first child to a chromosomal anomaly not unlike the one Hayden might have. The ultrasound revealed it, the amniocentesis confirmed it, and his wife carried the baby for nine months, delivered her without medication, and held her until she died, barely an hour after her birth. I added to these stories the ones I didn't tell, stories Katherine already knew and which hovered over my thoughts—Jeremy on his living room floor beside his father and brother, Matt beside the pool. It helped us to hear each other speak; our storytelling was a way of reminding ourselves that the worst can happen and had happened to people we know. Children died and their parents survived; if ours died, we would survive as well. But we also told these stories out of the more superstitious belief that if we could possess all the horror in the world, gather it to ourselves and identify it as part of us, we could dispossess our own narrative of its tragedy. We could convince God we hadn't been immune to suffering. We'd had our numbers called before. Let this one slide.

As the days passed, our stories began to change. At first we hardly noticed. The stories were as gruesome as ever—babies born with vital organs outside their bodies, car accidents, and plane crashes—except the people we were talking about weren't dead. They were alive. Katherine said the Neonatal Intensive Care Unit in Utah brought kids back in ways she never thought possible. Six months in the NICU, most of it in the dark, untouched by human skin to prevent infection or the transference of oil, eating and breathing through a tube, but in the end, alive. We began to see the possibility of a middle ground between dumb-luck avoidance of mishap and the suffocating darkness of our worst nightmares.

On the tenth day, the day we were to hear about the amnio, we lay in bed and whispered to each other the mother of all come-back stories. I saw it in the newspaper years ago, the story of a twenty-two-month-old boy who had wandered away from his babysitter in Rexburg, Idaho, and had fallen into a canal. He was underwater for thirty minutes and had floated more than half a mile before the police fished him out, cold and unresponsive. Paramedics at the scene and doctors in the emergency room performed CPR for more than an hour before finally pronouncing him dead. The boy's mother and stepfather spent more than an hour crying over him and kissing his cold skin and saying good-bye, and when they were finished, a nurse came in and wheeled him down the hall to prepare his body for the funeral home. It was then she noticed his chest was moving, barely, and realized he was breathing. He'd been pronounced dead, but wasn't. He was flown from Rexburg to the children's hospital in Salt Lake City, where Katherine learned more details firsthand. "He was breathing on his own but then had to go back on the respirator," she said. "About a week later, he was upgraded to fair condition. As far as I know, he made it." We practically giggled while we told it. We kissed. It could happen. Sometimes it did happen. Every now and then, someone makes it back from the dead.

The doctor called that afternoon. The results were negative. The baby didn't have Edwards or any other genetic anomaly. I told myself my fears were now behind me. I could calm down about the house, the plumbing, the irrational worries that had swallowed my thoughts for the last months. I'd finally bested my madness for good.

Through Christmas and New Year's and Valentine's Day, I lived in the tenuous hope Hayden would be born without complication, but tucked in the closet of my heart, and Katherine's too, festered the surreptitious expectation that complications awaited us. Problems could still occur: an organ, or two, or many, could grow abnormally. Something vital might not kick on when it should. I prayed, thought good thoughts, and when he finally came, on a day at the end of February when the rain was freezing and turning to snow, I watched the doctor and nurses for signs that Hayden was okay.

Initially he was cheesy and warm and spent his first hour wrapped in a blanket, in Katherine's arms and then in mine, but by the time the nurse returned to bathe him, his color had turned dusky, and his hands and feet were a deep, bloodless purple. When my mother-in-law, a specialized children's nurse, brought Galen to meet his new brother, she stood over the warmer with her bottom lip between her teeth. The delivery nurse thought he might be cold, but when she tested his oxygen saturation, it was lower than it should have been. She hesitated to take him from us, but finally she did, wheeling him down the hall to the nursery, where he was given oxygen and X-rayed and his heels were pricked to draw blood. "Probably a little fluid in his lungs," she told us, adjusting the prongs of the cannulas that delivered air through Hayden's nose. "Should drain out in a few hours. We've got him on 30 percent oxygen, which is hardly anything. A whiff. Room air is 21 percent. We'll wean him down, and when he's off it altogether, we'll wheel him back to your room. Probably later on tonight."

Katherine's mother took Galen home, and a nurse brought me a cot so I could stay the night. I went to bed beneath the two thinnest blankets on the planet. I slept poorly, shivering, waking every hour to see if Hayden was there. In the morning, he was still in the nursery. "Twenty-three percent," the nurse said in the morning, "shouldn't be long now." But he lingered there throughout the morning, and by lunch I accepted the fact that it was going to be another few hours. When Katherine's mother brought Galen to the hospital the next day, I volunteered to take him home so we both could nap. I wanted time to move faster while the fluid evaporated from Hayden's lungs. I wanted the world to reset while my eyes were closed. I wanted to wake up and call the hospital and hear that Hayden was in with Katherine, and that he'd been there for hours. At home I tried to sleep but could not and instead passed the afternoon watching the Discovery Channel. At three, the phone rang. Katherine's voice was higher and slower than usual, altered by the Percocet she'd been given to manage the pain of tearing during the delivery. It was also altered, I understood quickly, by her attempts to manage her concern. "The doctor's on her way back in," she told me. "Hayden's getting sicker. They've bumped him up to 50 percent oxygen, and he's still breathing hard."

"What's the problem?"

"The pediatrician says his lungs might be underdeveloped," Katherine said. "It could also be myocarditis."

"His heart?" I asked. I remembered myocarditis from the day Matt died.

"The doctor says they'll start by treating the lungs and see what happens. There's a NICU a half hour south, at a bigger hospital. They're going to transfer him."

"A NICU?" I asked. The terms, so long associated with Katherine's job, with other people's children and other people's misfortunes, were coming too fast. "Another hospital?"

"This place isn't advanced enough," she said. "There's a snow storm coming, and they don't want to risk having to rush him to the other hospital in bad weather. The helicopter won't fly if it's snowing. To tell you the truth, the nurses here are out of their league. They're making me nervous."

"He's that sick?"

"Yes," she said. She said it plainly, deliberately, so there could be no argument. Katherine had long told irritated accounts of parents defying doctors, thinking they knew what's best for their children by virtue of the fact that their children came from them. Even still, I couldn't help but fight the transfer. I asked if we should call another doctor. Should she call her former colleagues in Utah and arrange to have to test results faxed over? Could we drive Hayden ourselves down to the NICU? Surely he was well enough for a half-hour ride in the car. "He can't go off the oxygen," she said. "Plus, the ambulance is safer. In case something happens on the way."

In case something happens on the way. The words swirled inside me. "Something happening" wasn't an infinite list of improbable accidents, but a few very real possibilities. Katherine meant *in case Hayden stops breathing*, or *in case his heart arrests*, or *in case he dies.* We'd survived a confrontation with death before his birth only to arrive at another immediately after, and I wondered if the two were somehow related, if *this* was the dying within a week that had once been predicted. I'd been lulled into thinking each fate was singular, with only one road leading to it.

I hung up the phone and rose from the couch to shower and brush my teeth and head back to the hospital. All my months of angst and fretting were no longer mad but prescient. I'd been right. It was a feeling far worse than being dead wrong, for now every fear, even the most miniscule, felt rimmed with prophecy. In the shower the water poured over my head and neck and back, filling in my every opening. I felt an unexpected shot of empathy for the schizophrenic who lunged at Katherine. I, too, wanted a neck to squeeze. I beat my fists against the shower wall.

The nursery was empty when I arrived at the hospital. The other babies who shared Hayden's birthday were in with their mothers. I felt momentarily relieved by the possibility that he was already in the ambulance. I did not have to watch him go, and now all that was required of me was to travel to the next place. Around the corner I found a gaggle of nurses standing outside Katherine's room: three from this hospital and two from the next, and two mustached ambulance drivers in padded navy jackets. I recalled the hapless paramedics who ferried Matt from the pool to the hospital, and I wanted to threaten these men with my boundless ire if they so much as bumped the ambulance against the curb with Hayden inside. But these men weren't like those; they were fit and attentive, and between them was a stretcher with a yellow accordion-like base for moving up and down. Attached to the stretcher was a clear plastic Isolette, and inside the Isolette was Hayden, twenty-six hours old, stripped to his diaper, his eyes closed, his lungs retracting so hard that each breath revealed his ribcage, every last bone. He was up to 75 percent. Too much oxygen could cost him his eyesight. The transport nurse slowly told me the name of the neonatologist at the NICU and waited for me to repeat the name back to her. She opened the porthole on the side of the Isolette and told me I could touch Hayden, if I wanted. The empty hallway, the nurses, the darkening sky all felt too final, as though if I touched him now, I might never touch him again. So I didn't. I claimed my hands were cold. The drivers wheeled him away, and the nurses followed. I went with Katherine back to her room, where she gathered up her things and changed from her gown to her clothes so we could leave.

I've never taken a longer walk than I took that night: the length of the hallway from the room where Hayden was born, past the other labor and delivery rooms, where families gathered with flowers and balloons, past the nurses' station, where the women who'd delivered our son sat in a line behind a window with down-turned mouths and watched us leave without him, past the empty nursery, out of the unit, into the elevator, out of the hospital. I carried Katherine's bag over my right shoulder, her arm looped through my left elbow, her steps tiny in pink house slippers because her feet were too swollen for shoes. The bottle of Vicodin rattled in her jacket pocket. I helped her extend the seat belt — the movement required to reach across her shoulder still too painful for her to make — and then I climbed in behind the wheel and started the engine and drove. Snow fell like confetti in the streetlamps; it was dark, and the streets were wet. I kept my eyes fixed on the yellow lines. I had to remind myself to pay attention to the road.

~~~

I sat in a chair beside the Isolette, the Isolette beside the window, the window's glass reflecting the ever-flowing colored sine waves measuring Hayden's heartbeat (green), rate of respirations (yellow), blood pressure (red), and oxygen saturation (blue). Katherine's mother extended her trip to take care of Galen, I canceled my classes, and day after day, Katherine and I sat together before the monitor, following the nodes on the lines across the screen from right to left. I walked through the open door and disappeared almost entirely from time. In the morning, I'd watch the yellow school buses line up along the curb of the school beyond the hospital's parking lot, the crush of primary-colored coats moving across the whitened playground, and when I looked up again, dusk would have fallen, the playground left frozen and abandoned. I spent my lost hours impotently willing the lines into cadence with my own heartbeat, my own breaths. If I could slow my own breathing, gulp in enough oxygen to saturate my blood, maybe I could transcend the barriers between myself and Hayden, the attic of the plastic Isolette, the wires, the intubation hose joining his lungs to the gurgling oxygen canister on the wall. I could do something more than sit and wait.

I slept in spurts, with my arms crossed and my right foot propped on the heating vent, my mouth hanging open, jarred awake whenever the monitor toned. When the nurses and doctors rounded on the patients, I drove home to shower and change clothes, then turned around and drove back to the hospital. I steered on automatic pilot; several times I pulled into the parking lot and couldn't remember the last few miles. My body felt the way it did the day after Jeremy died, when I skipped school with my teammates and went driving around the neighborhood: the way we traveled in silence, the felt batting on the ceiling of the station wagon drooping over our heads, dipping into the dead-end cul-de-sacs to prolong the journey, steadily making our way, like a comet on a long, elliptical orbit, toward Jeremy's house. I'd felt a hole opening in my heart where my friend had once been, and the fear that rushed in to fill that hole had informed my life ever since. Though it directed me toward evangelicalism's promises of good fortune, it was that fear, far more than any radio show or sermon or fellowship, that had defined my faith, and had continued to do so long after I'd broken with the evangelicals. My faith had always been an attempt to evade the evil that had claimed my friend, yet all along I'd felt myself moving toward it, just as I'd felt the car moving toward Jeremy's house. All this time, I'd been waiting for the moment when I opened the door to a man holding a gun, or received a call informing me that the schizophrenic who'd lunged at my wife's neck had not missed, or looked over my child's bed as he breathed his last breath.

I covered my face with my hands. I heard the nurse's footsteps behind me, the taps at the sink turning on as she washed her hands, and for a moment I expected her to touch my shoulder and ask if I was okay. Instead she shuffled away, her rubber soles squeaking against the floor. How common I appeared to her, how many other fathers and mothers had sat in this chair and begged for their children's lives, as I begged for my child's. I promised God everything if only he would give me my son. I'd silence every personal objection and conviction and shout prophecies of doom from the street corners. I'd wander the globe dressed in sackcloth. I'd burn my house and everything inside it. Anything you say, just let Hayden live.

My faith, from the beginning, had been a series of bargains and impossible promises. I'd become an evangelical for the same reason I was now promising to return to it: because of a premature and unjust confrontation with mortality. In the wake of Jeremy's death, I'd pledged my obedience to a fundamentalist code and denied my body's desires in the hope that God would shield me from a similar fate. Now, sitting beside my son's Isolette, in the one place where bartering with God was warranted, even expected, I began to see how a life spent trading tangible happiness for the abstract avoidance of horror led to a kind of madness. It was a faith built on sand. *My* faith, despite its former rigidity, was built on sand. I'd run out of bargaining power; I'd traded in all my chips. If Hayden were to die, I'd at last arrive at the ultimate horror I'd spent my life begging God to save me from. The deal would be broken, faith and belief and hope all rendered pointless in a single stroke.

The hand that landed on my shoulder belonged not to the nurse but to Katherine. "I'm going home for a while," she said. She still wore her slippers, stained almost black from the dirty parking lot. "My mom says Galen's asking for us. I want to be there when he wakes up from his nap."

"Okay," I said.

"I'll be back before dinner. You want to come with me?"

"One of us should stay," I said. I couldn't bear the thought of Hayden's vitals crashing while we were home, drinking coffee and pouring milk for

Galen. But even if that happened, Galen would still need milk and would need my help to pour it. He'd survive and would need me to survive with him. I didn't want my fears to define his life or mine. "I'll come home tonight," I said. I drew an X across my shirt pocket. "Promise."

Hayden's monitor toned. The nurse squeaked over, opened the porthole on the Isolette, and detached the leads affixed to his chest. One by one the waves disappeared and then, as the leads were reattached, returned with a sudden, rhythmic burst of relief. "Stupid machines," she said. The nurse looked out the window toward the snow-whitened school playground on the other side of the parking lot. In the distance, the stacks of the paper mills fed the sky with smoke. "More snow's coming yet," she said.

Open Water

If I lean against the railing and squint, I can almost make it out: the orange buoy anchored a hundred yards off the end of the pier, a wanderer in the galaxy of wind and sea. My father and I stand together at the lookout point above La Jolla Cove. Behind us, in the shadow of the bougainvillea, Katherine spreads a beach towel for Galen and then kneels to unbuckle Hayden from the car seat carrier. He reaches for Katherine's hair as it brushes his face.

The bougainvillea's in bloom, though it's the end of summer, and the small violet flowers go all the way to the edge of the cliff. The rocky cove below is curled tight as a lowercase *c*. The hotels and condominiums on the hillside shadow the rocks and water, pushing the harbor seals toward the inland point of the cove where there is sunlight. My father sips coffee through the lid of a travel mug; it leaves a pencil-thin line of brown on the fringe of his white mustache. He sets the cup in the bougainvillea so he can scan the horizon with his binoculars, the heavy black Bushnells my mother gave him for Christmas when I was eight or nine. They're one of the few things he took with him, and seeing them returns me to the strange fact that we once lived together.

He passes me the binoculars, and I look north across the mile and a half of open water. The buoy bobs in the smoky haze, a twenty-foot tower of red-and-yellow balloons tethered to its northern pole, now horizontal in the breeze. The slightest shift of my wrist, a wiggle of my elbow, and it disappears. The binoculars fill with ocean. It looks like a long way to swim, and it is. And it's only halfway.

Each September, when I can scrape together the cash, I come to this tiny California beach to swim one of the oldest and most famous ocean races in America: the La Jolla Rough Water. There's a short, two hundred and fifty–yard race for children, the traditional one-mile, and the three-point-one–mile, or five-kilometer, "Gatorman." The Gatorman is my race. This day of swimming—as well as our breakfast before dawn and the

243

drive from my father's house in Laguna Beach along the coast through Camp Pendleton while the sun chalks the sky behind the Santa Margarita Mountains—is something we do together. Most years it's just the two of us, but this year, my sister Devin is here to race, and Katherine and Galen and Hayden have come along to watch.

The Gatorman runs from La Jolla Cove to the tip of Scripps Pier and back, a roundtrip distance three-quarters of a mile farther than the swimming leg of an Ironman triathlon. The cove sits at the far northwestern tip of a peninsula appended to the California mainland like an enormous ship docked against the coast. In the middle of the peninsula is Mission Bay, and tucked below the crook of the southern point is the North Island Naval Air Station, where two of the Navy's largest aircraft carriers, the *Nimitz* and the *Ronald Reagan*, sit docked against the coast. Across the bay is San Diego.

If the peninsula is a ship, then entering the ocean at La Jolla Cove is like jumping off the prow. The course points due north while land retreats to the southeast, dipping into the crescent of the La Jolla Underwater Park before meeting the mainland. By the time the beach appears off your shoulder during the race, it's nearly a mile away. A few swimmers enlist the company of a paddle boarder to mitigate the danger and the distance, and several more boarders paddle unaccompanied to corral the field. They ride kneeling, their eyes shaded by wide-brimmed lifeguard hats as they scoop their hands through the water. The paddle boarders are not lifeguards, only guides, and there are only about twelve of them for a field of five hundred. A true emergency, a swimmer on the verge of drowning, and they will summon the San Diego Lifeguards in their yellow speedboat. Short of that, short of your imminent demise, you're on your own.

Which is, of course, the fun of it, and one of the reasons I come back each year. The allure of the swim is that it traverses a path not everyone can follow, and most of those who can follow it dare not try. Challenging the ocean is a way of feeling significant in a Kantian sense: Man confronts Nature; Nature dwarfs Man; Man is awed by his smallness in the universe, and in his solitude feels unique. It's hard *not* to feel this way. And ocean swimming is different from other long-distance competitions. There's no bottom to stand on, no sideline to sit on, no port-a-potty or shady spot in which to rest. No first-aid tent. No police officer holding traffic. No line of spectators ringing cowbells. No volunteers offering cups of water and orange wedges. No one to shout your name. Stop running during a marathon or stop cycling during a tour and only time leaves you behind. The earth will wait beneath you. Stop swimming during an ocean race, and the world leaves you behind. Life leaves you behind.

Last night I stood at the kitchen window looking out over the glass table in the backyard patio where my stepmother and Galen constructed a pinecone birdfeeder. My stepmother showed him how to spread the peanut butter and didn't mind when he got it on his shirt or in his hair or on the chair cushion. While they worked, my stepmother told Galen the story of Jesus feeding the five thousand. "The crowds were amazed," she said, her chin lit by the ivory candle in the hurricane shade in the center of the table. "Who'd ever seen anything like it?" She rarely interacted with children, even mine, without linking the activity to the Bible, and children, she said, were most receptive when they were at play. She was better at telling Bible stories than anyone I knew. She had a way of transforming the tales into magic; they became fantastic and somehow plausible at once. It was the magic of reading the Bible literally, language handed down from heaven by God himself, the one instance I could name in which adults and children alike were encouraged to read as true history stories that in other contexts would be called fables. Disbelief wasn't suspended; it was challenged, mocked, spit upon. When I was younger—not as young as Galen but still a child—hearing how God had breathed life into dirt changed the way I looked at dirt. At any moment a fully formed adult might rise out of the flowerbeds and take a seat at the table. Listening to the same stories now, watching my son listen in awe, made me nervous. Such magical wonder doesn't occur in a vacuum but belies the politics lurking beneath the veneer, the antagonistic views of science and education, the repudiation of hard-won civil rights, the justification of war in the name of God's kingdom.

I'd already overheard my stepmother encouraging Galen to be "a warrior for God's love," and earlier in the day, I'd caught him playing with a plastic breastplate and helmet and sword—props left over from a past Vacation Bible School program—bearing the words "The Full Armor of God." In my college Bible studies, the full armor of God had referred to the Holy Spirit's protection against Satan, against temptation and malice. But the Crusaders as Christian heroes? Holy war as a Bible lesson during a time when American soldiers occupied two Muslim countries? No way. I'd ignored Galen's cries as I yanked off the battle gear and shoved it onto the top shelf of the closet, tamping down my urge to take the whole outfit to the trash. I leaned over the kitchen sink, waiting for my stepmother to utter the words—war against Muslims or gays or evolution—that would send me outside to put a stop to the conversation.

My stepmother continued, "After feeding all those people, Jesus asked his disciples who the crowds said he was. The disciples told him some people thought Jesus was John the Baptist, and other people thought he was Elijah. 'But who do you say I am?' he asked. And Peter said 'You are the Christ of God.'"

"Jesus is God's son," Galen said.

"That's right," my stepmother said. "Peter knew it before anyone else, and he wasn't afraid to tell the whole wide world. Jesus said to Peter, 'If anyone is ashamed of me and my words, the Son of Man will be ashamed of him when he comes in his glory.'"

I shut off the water and leaned over the sink. The patio was dark except for the candlelight. Backlit by the track lights in the ceiling above my head, my shadow fell across the grill and Spanish pavers and the table. My stepmother turned her eyes to me. She'd been aware of my presence all along. She was speaking to me as much as to my son. I saw in her face how far apart we'd grown. Once dinner conversations had lasted for hours as our debates ranged from politics to music to the four rivers that flowed through the Garden of Eden, and my stepmother brought her Bible to the table to settle disputes the way a Scrabble player referees a game with a dictionary. Now I said nothing about faith in her presence, neither her faith nor mine. Katherine and Devin and my stepmother had earlier that evening stood together in the kitchen. A few hours before that, I'd sat in the sand and watched my father carry Hayden into the ocean for the first time. I'd jeopardized such happy moments before and didn't want to do so again.

The rewards of silence are offset by its costs. I knew my stepmother no longer considered me a Christian, at least not in the evangelical definition, and the sword in the toy box along with the exhortation to Galen to be a warrior were exactly as the words implied: stabs aimed at getting me to say what I believed, whether or not I believed at all. She'd chosen the story of Peter's confession as a Bible lesson for Galen, Sunday school on the fly. But the question was for me.

This morning, my father was awake before six, his bag waiting by the door. Because it was Sunday, my stepmother was up early, too, dressed in pantyhose and a long plaid skirt, gathering her lessons for that morning's Sunday school program. Sundays were her busiest days: The first service began at eight, the last at eleven thirty. My father had once insisted I not compete on Sundays—church was more important, he said, and at least one day should be given over to something more important than swimming, which so completely occupied my attention the rest of the week. But our residual tensions—the argument we might have had but didn't—still hung in the air, a cloud left from a bug fumigator. We were all eager to escape it.

In the car the radio was tuned, as it always was, to the AM talk station. But since it was Sunday the talk was calmer, ambulatory, the hosts and the callers chatting over coffee rather than battening down the hatches for the impending doom. Katherine sat squeezed between the boys' car seats, doling out crackers and pacifiers. When the motion of the car finally lulled the boys to sleep, she leaned her head against the rest and closed her eyes. I rode with my feet propped on the dashboard, and for a few miles, it felt as though my father and I were alone. As we made our way south along the coastline, I recalled riding with him to his sales calls, his necktie looped around a hanger dangling from the hook behind the driver's seat, the seat tightening around my shoulders as he accelerated to change lanes. I'd always loved the intimacy of the car, the tempered glass a bubble around us. Inside my father's car, I was free to talk without fear of reprisal or judgment. I felt a similar intimacy whenever we surfed together, out of earshot of the shore, the waves crashing on the sand, the two of us floating together in a dangerous no man's land that often left us alone in the ocean. Riding shotgun that morning on the way to an ocean swim, I felt a double shot of that nostalgia. By the time my father exited the freeway and turned onto La Jolla Village Drive and began swooping toward the ocean through the eucalyptus trees, the heavy cloud under which we'd set out this morning had begun to lift.

We check in for the race. A line of folding tables has been set up at the edge of the park overlooking the cove, the aisles arranged by event and alphabet. Behind the tables is an archway of red and yellow balloons in the same helical twist as those tied to the buoys. The woman at the table uses her painted fingernail to isolate my name on a list. In exchange for my signature waiving my right to sue if something goes wrong, I'm handed a plastic sack containing a yellow swim cap, a Velcro ankle strap fitted with a digital timing chip, a PowerBar, a packet of PowerBar Gel, and a sample bottle of BullFrog Sunscreen. She lifts a white T-shirt from the stack beside her and hands it to me. The Gatorman logo is always the same: an alligator wearing a cap and goggles. Beneath the picture is the year and the word "FINISHER" in bold red lettering. The top three in each race receive cash prizes, but simply making it back to shore is an accomplishment worth displaying.

A race official in a khaki outback hat stands at the end of the row of tables, a black permanent marker pinched between his index and middle fingers like a cigar. He waves me over. I hand him my registration form, and he transcribes the numbers from the page to my biceps and shoulders with indelible ink. "These need to stay visible," he said. He slaps my shoulder to send me off, adding as I walk away, "Be safe out there."

"Swimmer 3022, ready for action," I say to Galen. I flex my arm and hold it down for him to punch. I'm proud of the numbers: The 3 announces that I'll be competing in the long race, and the official's command to keep the numbers visible makes the race feel dangerous, as though they might be used to identify my body.

After a coat of sunscreen and a short warm-up swim, I come out of the water with my numbers faded and smudged. Katherine darkens the numbers with a marker she keeps in the diaper bag. She writes slowly and presses hard, making sure this time the numbers won't rub off. Hayden lies facedown on the blanket in the shadow of the bougainvillea, his padded rear in a mound. His neck and ears are pink. "Is he okay right here?" I ask Katherine, holding out my palm. "Is it too hot?"

"He's in the shade," she says. "He's fine."

I kneel on the lawn and brush my hand across his glistening hairline. His skin pulses heat. I can smell his sunscreen baking. "You sure?"

"Put him in the stroller if you want," Katherine says. "But if you wake him up, he's all yours."

Kneeling over Hayden, I think of the day the neonatologist pressed her stethoscope to his chest and told us the medications were working.

His lungs were developing, and the infection was clearing; he'd had a rough start but was healing. The myocarditis had never materialized. A few days later, I watched the nurse disconnect the leads and withdraw the lines from his chest, the flowing waves on the monitor disappearing one by one. The doctor held him for one last picture before buckling him into his car seat and escorting us to the hospital's entrance. I shielded Hayden's face with my hand as I carried him through the icy wind between the sliding doors and the open car door. I felt as much terror leaving the hospital as I did going into it. Exiting the parking lot, my mother-in-law up front beside me, Katherine in back with Hayden's tiny hand clamped around her index finger and Galen's palm cupped over her opposite shoulder, I felt the weight of my worry pressing down on me, as heavy as ever. That night I paced the hallway between the boys' rooms like a sentinel on a castle wall, a murmuring voice vibrating the bones in my ears with tales of the worst. I thought of SIDS, sleep apnea, conditions I couldn't name, every half hour sliding open the boys' bedroom doors to make sure they were still breathing. Some time after one, exhaustion took over, and I crawled into bed. Katherine rolled over and put her hand on my chest. "Welcome back," she said, her voice sleepy but sardonic, a voice I loved. The house was quiet. She slid back into sleep, and soon, so did I.

I set my hand on Hayden's back now and feel his lungs expand, his good deep breaths, his ribs rising beneath my fingers. Seagulls circle the park overhead, diving for the crumbs the spectators throw over the rail.

Some nights Katherine and I lie in bed and remember the season of her pregnancy with Hayden. It's not the illness that haunts us, but the memory of having survived it. After two close calls with Hayden's life, it's hard not to brace for a third. Katherine admits that, like me, a part of her still sees Hayden's health as provisional. The spring after his birth, Katherine landed a job as the social worker for the NICU, in a different hospital than where Hayden was treated, but filled with the same monitors and Isolettes, parents bargaining with God with their faces in their hands. My own desperate bargaining continued for months after we brought Hayden home and continues, despite my best intentions and most rational self-talk, even today. By disavowing fundamentalist talk, I thought I'd also dispensed with the beliefs such talk signified; since I no longer read the Bible literally, its literal terrors no longer commanded me. But for many years, I'd held tight to the idea that faith was a kind of insurance policy against misfortune, as though God handed out coupons that could be redeemed for protection. Such an idea had been implanted in me early and deeply and had answered too great a need for me to change simply by declaring myself changed. It wasn't until I faced the possibility of losing Hayden that I saw just how unsustainable that brand of faith was.

Katherine pats the sweat on her forehead and digs into her bag for the Diet Coke she'd squirreled from the fridge this morning. "He's a hot sleeper, and it's hot out. Let him sleep or he'll be a pain in the neck." The can, frosted with condensation, crackles open with a soft applause. Katherine takes a sip, then holds it out. "Here," she says. "Have some."

I twist the can around until my palm is wet. I sweep my hand across Hayden's cheek and through the blond curls at the top of his neck. One eye slides open, examines me for a moment, and clamps shut again.

Meanwhile Galen dances on the grass in my cap and goggles, the rubber cap scrunching up his face like a baseball glove, a little like Sloth from *The Goonies*. He runs between the chairs to the railing at the edge of the cliff where a group of children play in the shore break below. The children chase each wave as it recedes and then scurry up the beach to dodge the next crash. The last boy pauses, taunting, his wet T-shirted back to the ocean. The next wave jacks over the top of his head, driving him into the sand and rolling his legs over his head. He comes up with his hair in his face, his knees and belly covered in sand, hollering and laughing. Galen watches him, his eyes mirrored by the goggles, the goggles fixed on the water. He's looking past the boy, past the group of children, his eyes set on the sea. He wants to go in. He wants to swim.

Though I've spent most of my life in pools, I've always gravitated toward open water. Whenever I come to a body of water, in the car or from the window of an airplane, I can't help but think about swimming across it. I try to estimate the time it would take to make it across and then turn around and make it back. It's the explorer's impulse: the urge to see how far out one can go and still make it back. How far a ship can sail, how high a climber can climb, the distance an untethered astronaut can float away from the space shuttle. The need to go out and return remains constant. To make it there is to take yourself beyond the boundaries of normal living. Beyond people, beyond shelter and comfort. To make it there and *back* is to bring the remote inside your radius of wandering, to make it a part of your home.

~~~

The announcer's voice booms over the park, calling the women one-milers to line up at the top of the stairs. Hayden opens his eyes, and Devin stretches her cap over her head, then touches the seams to make sure she's got all her hair tucked up inside it. She lets out a long breath, jounces her shoulders. "Ready?" I ask.

"One way or another," she says.

"Last year's winner squeaked in under twenty-three minutes. You can take her."

"No way," she says. "I haven't been in the water very much."

I pump my fist. "Don't let the bastards grind you down."

"That's a Harvard slogan," she says. "At Penn we used to cheer, 'Get up, bombs!'"

"What does that even mean?" I ask.

"I don't know," she says. "But say it loud enough and it gets the blood pumping."

She walks toward the stairs to the cove. "Get up, bombs!" Galen yells after her.

The years Devin and I spent together on airplanes flying between our mother in Texas and our father in California, and all the things we witnessed together, should have created a stronger bond between us. If only the plane could have circled the airport forever and never landed. But the planes had always landed, either in our father's city or our mother's. Whenever the plane landed in Houston, Devin pushed to the front of the line and ran down the Jetway while I hid out in the bathroom until the plane was empty, not wanting to face the fact that my visit to my father's was officially over and that I'd have to wait for months to see him again. The weary passengers who filed out between Devin and me only widened our separation. As adults we often visit our parents at different times, each choosing the other parent for the holidays, equitably parsing out time as though we've internalized the visitation rights decreed by our parents' divorce settlement.

Before our histories diverged, however, they were one. Devin was in the car with Jeremy's sister and mother at the exact time the murders were taking place. She didn't answer Jesus' call, and as a result has struggled to find her place in our father's life, but watching her line up with the other women for the one-mile and descend the sandy cement stairs to the cove, I'm sure she's wrestled with some of my fears. Surely she's wondered about the terrible fate that might have resulted had our mother, instead of Jeremy's, driven Devin and Bekki home from swimming that night. The murders occurred in such a small window of time that our mother, had she been driving, might have pulled into the Woodley's driveway just ahead of the killers. The few extra minutes it took to drive to our house and drop off Devin may well have saved the lives of Jeremy's mother and sister, even the lives of my own mother and sister. I haven't forgotten that.

On the sand, Devin finds a place in the middle of the pack. With the binoculars, I scan the other women around her, trying to guess who will go out fast and who will round the last buoy and come home strong. She lets out another breath as she palms the knob of hair beneath her cap. My father points his camera while Galen and I clap and yell. I shake my fist in the air and shout, "Get UP!" The boy beside us sounds an air horn, inches from my ear. Its deafening honk drowns out every other sound around us, as if all the noise in a twenty-foot radius has been channeled through the plastic horn. I have no way to compete with such a commanding blast, and this isn't the time for words. We're here, we're swimming. It's enough for now.

My father changes into his Speedo, a suit he wears one day a year, today. He squirts twin droplets of shampoo into his goggles to keep his lenses from fogging, and walks over to get in line. Katherine sets out lunch for the boys—apple slices and peanut butter sandwiches. I still have more than an hour before the Gatorman. I carry my father's binoculars back to the railing to look at the course I'm soon to swim.

Though 499 other swimmers go into the water with me, the swim is ultimately solitary. The last glimpse of the competition is on the beach before the gun goes off. Then it's all arms and elbows and nylon as we high-step into the surf and punch through the shore break and skim over the shallow rocks and sea grass and make for open water. It's a melee, a salmon run: Lift your head and you'll get an elbow in the eye; keep your head too low and the swimmer behind you will try to climb over your back. It's not personal. Everyone wants a clean line, and no one wants to pull up to let someone else go by.

After a hundred yards, we clear the shallow water and fall into line. I spot a swimmer to my right and resolve to stick with him or her. If we stay together we'll have a better chance of holding the pack, and the pack is our best chance for staying on course. The line on the map between the cove and the turnaround demarcates not only the route but also the distance; the course is five kilometers only if you swim in a straight line, and in open water, there's no such thing as a straight line.

As soon as my jitters settle and I find my stroke, we hit the part of the course I like the least—the kelp bed. A flotilla of stalks and leaves so slimy and heavy they cling to my skin like wads of wet toilet paper. Away from the shade of the coast, the kelp grows thick and close; trying to swim through it is like trying to ride a bicycle through a rain forest. Depending on the year, the bed ranges from one hundred to several hundred yards wide, and equally as far across. It's too far to go around, so the only way past it is through it. It's a slow, frustrating crossing, each stroke a reach into a primordial soup that retards my glide and requires me to frog kick to push my hips back to the surface. If the stalks get above my shoulders, they'll drag me under.

When the kelp ends and the water opens, the sea floor falls away. The view through my goggles goes from blue-green to pitch black. The door in the ocean becomes literal, a physical reality. The Scripps Institute of Oceanography is perched on the cliff above this coastline because of the two submarine canyons that bisect the continental shelf just off La Jolla, offering the rare opportunity to study deep-sea marine conditions without losing sight of land. The canyons form a V between the cove and the northern point of the coast. La Jolla Canyon runs south into the Underwater Park while Scripps Canyon goes north toward the pier. Both canyons are shifty and unsteady, constantly filling with and emptying out of sediment. Where the race crosses them, the bottom is more than nine hundred feet down. Between me and the floor of this ocean is enough water to swallow the Chrysler Building in New York, or the Transamerica Pyramid in San Francisco, or the Space Needle in Seattle. I could swim over their radio antennae and blinking red warning lights and never know they were there.

The depths of the trenches has allowed for the occasional rogue wave, generated by submarine seismic activity, to rise out of the deeps and wash out the shore. Migrating gray whales swim so close to land that a mask and snorkel and a bucketful of courage are all you need to look one in the eye. Leopard sharks are common in the Underwater Park, but now and then a larger species, a Mako or a Blue, will swim right into the surf. The pack offers only the illusion of protection, and I've lost long minutes imagining a shark circling toward the sunlight, its tail curled toward its snout, mistaking my hop-along stroke for a wounded seal. How easy it'd be for it to sink its jaws into my calf and pull me under. Who would notice? Every swimmer looks the same. We all wear the same yellow cap. If I disappeared, another body would take my place. Only hours later when I didn't return to shore would my family start to worry, and by then I'd be long gone.

By the time I've reached the buoy, the thought of a shark taking me out of the swim doesn't sound like the worst idea. The worst idea is swimming all the way back. I lift my head to spot the pier, navy gray and big as a warship, not the kind of pier from which to drop a fishing line. The surf slaps against the pylons, and I suck in air and put my face back in the water and move for the buoy. The field bottlenecks at the float, jockeying for the inside line as though gaining it makes a difference, and rounding it we steer for the two paddle boarders sitting saddle-style, resting their weight on their arms. Turning in front of them, we turn toward home. It's important to get pointed in the right direction. Out here, the variation between south and south-by-southwest makes an ocean of difference. A single degree off-course, and who knows where you'll end up. As soon as the buoy is behind me, the field of swimmers disperses like a meadow of geese spooked out of their thrushes. One minute I've got a swimmer to my right and another to my left, and the next minute there's no one on either side. I lift my head and see no one. I'm all alone.

But not alone. A mile and a half out to sea, stripped of protection, the sun so hot and bright it burns my eyes through my goggles, I feel closest to God. I feel his presence beneath me, holding me up, like the way I clung to my father's shoulders while he dove into the deep end of our neighborhood pool. Swimming is my oldest metaphor for faith. Paddling across a nine hundred foot trench, it's more than a metaphor—it's an act of faith.

I kick. I turn my head to breathe. I take one stroke after another. I trust the process to keep me afloat and pointed toward shore.

~~~

My first visit to California, the Thanksgiving I was twelve, my father borrowed wet suits from a coworker and took me swimming in the ocean. On that windy day, we swam at a deserted beach in Huntington across from an oil refinery because it was the first stretch of sand we saw when we hit Pacific Coast Highway. Simply going to the beach and looking at the water wasn't enough; we had to go in it. We had to swim. Swimming was my father's way of showing me he was still my father in spite of his abrupt and incomprehensible changes. I understood that much, even then. Now I see our swim that day was also his way of apologizing for leaving Texas without me or my sister, and a promise that we'd go on.

I often look back on my evangelical history with the sharp pinch of embarrassment. Even now it can be hard for me to admit, especially in my role as a college professor, that I used to sing with my hands in the air, or that I crossed the Pacific Ocean not to wander but to witness, or that I not only believed in but argued for the idea that women should be submissive to men or that homosexuality disqualified a person from a relationship with Jesus. How can I be in possession of an independent, questioning mind if I was once so persuadable?

On Sunday afternoons in the summer, Katherine and the boys and I like to drive into the country north of our house in Wisconsin—a road that inevitably leads past the big new evangelical church near the highway. The children's wing has a bank of windows four-stories tall and a marquee that looks like it belongs at Toys "R" Us. If we pass by it at the right time, we can hear the evening service starting up, the music pumping from its doors and windows, the drummer's foot stomping on the bass, four thousand hands all coming together in unison, over and over again, like the great beating heart of the world. Our neighbors down the street, our librarian, the woman who sold us a garlic press at the mall, are all clapping together, all calling out to God. The beat gets inside the windows and disrupts the radio. It's wild and rapturous and yanks me back to the carpeted rooms where I once sat, the speakers and pastors who once hefted their Bibles into the air as they proclaimed a need to "stand up for truth" or to "be in the world but not of it." In those moments I'm tempted to think of my former faith as a delusion, a departure from my moral compass, or else a kind of slow-burning post-traumatic stress disorder brought about by life-shattering events when I very young. I press the accelerator to the floor, hoping to outrun the sound.

But the truth is, there's a lot about my old faith that I miss. What looks like zealotry from the outside feels like passion from within, a conviction so strong even empirical science can't supplant it. My evangelical friends dared to believe big things were happening in their time on earth, that our small lives adhered to such hoary notions as Truth and Righteousness and Forever, and they believed in a life governed more by virtue than vice, more by good than bad, a life in which sex and love are inseparable. In Australia, my missionary team and I prayed with our foreheads on the floor, a surrender offering a release that felt to me mysterious and holy—a posture I'm still given to in private, in search of guidance or consolation. As hard as I've tried to separate myself from evangelicalism, it continues to define my faith, to shape its boundaries and limits, and I remain grateful for what it taught me. The peace and stillness I felt on the beach when I was fifteen, the voice that came to me on the wind, has been neither forgotten nor forsaken. The Lord hid his word inside my heart that night, and it's abided there ever since. I love church coffee and communion wine, stained glass and incense, Easter palms folded into crosses; I can still recite the Lord's Prayer, the Nicene Creed, the Apostles' Creed, the Benediction, and I believe every word. Giving up the mysteries of faith would mean exchanging one extreme for another—belief with no room for doubt, for doubt with no room for belief. I can, at last, answer my stepmother's question—Jesus' question—just as Peter did: I believe a holy death can atone for my soul's imperfections. I, too, believe Jesus is the Christ of God. The fundamentals endure, only without fundamentalism.

The numbers on my father's arms make him look younger despite his white hair and mustache. I come alongside him as he stands in line to go down to race. I ask him what time he has in mind. "I don't really care," he says. "I just want to have a nice swim." His back and neck are red with sun. He knows all about the start, the flying elbows, and wants no part of it. He's used to swimming in the ocean alone. He's made friends with the men around him, all of them graying and paunchy in the stomach, all of them over fifty. He's far enough removed from his days as a competitor that he no longer remembers his best times. Even if he did remember, they'd no longer matter. It pleases me to think that my time here today, like Time itself, will pass into nothingness. I take a picture of him and then hand the camera to a stranger. I take off my T-shirt so my numbers show beside his. We lean into each other. His skin feels like a towel left draped over a chair at the beach. We haven't seen each other since last year's Rough Water. For most of my life, we've lived in different states. "Father and son?" the stranger asks. We nod. He snaps the picture. "The family that swims together," he says, and passes the camera back to me.

After forty years of wandering in the desert, Joshua led the Israelites across the Jordan River and into the Promised Land. The river marked the line between exile and home. So it was to the river John the Baptist went to baptize, and to the river Jesus went to be baptized. They stood together in the water. Baptism is an act of exile and return, a metaphorical journey beyond the borders of your people, the same hands that push you out pulling you back in. The water isn't an accidental element in the rite. We're meant to live near water, not in it; in baptism we drown and return again to life. When I wash up on the shore at the end of the race, and dash the last fifty feet for the finish line, I'll feel a little redeemed. I'll have left the world and made it back. I'll have made room for my heart to grow. I'll move across the sand with the other swimmers who have endured this, too. A volunteer kneeling on the sand will strip off our timing chips as we walk away from the finish line. Another will hand out cups of Powerade, the color and temperature of urine, and PowerBars that have been in the sun all day, like flattened Tootsie Rolls with a little Gravy Train mixed in. I'll chow down on it hungrily. Before attempting to climb the stairs, I'll sit for a while in the sand, my chest pink, my feet in the tide as I look over the windswept waves, the paddle boarders, the swimmers still crawling in. I'll want them to see me when they run up the beach. The tide will wash over my ankles and retract, calling me back out.

All my stories lead to water. In my earliest memory, I'm padding toward the business end of a three-meter diving board, water wings on my arms, my father treading below as he calls to me to jump. On our first date, Katherine and I went swimming in the Great Salt Lake. Her legs bobbed against mine as we floated in the briny tide, the water a conduit for my courage, allowing me to touch her calf, her thigh, to reach around her back. The water wasn't simply a backdrop; it was an x in the equation. On dry land the outcome might have been different.

Jeremy and Matt return to me in the water more often, and more forcefully, than anywhere else. I'll look to the lane beside mine and see them there, our strokes in cadence, or one of them coming on hard. I pick it up to stay ahead, unable to resist the urge to compete, even with my ghosts. I find myself reliving old races, remembering old workouts, laughing at the old jokes—alone in the water, surrounded by time.

For most of my life, Jeremy has resided in me as an absence—a name conjoined with an event so horrible it split time in half, into Before and After. The rupture occurred when I was so young—Jeremy, along with his father Barry and his brother Greg, have been dead now for more than twenty years, half a decade longer than he lived—that it's sometimes difficult to remember that he was a real person: good sometimes, bad others, too young to be hardened by disappointment but old enough to wonder what his life would be like. But prowling about my house at night, listening to my sons squeak and wriggle in their sleep, I think of him lying in his bed, his water-filled mattress like a small lake in his room, thinking about swimming or his homework or a moment in his distant future. The melancholy that creeps in and follows me back to bed is the sadness of missing *him*—the boy who was my friend, not just his vanquished shadow. There's comfort in the hope that in some other dimension, on the other side of the door, he still exists. Maybe that other side is here, in the story, where he's remembered.

On the shelf behind my desk sits the one photograph I have of him, standing beside a pool in Katy, Texas. I don't know who took the picture or how I came by it, but weirdly enough, I remember it being taken. It was the District Championships, spring of our freshman year. The garage-style doors to the outside patio had been rolled up to let the chlorinated air escape, and in the picture, the left side throbs with humid sunlight. Jeremy was on his way to swim the one hundred breaststroke, the one event where we didn't compete against each other and therefore the one chance to be easy with each other, if only until our next race. He fished around inside his bag for his cap and goggles before pulling off his sweats. His skin was as smooth as a melon rind, though the dark scabs on his kneecaps and ankles and upper lip bore witness to how new he was to shaving. A girl he liked strolled by and made eyes at him, her long hair blown around by the warm breeze through the open doors. Jeremy stuck out his chest. "Down boy," I said.

"Arf, arf," he said. Then his laugh: honk, honk, honk.

"Better win," I said. "Don't want to look like a chump."

"I'm a lover not a fighter," he said. He slid over to the side of the pool to say hello to the girl, then turned and grinned at me. Devious and proud of himself, afraid of nothing. When he walked back toward me, he paused for the picture, his cap and goggles balled up in his hand, his hands on his hips. His mother or father must have taken it. The girl's in the picture too, in the background, wearing stonewashed denim shorts and a brown T-shirt. In a few months, she'll be his first kiss, on the balcony of a hotel in Baton Rouge, Louisiana, between sessions of a swim meet. He didn't know that yet, or that she'll break his heart the same afternoon and I'll find him crying in the bathroom. His whole life will be that one afternoon, and he had no idea about any of it. He just heard the water's slap and gurgle, heard the whistles and the horn, the hurrahs from the bleachers. His race was next. The look on his face says, now and forever, *I'm ready.*

It's after 1:00 PM when the Gatorman is called. I stand in the shade of a eucalyptus tree and wait for the stairs to clear. The last one-milers are still coming up. My father is dried and in his shorts, and stands against the railing overlooking the cove. Katherine holds Hayden while Galen stands with his back against my sister. I follow the procession to the stairs. We walk silently, solemnly, uncertain of whether we walk toward greatness or danger. On the beach I edge my way to the front left, just inside the reef that juts from the hook of the cove. The rocks push the swell to the south, revealing the line between the rocky shallows and clear water. I'll need to move to the right once I'm in the water, but I'd rather go in first and scramble than get caught in the scrum. The water is sixty-seven degrees, the top inch warmed by the wind and sun, that smoky Southern California smog. I search for the buoy, but I can't find it. The pier and the beach and the brown hills float away in the distance, pushed back by the sea.

The paddlers gather up their boards and head for ocean. The crowd around the railing cheers. The paddlers wave, and one by one slap their boards on the water, flop down, and head out. It's a long way even for them. Bodies press in tight. I can feel the anxiety in the swimmers around me, their adrenal glands wide open and throttling. Some bounce and jump, some suck in deep breaths of air as though hoping to squirrel away extra. They exhale long hot gusts against my neck and back. I splash in the shore break to rob the ocean of its initial paralyzing shock. Others do this, too. Together we sit in the water and pee, our last chance for a while.

I look up once more at the railing, at my father and sister, my wife and children. Everyone up there shares my last name. The sun shines on Galen's red hair and glares in Katherine's sunglasses. My father waves, and I wave back. *I see you, you see me.*

One last wave and then it's time to concentrate. I scoop a handful of water into my mouth, swish and spit. I scoop it under my arms and on my chest, and then I lower my goggles. I shake my arms. A man squeezes in beside me and goes through this same routine, the swish and spit, the splash, the lowered goggles. He's bronzed, hairless, not an ounce of fat anywhere. When he's finished, he turns and looks me up and down, sizing me up. He doesn't know me and can't possibly be intimidated by my wooly stomach, but I recognize him. He's an Olympian, a former American record holder. He swims open water races all the time, and today he's looking good for the cash. He'll beat me by a margin of seven to ten minutes, depending, and I know it, but standing with my shoulder against his, I can't help allowing myself the momentary delusion that when the gun goes off, I'll beat him to the water, and in the water, I'll beat him to the buoy, and who knows, maybe this is my day, maybe this will be the swim that has flowed dormant through my veins ever since a starter's gun first sent me into the water more than twenty-five years ago. How many times have I seen those races happen, nobodies becoming somebodies in just one swim? Maybe today it will be me.

He nods and I nod back. "Good luck," I say.

All delusions dissipate when I turn back to the sea. My story ends not in glory but in gratitude, my family waiting for my return. I take a deep breath and hold it and let it leak out slowly through my nose. I touch my forehead and chest, my right shoulder and my left, drawing on my skin the symbol of pain that the next hour will force me to appreciate. I pray for safe travel, for lessons learned. I lean forward and let my fingers dangle in the water. Beneath the surface the sea grass sways, the sand sparkles like gold in a miner's pan. An orange garibaldi drifts lazily in the tide's back-and-forth. A few feet farther out, the black abyss waits, unseen and unknowable. A wave sweeps in and engulfs my hand. I am ocean, I am salt and water. My heart is bursting. The harbor seals are barking, great deep woofs from the rocks. From the beach the woofs sound like cheers, calling out to me as I begin to run—as the Pacific takes hold of my ankles, my knees, my thighs, as I pull my hands together and throw them forward and dive—*go.*

    Go!

AUTHOR'S NOTE

A Door in the Ocean is a work of memory, and memory, like religion, is fallible and relies on faith. I've done my best to stick to the facts as I remember them, though in a few places, time has been compressed. For the sake of preserving their privacy and goodwill, I've changed the names and physical traits of some of the people in this story. Nevertheless, this is a work of nonfiction, which means that if you happen to recognize yourself in these pages, it's likely not an accident. For that I can only apologize.

ACKNOWLEDGMENTS

A Door in the Ocean went through several iterations before arriving at its final version. For much of that process, I felt, appropriately, at sea and adrift. I'd have never found my way were it not for the great and generous efforts of a number of people.

Earlier versions of several chapters appeared in different forms in *The Huffington Post*, *Southwest Review*, *Western Humanities Review*, *Fugue*, *The Literary Review*, *Image*, *The Missouri Review*, *Meridian*, and *The Best American Sports Writing* 2009. Thanks to the editors—especially, Mary Kenagy-Mitchell, Greg Wolfe, Barry Weller, Willard Spiegelman, Minna Proctor, Evelyn Somers, Mary Morgan, Glenn Stout, and Leigh Montville—for their sharp insights, and for giving the original essays a chance. Greg Wolfe and Mary Kenagy-Mitchell have championed my work from the very beginning, and I'm forever grateful for their enduring advocacy and friendship.

Melanie Rae Thon, Stephen Tuttle, Scott Blackwood, Megan Ward, Erin McGraw, and Alyson Hagy all read portions of the manuscript and asked hard, thoughtful questions. The Edenfred Arists' Residency provided a few bucolic days of writing, while David Wells provided good food and better company. Gail Hochman was an early advocate and foresaw the story's true form long before I did. Kathryn Lang showed enthusiasm when I needed to hear it and lent her acute, editorial eye later in the process. Debra Monroe arrived right as I was about to jump ship, and gave me, and this book, far more than I can ever hope to thank her for.

Kathleen Anderson and Adam Friedstein renewed my confidence in the manuscript and steered it into the hands of Dan Smetanka, who saw the book not only for what it was, but also for what it could be. He masterfully guided the revisions from the first word to the last, and made me laugh the entire time. The book you hold in your hands owes a tremendous amount to Dan's patience, intellect, and candor. Thanks also to Charlie Winton, Jack Shoemaker, and everyone at Counterpoint.

Rebekka Woodley Peltzman allowed me to make her family's story part of my own. Megan Ward, Tim Spurgin, Paul Cohen, Alison Guenther-Pal, and my father, Dennis McGlynn, provided wise counsel whenever I needed it, while Garth Bond, Celia Barnes, Faith Barrett, and

Karen Hoffmann kept my spirits buoyed throughout the long labor. Fr. Patrick Twomey and Rev. Dr. Steve Savides helped me keep the faith. Steve Van Tuyl always made sure beer was on tap. Thanks to my brilliant former students who have since become writers—in particular, Madhuri Vijay, Andy Graff, Callie Bates, Kelly Goss, and Jami Lin—for allowing me to take part in their work and for reminding me why storytelling matters. Thanks to all my students, past and present, for making my day job the best in the country. My family, Dennis and Linda McGlynn, Kerry Thompson, Devin McBrier, and Paul and Laura Sagers, were unfailing with their love and support.

Finally, Katherine McGlynn was my safe harbor throughout every storm. She gave up so many nights to talk me through the thorniest parts of this book and didn't flinch when her name appeared on the page. Without her, I'd have lost my courage long ago.

And without Galen and Hayden, I'd have no story to tell.

Printed in the United States
by Baker & Taylor Publisher Services